HARVARD HISTORICAL MONOGRAPHS

Published under the direction
of the Department of History

Volume LXXII

The Huguenots in America

A Refugee People in New World Society

Jon Butler

Harvard University Press
Cambridge, Massachusetts, and
London, England
1983

Library of Congress Cataloging in Publication Data

Butler, Jon, 1940-
    The Huguenots in America.

    (Harvard historical monographs ; v. 72)
    Includes bibliographical references and index.
    1. Huguenots—United States—History. I. Title.
II. Series.
E184.H9B87 1984   973'.088245   83-8547
ISBN 0-674-41320-2

For Benjamin and Peter

Acknowledgments

The paradox of historical scholarship is that it is an individual enterprise that depends on much cooperation among many people. I am especially indebted to numerous librarians for suggesting sources I would not otherwise have discovered. Among them are Esther Brumberg, Museum of the City of New York; Mrs. Edmund A. Burns, Huguenot Society of South Carolina; Samuel J. Hough, John Carter Brown Library; John Jensen, Special Collections, and Erike Linke, Interlibrary Loans, Wilson Library, University of Minnesota; Charles Marmoy, Huguenot Society of London; Gay Gibson McDonald, Beinecke Rare Book and Manuscript Library, Yale University; William H. McDowell, Jr., South Carolina Department of Archives and History; Philippe Monnier, Bibliothèque publique et universitaire, Geneva; Virginia Rugheimer, Charleston Library Society; John D. Stinson, New York Public Library; Allen H. Stokes, South Caroliniana Library, University of South Carolina; Larry E. Sullivan, New-York Historical Society; Denis Vatinel, Société de l'histoire du protestantisme français, Paris; and especially Zoe Ann Doyle, Interlibrary Loans, Library, University of Illinois at Chicago. Staff members of numerous libraries also proved uncommonly helpful. In the United States they included staffs at the Massachusetts Historical Society, the Newberry Library, the New-York Historical Society, the Rhode Island Historical Society, and the South Carolina Historical Society; and in Europe they included staffs at the Bodleian Library, the British Library, the Lambeth Palace Library, the library of the Société de l'histoire du protestantisme français, the library of the United Society for the Propagation of the Gospel, and the Dr. Williams Library.

Many friends and colleagues performed crucial miscellaneous tasks that included the coding of tax lists, censuses, and estate inventories; translating materials from German sources; obtaining microfilmed materials from European libraries; guiding quantitative materials through computers; and simply answering numerous bothersome questions: Mary Dunn, George Huppert, James Kettner, Richard Levy, Elisabeth Lewis, Norma Perry, Janice Reiff, Leo Schelbert, Daniel Scott Smith, Daniel Uchitelle, and Jan van den Berg. James Berquist, Russell

Menard, and John Modell commented on papers prepared for professional meetings, and Patricia Bonomi and Nancy Lyman Roelker kindly read all or large parts of the nearly finished manuscript and saved me from many embarrassing errors. A fellowship from the National Endowment for the Humanities permitted me to finish research in London and Paris and to spend a year writing. The Research Board of the University of Illinois at Chicago funded the work with numerous general grants, and the California State College, Bakersfield, Foundation provided small grants to get the project started.

Two friends deserve special mention. Darrett Rutman's suggestion for a senior thesis on Boston's French Church gave me a much larger project to come back to many years later. In a decade of Minnesota summers, Eric Monkkonen allowed me to talk on and on about my project and gave me good advice about methodology even when I know he would have preferred to "lag" tramps. I've always been glad for his friendship; now I know how glad I should be for his patience.

And Roxanne Deuser Butler not only made it possible for me to write this book but, as usual, improved every part of it.

Contents

Tables

Illustrations

Figures

The Huguenots in America

Dates are given in Old Style but I have begun the new year on January 1. Surnames and Christian names have been standardized following, where possible, George W. Baird's *History of the Huguenot Emigration to America,* 2 vols. (New York, 1885), or Arthur H. Hirsch's *The Huguenots of Colonial South Carolina* (Durham, N.C., 1928). Translations of French materials into English are my own unless otherwise indicated. The term "Huguenot" refers to all refugees of the 1680s and their descendants; thus, I have avoided using phrases like "French-surnamed persons," "descendants of the refugees," or "former Huguenots" even when these phrases might have been more accurate.

Introduction. The Huguenot Diaspora and the European Immigrant in Early American Society

Between 1680 and 1690, some 160,000 French adults and children fled their homeland to escape Louis XIV's vicious suppression of Protestant worship. Louis XIV began his drive against the Protestants in the 1660s and capped it in October 1685 when he revoked the Edict of Nantes, a decree issued by Henry IV in 1598 that granted France's Protestants freedom of worship under certain limited conditions. The 1685 Revocation, as it usually is called, produced the largest forced migration of Europeans in the early modern period. Braving crude transportation, incomplete knowledge of foreign places, and a countryside swarming with royal troops—in many cases escaping torture to elicit conversions to Catholicism—many French Protestants abandoned family businesses and farms to seek physical safety and freedom of worship in countries with a Protestant political leadership. Most of the refugees streamed into Europe's great Protestant cities—Geneva, Berlin, Amsterdam, and London—where they created large urban exile communities almost overnight.

The Huguenot refugees of the 1680s also settled in America. Indeed, they became the first major Continental European refugee group to settle in the British colonies of North America since the arrival of the Puritans half a century earlier. Most other immigrants in the British colonies between 1635 and 1680 came to America voluntarily to pursue their individual advancement; they were not captured to serve as forced laborers, as were Africans, nor were they forced out of their homes because they wanted to sustain a collective religious life, as were Huguenots. Little wonder, then, that Cotton Mather welcomed the Huguenots. In 1681, before even a dozen French refugees lived in Boston, Mather offered public prayers for France's Huguenots, hoping not only to relieve their "grievous persecution" but also to remind New Englanders that they too might lose their religious privileges, if not to persecution then to backsliding indifference to their grandfathers' still unrealized goals.[1]

This book marks the tercentenary of the settlement of Huguenot refugees in the American colonies. Sadly, it also marks a dearth of scholarship not only on the Huguenot diaspora but on the history of the Huguenot refugees in America and even on non-English immigrants in colonial America. The Huguenot dispersal thrusts up stimulating problems in the history of early modern Europe. The 160,000 Protestant exiles challenge historians to probe the social dynamics of an extraordinary forced migration occurring before the rise of modern industrial society. The experience of the exiled Huguenots raises important questions about national limits in late seventeenth-century Protestant cooperation and about the difficulty of sustaining religious and social cohesion beyond native homelands. The conversion of some 1,500,000 French Protestants to Catholicism between 1680 and 1700 underscores even contemporary doubts about the range and depth of lay religious commitment in early modern society, particularly after two hundred years of religious disputing.

The Huguenot diaspora and its causes have stimulated relatively little extended scholarly analysis, however, Jean Orcibal's *Louis XIV et les Protestants* (Paris, 1951) offers an intriguing explanation of monarchical policy toward France's seventeenth-century Protestants. Warren Scoville's *The Persecution of Huguenots and French Economic Development, 1680–1720* (Berkley, Calif., 1960) examines the technological and economic significance of the Revocation and diaspora. A superb new denominational history by Robert Mandrou et al., *Histoire des Protestants en France* (Toulouse, 1977), too little known in the United States, provides insightful if brief chapters on the Revocation and on French Protestantism in the next century.

Yet the diaspora remains an enigma. Elisabeth Labrousse and others have written brilliantly of Pierre Bayle's contribution to the eighteenth-century Enlightenment and on intellectual life in the Dutch exile community, but its social history remains unknown. Warren Scoville focused on economic development within France and was forced to depend frequently on often inadequate secondary materials to discuss the importance of the refugees outside France. Only in Germany has the diaspora and its effects in the eighteenth century attracted modern scholars, as in Stefi Jersch-Wenzel's recent *Juden und "Franzosen" in der Wirtschaft des Raumes Berlin-Brandenburg zur Zeit des Merkantilismus* (Berlin, 1978), although even this literature is often guided by antiquarian principles. Frederick A. Norwood's general study of forced migrations, *Strangers and Exiles: A History of Religious Refugees* (Nashville, Tenn., 1969), also depended on antiquarian histories to describe the diaspora of the 1680s and the subsequent life of the refugees in their places of exile. Robert Mandrou and the authors of *Histoire des Protestants en France* thus are not wrong when they complain that after three centuries historians still have not written a synoptic history of *le Refuge*.[2]

The dimension of the problem is revealed in the lack of histories about Huguenot refugees in Great Britain after 1680. At least 20,000 and perhaps as many as 50,000 Huguenot adults and children entered Britain between 1680 and the early 1690s. They arrived in a time of dangerously escalating political tension in England, much of which concerned Catholicism and France. In an overwhelmingly agrarian nation, the Huguenots were largely artisans, merchants, shopkeepers, and cloth-trade workers, and most of them understandably settled in London. If they knew prosperity in France, they frequently knew poverty in England. Now poor yet still skilled, they strained the national charity, stimulated angry debate about naturalization, and brought mobs of English artisans to the street demanding their deportation.

Voluminous sources exist to probe the experience and assimilation of the Huguenot refugees in Great Britain between 1685 and 1800. The Huguenot Society of London has published sixty quarto volumes of refugees' records and twenty-five volumes of its yearly *Proceedings*. London's major research libraries house several thousand seventeenth- and eighteenth-century manuscripts bearing directly on the history of the Huguenot refugees, sources only complemented by other extensive manuscript sources elsewhere in the nation. Yet we lack a single modern comprehensive history of the Huguenots' fate in eighteenth-century Britain. Thanks largely to the industry of the Huguenot Society of London we know a great deal about the refugees' arrival in the 1680s and about the history of their predecessors in the previous century. But we still do not possess a lengthy

systematic account of the rise and fall of Huguenot refugee
communities in eighteenth-century England, the pace of Huguenot intermarriage, the effect of occupational and residential
change on the refugees' social cohesion, and causes of decline in
the Huguenots' religious institutions.

One subtle measure of this neglect can be seen in George
Rudé's study of London politics, *Paris and London in the Eighteenth
Century: Studies in Popular Protest* (New York, 1970). Although
Rudé's subjects often are French-surnamed weavers from London's Spitalfields section, the lack of a modern comprehensive
history of Great Britain's Huguenot refugees prevents Rudé from
even linking the weaver's demands for political rights in the 1760s
to the Huguenots' flight to avoid French Catholic persecution in
the 1680s. Such a link would force us to revise our understanding
of the origins of London's 1760s protests, while its absence would
be an important measure of the weavers' assimilation in London
society and politics.

Historians have ignored the Huguenot diaspora for several
reasons. Nancy Roelker has suggested that modern Huguenots
cherish the "Desert" era between 1700 and 1787, when France's
remaining Protestants persevered as a persecuted minority, but
are embarrassed by the period between 1598 and 1685, when
Huguenots cultivated the favor of the monarchy to retain their
privileges of worship. They also exhibit little interest in the
diaspora itself, perhaps because the Huguenots who fled France
escaped the persecution of the Desert era and frequently abandoned their distinctive Huguenot religious institutions in exile
after 1700. Other historians of religion relegate the period of
significant Huguenot influence in European Protestantism to the
sixteenth century, slight Huguenots in the seventeenth century,
and find themselves lured away in the eighteenth century by the
problem of Enlightenment secularism. In contrast, immigration
and ethnic historians concentrate on the nineteenth and twentieth
centuries and, apparently, judge the flight of France's Huguenots
to be too early and too "pre-modern" to be interesting or
important.[3]

Huguenots have fared no better in America. They appear
briefly in most of the standard American history texts and in all
the histories of American immigration. But this appearance is

limited to one or two paragraphs. Never have the American refugees benefited from a detailed scholarly study tracing their experience in the century after their arrival. Charles Washington Baird's two-volume *History of the Huguenot Emigration to America* (New York, 1885) is a masterful survey of the Huguenots' geographical origins in France and of the Huguenot refugee settlements in New England. But Baird provided no treatment of the more important Huguenot communities in New York and South Carolina, something he apparently intended to do in additional volumes he never completed. The only scholarly local study, Arthur H. Hirsch's *The Huguenots of Colonial South Carolina* (Durham, N.C., 1928), is often undependable and now is outdated in both method and interpretation. Gilbert Chinard's charming *Les réfugiés Huguenots en Amérique* (Paris, 1925) reflected Chinard's incomparable knowledge of European emigration literature. But elsewhere he followed Baird, as he himself acknowledged, and, in any case, Chinard's work never appeared in English. It is scarcely surprising then that the Huguenots did not gain a separate listing in the most recent summation of American immigration and ethnic scholarship, the *Harvard Encyclopedia of American Ethnic Groups* (Cambridge, Mass., 1980), where they are briefly described in the general entry on all French immigrants.

Perhaps the American refugees' salient characteristic—their rapid social and religious disintegration—explains their absence from American scholarship. By 1750 only two weak French Protestant congregations still existed in the colonies, the vast majority of Huguenots were taking non-Huguenot spouses in marriage, and no discernible Huguenot strand existed anywhere in colonial political or economic life. Of course, these characteristics, if only for their pathological tenor, might also have intrigued historians. Indeed, if their main feature were added to the stereotyped images of Huguenots as rich merchants and skilled artisans and to the recent concern of American historians for social history, the Huguenot refugees should have furnished ideal subjects for historical study.

Yet Huguenots comprise only one of several colonial immigrant groups ignored by historians. Non-English Europeans accounted for about a third of the white settlers in the mainland colonies on the eve of the American Revolution, and they offer historians unusual opportunities to examine economic opportunity, political advancement, and cultural adaptation in pre-Revolutionary society. Two decades ago a sociologist, Gillian Lindt Gollin, contrasted Old and New World environments in *Moravians in Two Worlds: A Study of Changing Communities* (New York, 1967), and more recently Stephanie Grauman Wolf has used new techniques in family history to unravel a significant part of the German experience in early America in *Urban Village: Population, Community, and Family Structure in Germantown, Pennsylvania, 1683–1800* (Princeton, N.J., 1976). But other studies provide more limited information on colonial American immigrant groups. Jews, Scots, and the Scotch-Irish fare best. Works published since 1940 by James G. Leyburn, R. J. Dickson, and Duane Meyer on the Scots and Scotch-Irish and by Jacob Marcus, Edwin Wolf II, and David de Sola Pool on colonial Jews offer useful treatments of their respective immigrants, although they lack the greater precision of recent social history and now fit somewhat awkwardly into the picture of pre-Revolutionary society drawn by historians in the past two decades. The situation is desperate elsewhere, however. We still lack a sophisticated general history of German emigration to the American colonies. We are dependent on a 1936 study for our knowledge of Palatine emigrants and on a 1916 study for our knowledge of Swiss emigrants. Most important, we know almost nothing about the continuing emigration of English settlers to America after 1680.[4]

This book cannot remedy all the problems of early American immigration history. But it does attempt to widen our knowledge of the colonial American immigrant experience through a study of the first major continental European refugee group to arrive in the colonies after 1650. Readers will find limited references here to the first few Huguenots who arrived in New York in the 1660s and subsequently founded New Paltz in 1677 or to those who later settled at Manakin in Virginia in 1700 after living in exile in Europe for as long as two decades. Rather, the study concentrates on the refugees of the 1680s; these emigrants left Europe in the same decade under similar circumstances; they formed the bulk of the Huguenot emigration to America; and their surviving settlements in Boston and rural and urban New York and South Carolina placed them in the three major cultural regions of the eighteenth-century British mainland colonies—post-Puritan New England, the ethnically heterogeneous middle colonies, and the slave-holding societies of the colonial south.

This diversity in settlements makes the Huguenots unusual. Most other early American immigrant groups concentrated in the rural areas of the colonies, as with Scots, Scotch-Irish, and Germans, or resided exclusively in the colonial cities, as with Jews. It also makes the Huguenots more significant. The Huguenot experience in Boston, New York, and South Carolina offers a rare opportunity to capture the escalating regionalism of eighteenth-century America. That members of one immigrant group could so quickly adapt to such different societies not only suggests something important about the Huguenots but also points up the heterogeneity of the maturing mainland colonies before the making of the American Revolution. In this context, the Huguenot refugees emerge as the centerpiece of a very natural comparative history that follows the experience of the same immigrant group in three remarkably different American settings. What happened to the Huguenot refugees in Boston, New York, and South Carolina raises important questions about the relative importance of New World environment and Old World culture in shaping immigrant behavior—environment especially important if Huguenots remained cohesive in one society but not everywhere, the Huguenot past important if their cohesiveness waned and if they assimilated rapidly in each of their new and different societies.

Of course, the historian's principal task in discussing the Huguenot experience in colonial America is to explain their swift disappearance as a cohesive refugee group. Two models are especially relevant to this task. One achieved a classic formulation in Milton Gordon's *Assimilation in American Life: The Role of Race, Religion, and National Origins* (New York, 1964). Gordon emphasized the importance of "structural assimilation" in incorporating immigrants within their host societies. For the American Huguenots this involved their acquisition of legal rights through naturalization and denization, their participation in colonial politics, their economic activity and success, their pursuit of exogamous or endogamous marriage unions, their relations with English-speaking Protestant groups, and the pace and extent of their movement into non-Huguenot religious groups—characteristics that also measured the social malleability of the colonies Huguenots entered as much as they measured the Huguenots' interest in assimilation.

A second model for probing the Huguenots' demise is found in Kai Erikson's *Everything in Its Path: Destruction of Community in the Buffalo Creek Flood* (New York, 1976). This book raises central questions about the internal causes of social disintegration through an analysis of a modern event, the consequences of a 1972 dam collapse in Buffalo Creek, West Virginia. The long-term devastation of this catastrophe proved as appalling as the immediate property loss and the drowning of 125 individuals. Old antagonisms, insecurities, and internal tensions previously constrained in the social structure broke loose in the aftermath of the flood to ravage survivors with fear, paranoia, and anomie. Media sentimentalism to the contrary, survivors of the Buffalo Creek flood found it impossible to salvage their old human community, however imperfect, from the destruction of their physical community despite valiant efforts to reconstruct both.

Disaster descended upon France's Protestants in the Revocation. Like Erikson's West Virginia miners, they too attempted to reconstruct familiar social and religious patterns in the aftermath of the Revocation, and the traditions of the previous century became their principal storehouse of examples and precedents to guide this effort. But also like Erikson's miners, the earlier Huguenots' experience rang with antagonisms, insecurities, and internal tensions only poorly constrained within the social interstices of the Ancien Régime. The Revocation did not free up every affliction common to France's seventeenth-century Protestants. But it loosened a sufficient number of them to make the refugees' task of religious and social reconstruction all the more difficult. Nowhere did Huguenots escape the burdens of their past. Despite major advantages of size and concentration, the larger exile communities in Great Britain, Holland, and Germany as well as the smaller exile communities in colonial America all learned that the pre-Revocation Huguenotism they sought to preserve often undercut the religious and social cohesion reinforced and forged by the Revocation.

Of course, assimilation and waning cohesiveness typified the Huguenot experience everywhere in America. Yet these characteristics should not advance the Huguenots as models of a neo-orthodox interpretation of the American past. So many different immigrants entered so many different New World societies between 1607 and the 1980s that no single interpretive mode can encapsulate their many experiences; the story of one group was not necessarily that of another group arriving in a different time or place. Only by revealing the full spectrum of immigrant experiences can historians appreciate the range and depth of their common patterns, whether these reflect old melting pot theories, reasonable if not complete political and social assimilation, or the persistence of ethnic consciousness among immigrants—the interpretation that has dominated most recent immigration histories. The story of Huguenot refugees in colonial America is offered here by way of gaining a more sophisticated perspective on two important problems—the early American immigrant experience and the development of eighteenth-century American society.

PART I

Flight from Terror

It is now fifty years since we landed at Dover
and I doe find that time doth wear out matters
after such a manner that all that is past is now as a
dream, . . . the generallity of Christians even the
reformed ones are like the Israelites, noe sooner
past the sea but they forget their deliverance and
goe a Stray.

—*Isaac Minet's Narrative, c. 1730*

1 / French Protestantism and the Revocation of 1685

In 1685 Louis XIV dramatically reshaped the religious configuration of late seventeenth-century France by revoking the Edict of Nantes of 1598 and thereby abolishing the Protestant liberties of worship it protected. The effect of his action is measured in simple facts. In the decade between 1680 and 1690, Huguenots declined from about one million to fewer than 75,000 of France's total population of some twenty million. Most Protestant congregations disbanded, and Catholic authorities demolished their church buildings or "temples." Two-thirds of the Protestant laity converted to Catholicism, under duress, of course. Less than a fifth of France's Protestants successfully escaped from the country. A surprising 20 percent of the ministers followed their laity into Catholicism, while the departure of the other ministers into exile stripped the few remaining lay Protestants of any significant ministerial leadership. Even dead Protestants abjured. Catholic partisans uprooted Huguenot graveyards to prevent the dead from mocking Europe's "most Catholic King."[1]

How could France's Protestants have been so thoroughly uprooted? The movement once claimed numerous followers among the nobility and lesser aristocracy, took deep root among artisans and merchants, and turned some Protestant cities into military strongholds. The French movement gave social meaning to the theology of Jean Calvin, and shaped international Protestantism in major ways in the century of the Reformation. But many difficulties also afflicted the movement, especially lack of popular support, problems in church government, internal discord, and Protestantism's inability to resist Catholic coercion and persecution. These problems hastened the fall of French Protestantism in the last half of the reign of Louis XIV. They also shaped the Huguenot diaspora in Protestant Europe, the history of the exile communities there, and the history of the French Protestants in America.

From its first appearance in France, the Protestant Reformation sustained deeply symbiotic links with French politics. Its principal spokesman, Jean Calvin, directed much of France's religious reform from the safe haven of Geneva in Switzerland. His message spread quickly, and by 1560 Protestant congregations dotted the French countryside. Neither monarchy nor Church proved able to contain the Protestant challenge. One major problem was the monarchy's difficult relationship with nobles, of whom as many as a third had adopted Protestantism by 1580. The ensuing series of quarrels carried France into larger European struggles known as the "Wars of Religion." Yet, perhaps true to the shallowness of the nobles' spiritual commitment, the wars in France ended in 1598 when the Protestant Henry of Navarre took communion as a Catholic to become Henry IV, King of France. "Paris," he reportedly said, "is worth a Mass."[2]

Henry IV's return to Catholicism was a Protestant defeat, mitigated by the famous Edict of Nantes of 1598, which granted liberties of worship to France's Protestants. Yet the Edict limited the privileges severely: freedom to worship was confined to some two hundred fortified villages, towns, and cities; Protestant congregations were forbidden in towns where a Catholic bishop resided; and Protestants were prohibited from organizing new congregations after 1598. Thus the Edict deftly circumscribed Protestant growth in exchange for immediate freedom of worship. Yet even these gains had an illusory character. The Edict's validity depended on a monarchical stability Henry IV could not guarantee and on the willingness of later monarchs to oppose unending Catholic demands to suppress French Protestantism.[3]

The story of the Edict in the next century was one of constriction and, finally, revocation. The fortified Protestant towns, "states within the state," lasted only two decades. After the death of Henry IV in 1610, Cardinal Richelieu ordered their destruction, and royal troops reduced the port of La Rochelle to burning rubble when its inhabitants resisted. Thousands were killed, others converted to Catholicism, and some migrated to new towns. For the next thirty years, however, the monarchy used less violent means to control the Protestants. Instead, the Edict's already limited Protestant liberties fell victim to increasing restrictions. This trend accelerated after Louis XIV assumed his personal rule of France in 1661. Royal officials closed new congregations formed after 1598, allowed Protestants only one teacher for each Protestant school, and banned Huguenots from the more important professions.[4]

After 1675 Louis XIV abandoned the policy of merely restricting Protestant liberties and began to suppress the movement altogether. Squads of royal troops (*dragonnades*) marched into Poitou to "preserve" Catholicism in a solidly Protestant province. Murder, beatings, jailings, rape, and torture all served religious ends: as one bishop wrote, "the dragoons here have been good missionaries." Despite resistance, the violence worked, and half of Poitou's 100,000 Protestants renounced their faith. Church and royal officials occasionally expressed qualms about the brutality but welcomed the converts it produced from the shrinking Protestant ranks. Whereas about 750 Protestant congregations existed at the beginning of Louis XIV's rule in 1661, only 350 remained by 1680—an ominous decline in French Protestant strength even before the Revocation.[5]

Many historians trace the destruction of seventeenth-century French Protestantism to its increasing vulnerability after 1650. Here, the most emphatic judgment is that of Emile Léonard, author of the three-volume *Histoire générale du protestantisme* and an associate of Lucien Febvre and the "Annales school" of French social historians. Léonard uses a pathologist's vocabulary to describe French Protestantism after 1600: "Persecution like sickness only strikes weak bodies, and it is first in the internal and utmost weaknesses of the Protestant body that the reason for its fall must be sought." To back his hypothesis, Léonard catalogues Protestant defects. Ministers were poorly trained and lost their zeal after 1610. The movement's Calvinist thrust was compromised by Arminian notions advanced by Moise Amyraut and denominational authority and organization weakened. The national Protestant synod did not even meet after 1659, while provincial synods wallowed in trivial local disputes and individual congregations ignored their advice. The result was a dangerous flabbiness in Protestant discipline. Whereas we have come to think of French Protestantism as stoutly Calvinistic and rigidly ordered, it was, in fact, ecclesiastically disordered and latitudinarian in theology.[6]

If Louis XIV savaged a sick body when he attacked the French Protestants in 1685, it might be remembered that the disorder among French Protestants probably was no more severe than that among other European Protestant groups. Poor clerical training, lack of ministerial zeal, heterodoxy in theology, lax ecclesiastical discipline, and attacks from the state afflicted Protestants in many countries. They stood at the center of English Protestant disagreement about reform in the Anglican church and were an indirect cause of the Puritan migration to America.[7] Moreover, although the institutions of French society were Christian, much of the population was only nominally so. A. N. Galpern, William Monter, and Emmanuel Le Roy Ladurie have shown that before the Reformation, Catholicism was only one source of religious ideas and practices for French men and women. Others included astrologers, fortune tellers, wise men and women, and occult medical practitioners. The Reformation confused this religious mix further. After 1530 the people did not merely choose between Catholicism and Protestantism but often shifted among different styles of Protestantism, Catholicism, and occultism. In this context, the defections from French Protestantism after 1680 and the earlier ecclesiastical and theological disarray should, in part, be seen as a consequence of turbulent popular religious practice under the Ancien Régime.[8]

Anomalies characterized many aspects of seventeenth-century French Protestantism. As in Germany, the Protestant population was unevenly distributed. It was draped across France like a sling. It had some supporters in Brittany and Normandy in northwest France, many in Poitou, Aunis, Saintonge, and the port city of La Rochelle, and large numbers in Languedoc and the Cévennes mountains. Then it thinned out in northwest and central France although a small but significant Protestant population always existed near Paris.[9]

In western France—Normandy, Brittany, Saintonge, and Poitou—and much of Languedoc, merchants, craftsmen, artisans, and moderately prosperous farmers comprised the bulk of congregational membership, while peasants remained almost entirely

outside the movement. But in the Cévennes mountains of Languedoc, artisan conversions were followed by a Protestantization
of the peasantry. Some rejected Catholicism while others rebuffed
sorcerers and diviners to embrace Calvinism. In either case, they
became zealous Protestants. Calvin had to warn them against
extremism in the 1560s, and a century later they led the most
significant and armed resistance to Louis XIV's attempt to crush
Protestantism found anywhere in France.[10]

The general lack of peasant support for Protestantism everywhere except Languedoc did not mean that the movement did
not appeal to and care for the poor. Huguenot congregations
regularly organized poor funds. At Calais, the fund was sustained
by money dropped into the poor box, by contributions made at
marriage ceremonies, gifts of cash, property, and objects, and by
money given to mark the conclusion of business transactions. The
range of recipients was equally broad. It included refugees fleeing
to Holland and England, orphans, widows, indigents, workers in
need of tools, and workers with tools in need of cash. In fact, for
some, the congregation became a kind of pawnbroker. The poor-
fund trustees accepted valuable objects or personal mementos in
exchange for loans or direct charity.[11]

Even within the relatively homogeneous Protestant population,
perceptions of social class clearly affected congregational life, as
Pierre Bolle describes in his study of Mens-en-Trièves in
Dauphiné on the eve of the Revocation. This was a Protestant
market town of about one thousand, including nearby country
residents. No powerful local noble lived there, and peasants made
up less than 3 percent of the population. Two-thirds of the residents were artisans, 15 percent were businessmen—merchants,
bakers, and inkeepers—and 12 percent were "notables"—lawyers,
doctors, schoolteachers, *rentiers,* and, of course, bourgeois.[12]

These persons did not share equally in church office-holding,
however. In the three decades prior to the Revocation, businessmen and notables provided 56 percent of the church elders
or about twice their proportion in the population, while the
artisans constituted only one-third of the church elders. The
poorest artisans and laborers never were named church elders at
all. The same pattern occurred in Protestant congregations in the
ports of Bordeaux and Rochelle in western France. Church elders

there came from the ranks of the prosperous merchants, businessmen, and lawyers. None were artisans, who composed most of the membership in the congregations, or laborers.[13]

The upper-class and bourgeois domination of local congregational life was complemented by a hierarchical national church government dominated by ministers. Although historians traditionally have argued that this church government was democratic, it is now clear that such was never the case. In practice, authority flowed down from the national and regional meetings to the local congregations, in a manner analogous to Presbyterianism. As was true there, a national synod determined broad denominational policy. Regional synods and smaller provincial "colloquies" handled special local problems, and consistories of prominent laymen managed the congregations. Bourgeois and upper-class laymen played significant roles in the consistories and colloquies because of their importance in congregational finance. Ministers clearly dominated the regional and national synods out of their position as expositors of God's Word. In none of these gatherings did artisans, small merchants, or peasants exercise significant influence despite Protestant rhetoric about the power of the laity in a true, reformed church.[14]

This oligarchical French Protestant church government was never effectively centralized, however. The contrast with England's Quakers is particularly striking. Between 1660 and 1685, the originally individualistic Quakers responded to monarchical suppression by perfecting centralized committees in London that directed all aspects of Quaker resistance. The Huguenots responded to more severe attacks in almost opposite fashion. After the last national Protestant synod met in 1659, regional synods and colloquies coordinated resistance to the Crown as best they could. Congregations slowly crumbled, efforts to control heterodoxy waned, and by the mid-1670s, France's Protestants had in effect drifted toward English Congregational practice. Thus, in contrast to previous theory and practice, after 1660 Huguenot church government increasingly rested on local congregations rather than on superior presbyteries and synods.[15]

One reason why French Protestants failed to resist Louis XIV's challenge was their already prominent regionalism. Another reason resided in the domination of congregtional office-holding by bourgeois and upper-class laymen, who were content to retreat to a *de facto* congregationalism that heightened their already important power in local matters. Still another explanation lodges in what one historian has called the French Protestant "monarchical cult" (paradoxically, increasing royal pressure stimulated Protestant veneration of the monarchy). For one thing, the monarchy had guaranteed Protestant worship through the Edict of Nantes; moreover, French Protestants venerated patriarchical authority as did most other Protestants. Orthodox French Protestants had long ago rejected the notorious theories of François Hotman, the sixteenth-century Huguenot who advocated resistance to the monarchy as one means of advancing religious reform. In this setting, France's leading Protestants feared that resistance and rebellion would only provoke Louis XIV. Even after the dragonnades entered Poitou, Protestants continued to believe that Louis XIV would uphold their liberties.[16]

Louis XIV revoked the Edict of Nantes on October 22, 1685. The ensuing effort to enforce the Revocation became a spectacular, if perverse, social ritual even in a reign renowned for pageantry of all kinds. For a year prior to the Revocation, royal troops circled through the French countryside destroying strategically placed Protestant congregations. Then, on the day of the Revocation, these troops struck at the great Protestant temple at Charenton, then a Paris suburb where the nation's Protestant elite worshiped. In a day it was demolished. For a decade thereafter, royal troops marched from village to village carrying the banner of the monarchy before them. They arrested known Protestants, paraded them past jeering Catholic partisans, and delivered them to local Catholic authorities who used violence and the threat of violence to obtain quick public abjurations of their Protestant faith.[17]

This vivid public attack on the Protestants preyed on the fleeting character of religious allegiance in early modern Europe. Although many Protestant abjurations were hypocritical and were obtained under duress, this royal oppression still met with long-term success. One graphic acknowledgment of this success comes from the anonymous Protestant who eventually settled in Virginia and has ever since been known as "Durand of Dauphiné." Traveling toward Marseilles from Dauphiné with Protestants who had refused to convert, Durand passed through village after village that had been visited by yellow-clad royal troops looking for Protestants. Finally, after coming upon the troops themselves, he passed himself off as a simple traveler and engaged them in a casual conversation. He found them jovial. Their task was proving easy, they said, for most Protestants displayed so little attachment to their religion that

> no sooner did they hear the beating of their drums than they rushed en masse to the churches to make their abjurations. It was true, my informants continued, that the first towns they visited upon entering the province made resistance for three days, and they had settled up well with them in consequence; but as for the rest, [the soldiers] had not been suffered to unbridle their horses in one of them, or take so much as a fowl from the roost.

Durand found residents in another town "in a lamentable state. Their consciences had begun to reproach them with the crime they had committed so precipately in abjuring." But, significantly, the residents failed to renounce their abjurations. Nor did Durand ask them to do so.[18]

Louis XIV hoped not only to cripple French Protestantism but to keep rebellion minimal and ex-Protestants working in France. To accomplish this aim, the government designed the Revocation so it would split the Protestant movement. The decree ordered all Protestant clergymen to leave France or conform to Catholicism; in fact, it encouraged them to migrate. At the same time it required lay Protestants to remain in France or risk having their properties confiscated. The plan worked. At least 650 of France's roughly 800 Protestant ministers left the country, and most of the rest abjured, while at least 80 percent of the laity remained in France, most of whom also abjured.[19]

The Protestants who remained in France responded in many different ways to the Revocation. Armed rebellion occurred only in Languedoc and the Cévennes mountains, where it reached a climax in the so-called "War of the Camisards" between 1695 and 1705. Although historians have emphasized peasant dominance in this resistance, much of this lower class support has been romanticized and removed from its social context. In fact, the Languedoc resistance was linked to the broad strength Protestantism enjoyed in the province, as whole communities of peasants, artisans, small farmers, merchants, and lesser nobles rebelled against the monarchy collectively rather than as single classes.[20]

Other Protestants resisted passively. Some of the laity signed papers of abjuration but continued private Protestant worship in the family. A few ministers remained in France and preached among small clusters of Protestants but soon fled when their work became known to government officials. This essentially passive resistance, which was supported by most exile ministers, meshed nicely with the emphasis on family worship, which had been encouraged in French Protestantism. Together, they allowed artisans, skilled laborers, merchants, and lawyers to preserve their faith as well as their occupations simultaneously, though each in his own way.[21]

To an important degree, our view of the Huguenots who fled to England and America is linked to the history of those who stayed in France. Therefore, it is important to understand how the Revocation permanently altered the size and social composition of France's Protestant movement. When it reemerged after Louis XIV's death in 1715, it remained weak even where it once had been strong, demonstrating the ability of coercion to reshape religious belief, practice, and allegiance in seventeeth- and eighteenth-century Europe. In La Rochelle, Protestants in 1685 still constituted 25 percent of the port's population although their numbers had been declining steadily since 1620. But by 1724 Protestants accounted for only 5 percent of the population. Georges Frêche's study of five villages in Puylaurens reveals similar declines in Protestant strength after 1685. In Castres, Protestants dropped from 43 percent in 1665 to 14 percent of the population in 1744. In Sorèze, they declined from 59 percent to 11 percent, in Briatexte from 55 percent to 4 percent, and in Lacrousette from 39 percent to 6 percent.[22]

The shrinkage in the Protestant following was matched by a narrowing of the movement's social composition. The shift is difficult to measure but is best seen in the disappearance of artisan Protestants. In many places they had comprised the largest occupational group in the movement. But so many either fled France or converted to Catholicism that this was not true after 1685. In the Puylaurens villages, artisans had comprised 41 percent of the membership in Protestant congregations before 1673. But by 1750 they became only 23 percent of the members in much smaller congregations. At the same time, the percentage of lesser nobles rose from 1.8 percent to 15 percent, and the percentage of bourgeois Protestants climbed from 17.8 to 33.7. Studies of other congregations by Daniel Ligou, Pierre Channu, and Emile Léonard confirm the same trend. The result was clear. The class effects of the Revocation forced eighteenth-century French Protestantism into a more bourgeois mold as the movement lost the significant lower-class following it often enjoyed in the first 150 years of its existence.[23]

Enormous numbers of French Protestants clearly preferred to convert to Catholicism rather than resist, revolt, or flee. The small proportion of Protestants who left France does not account for the dramatic decrease in the Protestant population after 1685. Instead, studies of post-Revocation Protestant communities reveal that the number of children baptized as Catholics rose significantly just at the time when the Protestant congregations were being demolished. Many of the new Catholics may have intended to rejoin the Protestant movement. Yet whatever their feelings in 1685, most of them never embraced Protestantism again; their hopes and desires to do so were thwarted by continuing persecution, family needs, and economic and political realities.[24]

A careful study of the Huguenot clergy at the time of the Revocation by Samuel Mours reveals striking regional variations in their rates of exile and abjuration that parallel anomalies in lay behavior. Almost half the ministers (sixteen of thirty-four) abjured in Béarn in southwest France, and even in the Cévennes mountains, where Protestantism was especially strong, 25 percent of the ministers abjured (nineteen of seventy-seven). Of those who fled, ministers from western France settled in Holland and England while ministers from eastern and southern France generally settled in Germany. Only ministers from Upper Languedoc did not appear to seek the most convenient place of refuge. Twenty-two went to Holland, thirty-four to England, and only seventeen to Switzerland and Germany, perhaps because the resistance in the Cévennes mountains blocked otherwise obvious routes of exile east and north.[25]

The number of lay Protestants who left France is subject to much debate. The refugees never were counted, and both contemporary estimates and later calculations vary widely. Antoine Court, the great mid-eighteenth century Protestant leader, believed that over 2,000,000 fled. Jean Orcibal, writing in 1948, estimated that only 100,000 Protestants left France. Since overestimation is the most common flaw in analyzing such migrations, the careful, conservative figures of Samuel Mours found in Table 1 will serve us well. Mours believes that about 160,000 Protestants left France. Paradoxically, the relative size of the migration from a particular province was inversely related to the size of its Protestant population. In northwest France, where the Protestant population was small, between one-third and one-half left. But in

Table 1. France's Protestants in the reign of Louis XIV, 1660–1690

Province	Protestants in the 1660s	Refugees by 1690	
		N	%
Normandy	59,000	21,000	36
Brittany	6,000	3,500	58
Anjou, Touraine, Maine	13,500	7,800	58
Poitou	90,000	18,000	20
Saintonge, Aunis	98,000	25,000	26
Lower Guyenne	100,000	11,000	11
Béarn	30,000	500	02
Upper Languedoc, Upper Guyenne	80,000	6,000	08
Lower Languedoc	88,000	6,400	07
Cévennes	82,000	4,600	06
Vivarais	45,000	3,500	08
Provence	9,000	1,500	17
Dauphiné	72,000	18,000	25
Burgundy	17,000	10,000	59
Berry, Orléanais	15,500	4,000	26
Île-de-France, Picardy, Champagne	48,000	20,500	43
Total	856,000	161,300	19

Source: Samuel Mours, "Essai d'évaluation de la population protestante réformée aux xviiᵉ et xviiiᵉ siècles," *Bulletin de la société de l'histoire du protestantisme français,* 104 (1958): 1–24; Mours, "Essai sommaire de géographie du protestantisme réformé français au xviiᵉ siècle," ibid., 111 (1965): 303–321, and 112 (1966): 19–36.

Lower Languedoc, Cévennes, Vivarais, and Guyenne, where half
the nation's Protestants lived, only 6 to 10 percent fled. This
probably happened because Protestants in northwest France were
both more vulnerable to attack as a distinct minority and closer to
places of refuge like England or Holland. The more numerous
Protestants in southern France were farther from potential places
of exile, and their numbers made armed resistance to persecution
possible.[26]

Many French Protestants settled in Germany's Protestant principalities, which welcomed them eagerly. Within two weeks of the
Revocation the Great Elector of Brandenburg, Frederick William,
issued a remarkable document called the "Potsdam Decree" that
encouraged French Protestant settlement and became a model for
terms offered to the Huguenots in many principalities. Government agents were ordered to help Huguenots secure transportation, passports, and housing, and to assist them in resuming their
occupations. It promised Huguenots direct financial aid and the
rights of native citizens. The decree even guaranteed privileges of
the nobility to those who had enjoyed them in France.[27]

About 30,000 refugees settled in the Protestant principalities.
Prussia received nearly half of these refugees, and about 5,000 of
them formed a "new city" outside Berlin. Most were married men
and women between twenty and fifty years of age who came with
families from the eastern and southeastern French provinces. A
surprisingly large number came from Languedoc, however,
which was another testament to the resilience of Protestantism in
the province and to its isolation from routes of exile to England
and Holland. Probably half the refugees engaged in farming—the
same proportion as in America. Many took up land offered in
special agricultural settlements established by some governments,
including Prussia. These governments hoped that the Huguenots
would revitalize an agricultural economy that had suffered from
frequent wars and backward technology. In the cities, the
Huguenot artisans had a salutary effect on the German crafts and
trades. Their achievement was as much a comment on the general
backwardness of the German economy as on their skills. Their
contributions were especially important in the silver and gold
trades, in banking, jewelry-making and glass-making, and, of

course, in the cloth trades, including weaving and tapestry-making.[28]

The Huguenot refugees in Germany also sustained some significant religious and social cohesion. Refugee congregations still functioned with some vigor in Germany in the 1740s in both rural and urban settings, and endogamous marriages long remained commonplace among Germany's rural Huguenot refugees. Yet rural isolation probably sustained these marriages, while economic success and even the religious cohesion of the refugees bore the strong imprint of state support. In Prussia and elsewhere the law recognized traditional Huguenot methods of church government and gave Huguenot congregations special legal standing in the refugee communities; refugee farmers, artisans, and craftsmen all received significant special economic privileges; and in some places, special courts handled refugee legal affairs. As in pre-Revocation France, the law may have stimulated a cohesion that was not inherent in the community.[29]

Holland received about 50,000 refugees, a few of whom finally settled in America. Most apparently came from northern and western France, and many arrived with surprisingly large family groups. A census of ninety-eight households taken in the congregations at Cazand and Groede in 1685 reveals that only twenty-nine contained single persons—fourteen males and fifteen females. Twenty households contained adults only, usually married couples with no children, groups of brothers and sisters, aged parents and their adult children, but also apparently unrelated adults who were sharing housing. Most surprising was the fact that nearly half the households—forty-three of ninety-eight—included children under the age of sixteen.[30]

Unlike other places of refuge, Holland already contained a religious institution into which the new refugees might fit. This was the Walloon church, which had received French Protestant members earlier in the sixteenth century. Although the church had been strong in the 1590s, it had grown weak in the seventeenth century, and by the 1680s it faced both a shortage of ministers and a shrinking lay following. Seventeen of forty-three congregations had disbanded, and those that still existed were small. Paradoxically, the renewal stimulated by the Huguenot diaspora after 1680 created a surplus of ministers. The thirty-nine French Protestant congregations organized within Holland's old Walloon church after 1695 simply could not provide livings for the 350 exile Huguenot ministers living in Holland by 1700.[31]

In addition to excess numbers, the ministers compounded their troubles with severe internal conflicts. Some of them revived arguments about Arminianism and the theology of Moise Amyraut. Others adopted chiliastic views that irritated the refugee laity and strained relations with the old Walloon church and the powerful Dutch Reformed church. The most spectacular debate occurred between Pierre Bayle and Pierre Jurieu, two of the most distinguished Huguenot theologians of the seventeenth century. Bayle urged patience in the face of the Revocation and so did Jurieu, but only temporarily. He embraced radical millenarianism, predicted the downfall of Louis XIV, and all but advocated the direct use of force against Louis as was already occurring in Languedoc. The Bayle-Jurieu debate actually was more significant in theology and philosophy than in politics since, except in Languedoc, most French Protestants followed their traditional respectful approach toward the French monarchy. But the controversy did point toward serious social and religious tensions inside Holland's French Protestant exile communities.[32]

The Huguenot flight to England takes us directly to the history of the Huguenots in America. Most refugees who eventually settled in America first lived in England. They often traveled to America with British help, left relatives behind in England, and used the English exile communities as resources after they arrived in America. On the other hand, England, as the center for the transatlantic empire of which the American colonies were part, viewed the problem of peopling the American colonies from a political perspective. The number and kind of refugees who would settle in America was as much a matter of state concern as of individual interest, and Huguenots thus became subject to two sets of government immigration policies: those directed toward the Huguenot refugee communities in Britain and those pertaining to the American colonies.

The problem of the refugees in Britain begins with an assessment of their numbers. Again, estimates of Huguenot immigration vary wildly and no censuses are available to solve the problem easily. An emissary of Louis XIV in London in 1686 claimed that only 4,500 refugees had arrived there by then. But a 1719 French report on the British economy claimed that over 90,000 refugees then lived there. Historians have settled for an estimate of 50,000 refugees, a modest figure first suggested by the Anglican Bishop Gilbert Burnet. But even this may be too high. If by "refugees" we mean only those French Protestant men, women, and children who traveled from France to England between 1680 and 1695, the more accurate figure might be 20,000 to 30,000 persons, perhaps even fewer. The committee that administered aid to the French refugees in England in 1688 claimed that only 20,000 Huguenots lived there then, and in the 1690s the same committee and its successors never claimed that they were helping more than 10,000 refugees in the nation.[33]

The refugees came to England in several waves. As in Holland, Huguenots had been entering England since the 1550s, and by 1650 seven Huguenot congregations existed in England, all but one in the countryside. The post-1680 migration altered this pattern. Some of the refugees settled in rural areas; others went to reasonably large port cities like Bristol; and the vast majority took up residence in London. Thus by 1685 the English Huguenot refugee population was largely urban. As a result, while the number of Huguenot congregations in rural areas expanded from six to about fifteen between 1680 and 1700, they grew from one to twelve in London and its environs. In addition, the new London congregations were larger than their old country predecessors. The important Threadneedle Street congregation alone admitted some 1,000 newly arrived refugees as communicants in 1686. By comparison, the rural congregations, including one at Canterbury that dated from the 1550s, collectively failed to admit that many communicants in the entire half-century after 1650.[34]

The vast majority of the French refugees came from western and northern France. Irene Scouloudi's important study of London's large Threadneedle Street congregation reveals that of 1,867 heads of families who arrived between 1681 and 1687, 47 percent (878) came from western France, 28 percent (536) from central France, 23 percent (423) from northern France, and only 3 percent (30) from southern and eastern France. Baptismal and marriage registers of other congregations support Scouloudi's

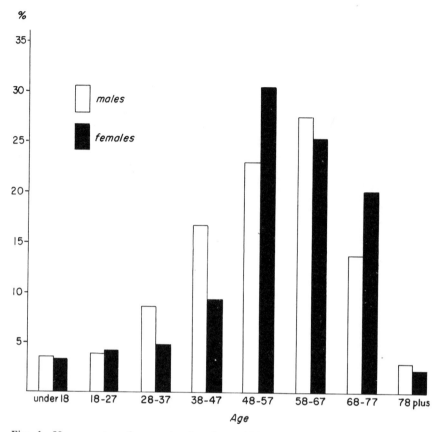

Fig. 1. Huguenot refugees in London, 1689 (age distribution, heads of household). *Source:* Royal Bounty ms. 7, Nov. 20, 1689. Huguenot Society of London.

conclusion. About 37 percent of the refugees in London's La Patente de Spitalfields congregation came from Poitou, 25 percent (362) came from Normandy, 8 percent (109) from Saintonge, and only 3 percent (35) from Languedoc. In the Leicester Fields congregation, 48 percent (418) of the refugees admitted between 1688 and 1783 came from Saintonge, Aunis, Normandy, and Poitou, and only 6 percent (50) came from Languedoc.[35]

The London refugees differed remarkably from immigrants who typify voluntary population movements in modern times. A rare contemporary measure of their social composition occurs in an account of aid given to London refugees between April and

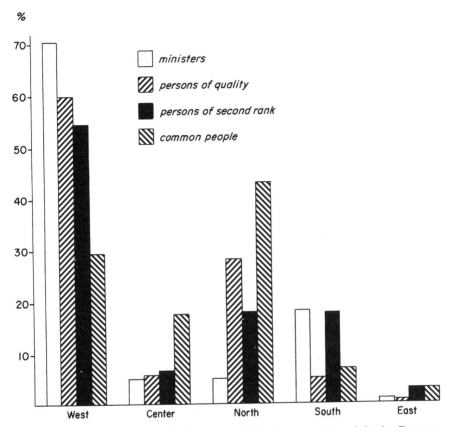

Fig. 2. Huguenot refugees in London, 1689 (geographic origin in France, heads of household by social class). *Source:* Royal Bounty ms. 7, Nov. 20, 1689. Huguenot Society of London.

November 1689 that describes their social class, ages, occupations, even their diseases and afflictions (Figs. 1 and 2).[36]

London's refugees represented that segment of France's Protestant population most vulnerable to Catholic persecution. Many were old, very old. Of 761 heads of households listed on this account, 46.6 percent were over 55 years of age. Fully 11.8 percent were 71 or older, but only 15.3 percent were between 21 and 40. Moreover, 55 percent of the household heads were women, most of whom also were significantly older than the males who headed households. Whereas 78.3 percent of these women were over 48 years of age, this was true of 67.2 percent of the men. In contrast, 29.1 percent of the men but only 18.3 percent of the women were between 18 and 47. And, as one might suspect, most of the women—46 percent of those who headed house-holds—were widows.[37]

Class and sex had important effects on the origin and condition of the refugees. Women and lower-class males had traveled shorter distances to get to London than males who came from bourgeois and aristocratic backgrounds. Whereas 32 percent of female household heads came from France's northern provinces, only about 20 percent of the male household heads originated there. In contrast, 7 percent of the female heads and 18 percent of the male heads came from the more distant southern French provinces. Similarly, larger percentages of refugees from the lower classes came from the center and north of France than from the south. Class also affected the distribution of widows in the refugee population. Only 27.9 percent of the women in aristocratic households were widows, but widows comprised 52.6 percent of the women in lower-class refugee households and 61.5 percent of the women in bourgeois households.[37]

Class also affected the prevalence of disease among the refugees. Sixty-eight percent of all reported diseases, illnesses, and detrimental physical and mental conditions occurred among refugees identified as members of the common classes although they comprised only 34.8 percent of the households described in the aid account. Considering the age of the population, it is scarcely surprising that infirmity was the most common affliction, occurring 52 times or in 6.8 percent of all households. Mental illness, crippling conditions, and blindness were reported in 45 households. (5.9 percent).

Occupation rather than class affected household size most directly. Ministerial households were significantly larger than all other households. On the average, they contained 2.6 persons. In contrast, aristocratic households contained 1.7 persons, and bourgeois and lower-class households each contained 1.35 persons. Thus, 298 persons lived in the 115 households headed by ministers, while only 291 persons lived in the 215 households headed by bourgeois refugees.

Class determined the amount of aid that the London refugees received. Common people got 38 percent less per capita aid than did members of the Huguenot aristocracy, even though common people were more often sick, disabled, maimed, or mentally disturbed than aristocratic refugees. In the 1687 aid account, common people received £0.37 in aid per person, whereas members of the aristocracy received £0.55, and ministers received £0.42. Thus, as *personnes de qualité,* sixty-year-old François Gua and his forty-two-year-old wife of Rochebrueille in Saintonge, both of whom were sick, received £1.50 from the committee. But a commoner, the blind Judith Pillet of Lunere and her seven-year-old child, received £0.50, while an eighteen-year-old woman with a child received £0.60. Clearly, living on less in pre-Revocation France was proving a good model for living on less in refugee London.

Most historians have been impressed by the breadth and depth of anti-Huguenot prejudice in late Stuart England. In fact, however, the government pursued erratic policies with regard to the refugees, and the Huguenots angered or worried only certain segments of the English population. Royal policy toward Huguenots between 1680 and 1690 proved as fitful as the course of the monarchy itself. In common with his handling of other problems, James II never developed a consistent policy toward the Huguenots. As a Catholic monarch in a Protestant nation, he was both eager and under pressure to maintain close ties to Louis XIV. This may explain the extraordinary shifts in his attitudes toward Huguenots. During his brief reign from 1685 to 1688, James II ordered royal printers to issue pamphlets denying the existence of any Huguenot persecution in France. He also ordered authorities to burn all copies of Jean Claude's well-known *Account of the Persecutions and Oppressions of the Protestants in France* (London, 1686) and worried so much about Huguenot retribution that he refused to allow foreigners to become royal guards.[38]

Because James justified his attempted repression in ugly language—"Dogs defend each other when attacked, why should not Kings do as much?"—his words are well remembered. Yet fortunately for the refugees, James did not live up to them. He never forbade Huguenot refugees to settle in England or its colonies, he established committees to provide them with financial aid, and he allowed them to form Huguenot congregations that were at first independent; then, after being pressured by Anglican bishops, he required them to conform to the Church of England. His Protestant successors, William and Mary and Mary's sister Anne, continued and expanded on James II's record. They increased royal donations to the Huguenot aid committees and encouraged the committees in their attempts to raise public funds. But empathy had its limits. When the Treaty of Ryswick was signed in 1697, they made no effort to force Louis XIV to restore the Edict of Nantes despite pleas from exiled French Protestants to do so.[39]

James II and William and Mary also offered legal privileges to the refugees. These privileges came to foreign-born residents in two forms, naturalization and denization. Naturalization gave its recipients the legal rights of native-born Englishmen, including those of voting and office-holding. But it was granted only by Parliament, and Parliament never passed a general naturalization act for Huguenots although it did pass private bills to naturalize a few prestigious refugees. Refugees obtained denization through "letters patent" issued by the Crown and obtained upon application. This procedure cost less than parliamentary naturalization. It allowed recipients to engage in business and to own some kinds of property in England and its possessions, including its American colonies. Hence a refugee of 1682, resident in Boston, urged prospective Huguenot colonists to obtain denization in London before coming to America. Yet denization proved tedious to obtain, still cost more than many refugees could afford (large groups tried to crowd their names on to a single denization grant to share costs), and did not entitle refugees to own land, inherit property, or designate heirs to their own property. Despite these limitations, several thouand Huguenots received "letters patent" from the Catholic Stuarts and from William and Mary that guaranteed them at least some legal privileges. Equally important, the Crown ignored the legal problems of other refugees who never received parliamentary naturalization or even denization. These Huguenots could have lost "illegally" acquired property, while their children or other heirs could have been prevented from inheriting it or anything else. Yet the English courts failed to wield the law against the Huguenots despite the English reputation for bigotry or even James II's personal dislike of them. Indeed, through their silence, the courts gave Huguenots an invaluable *de facto* residence status that at least bypassed the fees of London's notoriously greedy lawyers.[40]

Popular reaction to the Huguenot refugees is more difficult to assess. Seventeenth-century England was a bigoted, ethnocentric society. The English disliked the Scots, Welsh, and Irish only somewhat less than Spaniards, Germans, and the French, and were in the process of enslaving thousands of captive Africans in America. In contrast, the reception of the Huguenots by the general public was amazingly positive. The royal committees collected over £200,000 for Huguenot relief between 1685 and 1700. Although they may have hoped that this aid would induce Huguenot conformity to the Church of England, all their many contributors could have had no such collective notion. Indeed, social pressure to provide visible support for the refugees was so strong that it induced some hard-pressed Englishmen to drop counterfeit money into the collections in 1689 to avoid the embarrassment of having to ignore pleas to support the refugees.[41]

Local authorities also provided temporary aid to many Huguenots. Corporation officials in Bristol, Barnstaple, Norwich, Exeter, Southampton, and Portsmouth arranged for money or shelter for newly arrived refugees. At the same time, local governments also complained that the Huguenots strained town resources: Portsmouth officials encouraged refugees to depart for London; Lincoln officials reported that efforts to raise additional funds would be "but a prejudice to them and all others" needing charity; Bristol town officials tried to move the refugees elsewhere. As early as 1681 the Bristol mayor informed the Privy Council that the town could not absorb more Huguenots and asked for its advice on "how to dispose of these French already come, and those that may hereafter arrive."[42]

Sometimes the refugees did evoke popular hostility. In a society that was rife with rumors about Catholic plots and still torn by religious dissension, it is scarcely surprising that Huguenots at times became targets of popular ridicule that had a religious and cultural focus. For example, some people gossiped that the refugees really were Catholics, or that they denied the Trinity, and that their "cabbages and roots" and especially their garlic polluted London's streets. Most of the popular hostility understandably centered on economic issues. Before 1700 one of the issues that brought English citizens to the streets was the intrusion of French refugees into specialized occupations and crafts, especially weaving. The Huguenot weavers undoubtedly strengthened the industry in England because they were more technologically advanced. That is why they threatened the English weavers' security. A 1683 report to the Privy Council warned that London's weavers threatened violence against the French immigrants. "They say, if they can get a sufficient number together, they will rise and knock them in the head." This happened in Norwich, where worry about potential job losses and rumors about the Huguenots' hidden Catholicism produced a vicious riot. Huguenots were dragged from their lodgings, some were beaten, and one French woman was killed. Later, rioters in Southwark and Westminster destroyed looms owned by refugee weavers.[43]

Even the riots, however, point out the positive treatment of Huguenots in economic affairs by the British government. Laboring men and women attacked Huguenots because government officials refused to use traditional economic regulations to prevent Huguenots from competing with English craft workers. For example, the semimonopolistic Livery Companies in London governed many of the crafts in which Huguenots were so highly skilled—goldsmithing, silversmithing, and all the cloth trades including the important silk trade. The government could have allowed, even encouraged, the Livery Companies to strangle Huguenot competition; instead, it encouraged them to admit Huguenot craftsmen despite complaints from English workers. Here Huguenots benefited from government policies moving England toward a more modern economy in which workers sold skills and labor in an increasingly open market.[44]

The Church of England proved illiberal, however. For more than a century before 1680 Anglican authorities allowed French Protestants to form independent exile congregations. The first such church, on Threadneedle Street in London, was formed in 1550. Of the five additional congregations formed by 1640, only the congregation at Canterbury conformed to the Church of England. After 1680, however, Anglican authorities abandoned their permissive policies toward the growth of Huguenot congregations. At that time Anglicans became worried about a potential Huguenot-Dissenter alliance, particularly with Presbyterians, since Presbyterians and Huguenots presumably shared a common theological and ecclesiastical heritage. English Dissenters long used the French Protestants as models of reformed religious activity and took special interest in Huguenot polity. The Separatists who later settled at Plymouth in Massachusetts noted carefully how fully they followed the French Protestant model of church government. Later Dissenters translated various Huguenot publications, including the 1623 French Protestant synod proceedings at Charenton; *The Ecclesiasticall Discipline of the Reformed Church in France* (London, 1642), published as the Westminster Assembly debated the restructuring of England's national church; and John Quick's two-volume edition of France's sixteenth- and seventeenth-century Protestant synod proceedings, *Synodicon in Gallia Reformata* (London, 1692), published to guide Dissenting groups after passage of the 1689 Act of Toleration. There was some evidence, then, and much anxiety that the relationship had gone beyond mere intellectual contact. Sometime in the early 1680s the mayor of Southampton complained that Huguenot refugees who had been given a building in which to worship were illegally allowing Dissenters to use it as well, and Bishop George Morley was among the several Anglican bishops who urged Henry Compton, the Bishop of London, to redirect Huguenot refugees to Holland or Germany to frustrate the burgeoning Huguenot-Dissenter alliance.[45]

In addition, England's growing political instability, as evidenced by increasing riots and political plots, stimulated a powerful demand within the Church for political and religious order. Since government officials traditionally viewed religion as an important basis of national, social, moral, and political stability, they viewed the French refugees with alarm despite their Protestant identity. Thus the Church of England hierarchy moved to forestall their possible organization of a refugee denomination in England and, instead, acted to incorporate them within the Anglican church. They used two forms of coercion to do so. First, they attempted to force refugees to accept Anglican ecclesiastical authority. In 1661 the Crown chartered a new Huguenot congregation in London's Savoy district with the stipulation that it use an Anglican liturgy translated into French, accept the authority of the Anglican bishops, and hire only ministers ordained or reordained by Anglican bishops. Later, between 1680 and 1690, James II and William and Mary used the Savoy charter as the model for allowing the incorporation of new congregations, even though they granted some exceptions. Anglicans also demanded obedience from refugee ministers. They required the reordination of all Huguenot clergymen whether or not they served conformist or nonconformist congregations, but they also trained new French ministers. Although refugee ministers far exceeded the number of refugee congregations, Anglican authorities had young, newly ordained ministers available when a pulpit became vacant.[46]

In another form of coercion, the Huguenot aid committees were used to entice refugees into the Church of England. The committees allotted special funds to support unemployed French ministers and, after 1690, aided the new French ministers trained and ordained under Anglican auspices. They also denied aid to refugee ministers who refused Anglican reordination. A parallel policy guided the distribution of aid funds to the French laity. No refugee who had not taken communion in a conformist French congregation could receive funds. To implement the policy, conforming congregations issued tokens to communicants who, in turn, presented them to the aid committees. Since the committees were the only source of financial aid for most refugees, Anglicans knew well that the aid might promote Anglican conformity. As one Anglican bishop put it in 1686, Anglicans might expect that refugees receiving help would "bring along with them good Inclinations . . . to Conformity to the Church of England."[47]

This Anglican pressure worked best among the isolated rural congregations, and twelve of the fifteen refugee congregations beyond London had conformed to the Church of England by 1700. But in London, where most refugees lived, a quite opposite pattern emerged. Many Huguenot congregations founded there before 1690 conformed to the Church of England. But several of them disbanded quickly, while nearly all the congregations formed in the next decade remained independent. As a result, an Anglican survey taken about 1700 revealed that only eight of the fourteen Huguenot congregations in and around London then conformed to the Church of England and that all the conforming ones were small and weak except the so-called Savoy Church. In contrast, London's six independent Huguenot congregations were large, with the mammoth Threadneedle Street Church claiming something close to 3,000 members in 1700.[48]

London's Huguenot laity rejected Anglican conformity because the Anglican liturgical emphasis contrasted sharply with traditional Huguenot worship. Like England's Puritans, France's Huguenots stressed scripture reading and preaching in their worship and minimized the liturgical pomp that they believed symbolized Roman Catholic corruption. The Anglican "middle way," successful for many Englishmen, represented an unacceptable compromise to many lay Huguenots. In 1662 the London exile minister John Durel attempted to resolve obvious language problems in the way toward an Anglican-Huguenot alliance by translating the *Book of Common Prayer* into French. Durel's work appeared under the unfortunate title *La Liturgie* and encountered immediate criticism. In a 1662 sermon Durel addressed himself to complaints by London's Huguenot laity against Anglican conformity and his own translation, *La Liturgie*. Many Huguenots objected that too much Anglican ritual was "taken out of the *Mass-Book*." Anglicans used the sign of the cross in baptism; they celebrated holy days and knelt to take communion; their ministers wore gaudy vestments and used them in too many ritual processions. Durel answered these complaints by arguing that such things were matters of taste and mere national tradition. But he obviously convinced only a minority of England's refugee Huguenots then or later that the worship outlined in *La Liturgie* conformed to Huguenot tradition.[49]

London's large nonconformist refugee congregations could have been the foundation of a French Protestant denomination-in-exile. Yet none ever emerged in late seventeenth- or early eighteenth-century England. One reason for this failure stemmed from the limited relationship between England's Dissenters and the Huguenot refugees in the three decades before 1700 despite deep Anglican worry about this potentially rich association. In fact the Dissenters, still reeling from their Restoration losses even after passage of the Act of Toleration in 1689, never pursued the relationship. Bristol Quakers aided some refugees there in the 1680s but only on an individual basis. Presbyterians asked three

Huguenot ministers to join the Essex Association in 1691—only one did so—and records of other Presbyterian associations and ministers reveal no significant Huguenot-Presbyterian alliance anywhere in the several decades after the Revocation.[50]

The major cause of the Huguenot failure to form a denomination-in-exile turned on effective Anglican control of the Huguenot clergy. The Huguenot laity supported traditional Huguenot worship, as evidenced by the large membership of London's nonconformist French congregations in 1700. But even the ministers of these congregations had been reordained in the Church of England. They used the traditional French Protestant form of worship because Anglican authorities were willing to tolerate it in exchange for their silence on the question of an independent denomination. Although an association of Huguenot ministers was formed in London in 1700, it only arranged speakers for vacant pulpits and, after 1720, usually met only to congratulate British monarchs on their coronations. It never enforced a collective ecclesiastical discipline and, above all, never ordained new ministers. Tellingly, its members came from *both* London's conformist and nonconformist congregations. It was a fraternal rather than a denominational gathering, whose existence revealed how fully the refugee clergy had abandoned any plans to sustain an independent Huguenot denomination in England.[51]

Although the lack of studies of Huguenot assimilation in eighteenth-century England makes it difficult to assess Huguenot refugee life after 1700, a few salient facts emerge. At least through 1720, class differences divided Huguenots in London just as they had done earlier in France. The conformist Savoy congregation contained few weavers and many rich London merchants, goldsmiths, and silversmiths. But the congregations in Spitalfields, both conformist and nonconformist, contained enormous numbers of weavers and only few wealthy members. As was true in 1689, these class differences affected the distribution of aid to needy Huguenots. After 1690 poor refugees continued to receive far less per capita aid than did bourgeois refugees or clergymen. Between 1689 and 1693, for example, clergymen and London's so-called Huguenot "nobility" received nearly £8 in aid per person, while lower-class refugees received only £2.47 in aid per person. These discrepancies fueled bitter debates among the London refugees from the 1690s through the 1720s and severely undercut refugee cohesion in the city.[52]

Religious differences also afflicted the refugees. As in France, the London congregations argued frequently about moral discipline, money, distribution of poor funds, and personal matters. Between 1705 and 1712, these divisions were further complicated by the arrival of the "Cevenol Prophets," later termed the "London Prophets" or the "French Prophets." These were new religious refugees who had been defeated during the War of the Camisards in France's Cévennes mountains. Their millenarian radicalism frightened leaders of London's refugee congregations, in part because the Prophets appealed directly to London's poor refugees. In fact, they attracted their greatest support outside the refugee community. The Cevenol Prophets joined English and German millenarians in a "Philadelphian Movement" whose leaders claimed they could predict the future and raise the dead. The strenuous opposition of London's leading Huguenot laymen and ministers, conformist and nonconformist alike, together with the failure of the Prophets' major claims, kept their Huguenot following small, however.[53]

Yet the Huguenot laity was turning away from its own refugee congregations even as it was rejecting the radical Cevenol Prophets. This is made obvious in the declining use of the London refugee congregations as ritual centers for the performance of baptismal and marriage ceremonies, especially after 1700. At La Patente in Spitalfields marriages declined from 98 in the 1690s to 42 in the 1720s, while baptisms declined from 719 between 1701 and 1710 to 356 in the 1720s. At the conformist Savoy Church marriages declined from 143 between 1701 and 1710 to 72 in the 1730s, while baptisms declined from 407 to 278 in the same decades. Unfortunately, only fragmentary marriage records of London's massive Threadneedle Street Church have survived, but the course of the better-kept baptismal records reveals the rise and fall of the congregation between 1670 and 1740. The Church baptized 1,144 children in the 1670s, 2,591 in the 1690s, and 1,672 in the 1710s. In the 1720s baptisms rose to 2,001 but then dropped to 1,427 in the 1730s and to 1,006 in the 1740s, although most of the city's other Huguenot congregations had disbanded by then.[54]

Thus as early as 1710 the French Protestant community in England offered no better model for refugee cohesion than did the other exile communities in Holland or in Germany. The approaching decline of the refugees' religious institutions could be traced in good part to the failure of Huguenot ministerial leadership amidst an active Anglican campaign of clerical cooptation. The behavior of the Huguenot laity is more difficult to assess, however. Although their abandonment of London's refugee congregations is obvious, its causes and implications remain perplexing. The fate of the refugees after 1700 never has been studied in depth, and we do not know if most refugees moved into the mainstream of English society, joined other Anglican or Methodist congregations, or abandoned organized religion as the refugee congregations disintegrated. Nor do we know if Huguenots took English spouses, moved out of ethnic ghettos like London's Spitalfields, or took employment in new occupations. Still, although the causes of the Huguenot decline in England remain unknown, the obvious decay of community among London Huguenots offered an ominous model for refugees in the British colonies in America.[55]

2 / The Huguenot Emigration to America, 1680–1695

Between 1680 and 1695, British colonists on the North American mainland witnessed the arrival of the first of several European immigrant groups to settle there in significant numbers in the century before the American Revolution. To the colonists who received them, the emigration of the Huguenots might simply have seemed a natural spillover of the massive Huguenot diaspora of the 1680s, bringing at least some survivors of religious and political debacles from the Old World to the New. But for Huguenots, New World emigration significantly complicated the original, seemingly simple flight from religious persecution. It took them across an ocean, not merely to a nearby country, and into new societies, the oldest of which was still just taking shape. It was more dangerous, challenging, and irrevocable. In short, flight to America represented a significant and dangerous new choice to France's beleaguered Huguenots. It transformed refugees into emigrants. Potentially, therefore, it might transform Huguenots as well.

Actually, Huguenots had been coming to America for a century before the Revocation. Between 1550 and 1620, Protestants actively participated in France's national effort to colonize the New World. In 1557 the Protestant Admiral Gaspard de Coligny sponsored a settlement in the bay of Rio de Janeiro, which survived only a year. Its demise stemmed from fears of attacks by Portuguese soldiers and natives; tension between settlers and the colony's eccentric leader, Durand de Villegagnon; Villegagnon's peculiarly timed conversion to Catholicism; his return to France with many colonists; and the Portuguese capture of settlers who remained behind. In 1562 Coligny sponsored another settlement that was intended for Florida but was finally located near what later became southern South Carolina. It too failed, for reasons similar to those that destroyed Jamestown a half-century later—poor planning, concern for gold rather than agriculture, bitter relations with American natives, and leaders with little capacity to lead. In 1564 Protestants established a third settlement called La Caroline at the mouth of the St. Johns River in Florida. This colony also included women and children. But signs of permanence and success made it a Spanish target. In an attack in September 1565 the Spanish butchered Huguenots who surrendered and enslaved those who unsuccessfully resisted. The massacre ended French Protestant efforts to settle in America as part of the national French policy of New World colonization.[1]

The collapse of the sixteenth-century Huguenot colonies and the failure of an apparent plan to settle Huguenot refugees in Virginia in the 1620s, about which nothing else is known, reduced Huguenot emigration to the New World before the Revocation to a trickle of individuals. Between 1560 and 1680 small numbers of Huguenot merchants, tradesmen, and artisans drifted into French America where they intermixed with Catholic settlers. Their small numbers gave Catholic authorities little concern. In Canada they never formed separate settlements of their own nor, apparently, did they form separate organized communities within Catholic settlements. No Huguenot ministers lived or preached there, and no Huguenot congregations were formed. French authorities in Canada never even reported rumors of organized worship among Huguenots despite Catholic paranoia about Protestant secrecy. This social situation had paradoxical consequences. Although isolation forestalled persecution of Canada's few Huguenots, the lack of congregational worship also dissipated their faith. Thus through the 1760s, French Canadian authorities each year obtained small numbers of Protestant conversions to Catholicism without resorting to the repressive means still being employed in France.[2]

Other French Protestants lived in the Caribbean although just how many is not known. St. Christopher had the largest Huguenot population. Charles Washington Baird found that seventy-one Huguenots were reported on a 1671 St. Christopher's census; they settled in the British colonies after the Revocation. Huguenot clergymen may have visited the island as early as 1650, and the colony apparently supported a Huguenot congregation in the 1670s. Smaller numbers of Protestants lived on Guadeloupe and Martinique—Baird counted twenty-one from Guadeloupe and thirteen from Martinique who later came to America—although apparently they formed no congregations there. Between 1680 and 1685, nearly all these Protestants fled to British America as the repression at home spread to the colonies. Thus the governor of Canada reported, with some exaggeration, that between fifty and sixty Protestants from St. Christopher and Martinique had already settled in New York.[3]

Between 1686 and 1689 Louis XIV tried out a policy of deporting French Protestants to the colonies. Government documents indicate that as many as 500 Huguenot adults and children were shipped there, most of them from Languedoc, Saintonge, and Poitou. What happened to them is not fully known. Many apparently died on the voyage to the Caribbean or soon after they arrived; some escaped by finding captains willing to return them to Europe and even France; others remained. The "Code Noir" of 1685 stipulated that Protestants would be punished for expressing their religious views publicly, but it did not require them to convert to Catholicism. This anomaly reflected the indolence of French colonial officials, who allowed many deportees to retain their Protestant faith. Again, however, isolation and lack of organized worship took their toll of Protestant allegiances as children of the original deportees frequently became Catholics. As a result, although colonial officials had granted the deportees *de facto* toleration, few of their children retained their Protestantism after 1730.[4]

French-speaking Protestants also settled in New England and New Amsterdam before 1680. Although many historians term these settlers Huguenots, most of them were French-speaking residents of the Channel Islands of Guernsey and Jersey or Walloons from what now is Belgium and parts of northern France. Few were from the traditional areas of Protestant strength in western and southern France. Between ten and fifteen such families from Jersey and Guernsey settled in Salem between 1650 and 1680. They included the well-known merchant Philip English, who anglicized his name from "L'Anglois," and others named Beadle, Brown, Feveryear, and Muzury. As one recent historian describes them, most had lived in the Channel Islands for at least a generation before their American arrival. But a few had more immediate French origins. Rachel Dellaclose, for example, left La Rochelle in 1660, lived in Jersey for a decade, and then moved to Salem, where she joined the First Church on the basis of letters she brought from Protestant ministers in France.[5]

The Walloons were concentrated in New Amsterdam. A Walloon, Jean Vigne, was apparently the first white child born on Long Island, and Walloons probably constituted a fifth of New Amsterdam's population by 1650. Thereafter the French-speaking population of the colony become more mixed. Between 1650 and 1660 Waldensians from eastern France settled on Staten Island—how many is unknown—while in 1658, Protestants from northwest France, who first had moved to the German Palatinate, migrated again to America and settled in the Dutch town of Kingston, sixty miles north of New Amsterdam on the Hudson River.[6]

The earliest Huguenot refugees in the colonies did not form significant refugee communities. David Konig argues that the "Essex 'French,'" the Channel Islanders who settled in Salem in Massachusetts's Essex County, maintained at least some degree of ethnic cohesion and exclusivity in the seventeenth century. They lived together on the south side of Salem, imported their indentured servants from Jersey, and sustained a special reputation for sharp business practices, one sign of which was their frequent resort to lawsuits to enforce contracts and to collect debts. Indeed, bitterness over the business practices of Philip English (formerly L'Anglois) may have encouraged Salem village residents to accuse English's wife of witchcraft during the 1692 Salem witch trials. But the number of refugees in Salem was small, and their distinctiveness is more apparent than real. Granting that Philip English's business reputation may have extended to that of his fellow Jerseyans, we still would need a study of business practices among all Salem merchants to know whether his behavior was in fact unusual. Moreover, other evidence suggests that the ethnic cohesion the group attained was fragmentary at best. For example, the Essex French exhibited little exclusivity in choosing spouses. Those we know about divide almost evenly in their choice of English or French spouses. Hence the settlers seem

to have rejected the endogamous patterns in marriage traditionally associated with ethnic or religious cohesion. Even more
important is the simple fact that they never organized a separate
Jersey or Guernsey congregation.[7]

In New York national or ethnic cohesion flourished best among
geographically isolated settlers. New Amsterdam's French-
speaking residents exhibited little inclination toward exclusivity
before 1680. Some of the town's Dutch ministers apparently
preached in French occasionally, although it is not known how
often. But they never encouraged formation of a separate
congregation, and the relatively small population of French-
speaking laity apparently never asked for one. In fact, these
French-speaking Walloons may have been no more religious than
New Amsterdam's Dutch residents. The only one whose personal
religious views are known to us appears to have moved past
Protestantism to skepticism. A traveler described Jacques
Cortelyou as a multilingual Walloon who had studied philosophy,
mathematics, and surveying. Reputedly he was "a good Cartesian
and not a good Christian," who lived "by reason and justice only"
and did "better by these principles than most people in these parts
do, who bear the name of Christians or pious persons."[8]

By contrast rural French-speaking settlers sustained greater
interest in things French. The Walloons and Waldensians living
on Staten Island in the 1660s asked the Classis in Amsterdam for
a bilingual minister who could preach in French and Dutch. By
the mid-1680s Staten Island's French-speaking population had
grown sufficiently from natural increase and the arrival of new
refugees to sustain a separate French congregation. It is not
known when the congregation first met, but it existed by at least
1696 when David de Bonrepos left New Rochelle to become its
minister.[9]

The Walloons who first settled in Kingston in 1658, purchased
40,000 acres twenty years later in 1678 and moved up the Hudson
River valley to form the settlement of New Paltz. Most of the
founders originally came from northwest France and first had
fled to the Palatinate before migrating to America. Although
they left France long before Louis XIV began his final drive
against the Protestants, they did not have a French minister until
the eve of the Revocation. Until then they used Dutch ministers

sent by the Amsterdam Classis. But in 1683 they acquired the part-time services of Pierre Daillé, who was serving a new French congregation at Fort George in New York City. Daillé's patronymic was well known in French Protestant history, and he may have been related to the great mid-seventeenth century theologian, Jean Daillé. He was a graduate and faculty member of the French seminary at Saumur and visited the New Paltz congregation twice a year between 1683 and 1692 to preach, perform marriages, and administer baptisms. Yet these settlers remained spiritually and physically distant from the refugees of the Revocation arriving after 1680. No new refugees settled in New Paltz, and the village's old Walloon and Waldensian residents maintained ecclesiastical ties with the Dutch Reformed Church of New York City and the Amsterdam Classis; they never established new cooperative relationships with the new French congregations in New York City, New Rochelle, and Staten Island.[10]

It is difficult to determine how many Huguenots settled in America between 1680 and 1700. Much evidence of their emigration, especially shipping and arrival lists, has been lost. Only one early shipping list remains, naming some ninety adults and children about to sail for South Carolina in 1679 on the *Richmond*. The only other significant lists describe the later refugees who settled in Manakin in Virginia in 1700 and whose long residence in Europe after the Revocation made them considerably different from their predecessors. But there are no shipping or arrival lists describing the great bulk of Huguenots who arrived in the 1680s in the decade immediately surrounding the Revocation. It is thus necessary to use other means to find out how many refugees came to America, what kind of groups they traveled in, and from what French provinces they originated.

The lack of direct evidence about the Huguenot migration has encouraged historians to exaggerate its size. Baird's antiquarian proclivities probably saved him from making such an error, however. He devoted nearly half of his *Huguenot Emigration to America* to a detailed listing of individual Huguenots whose names appeared on colonial tax lists, deeds, and other documents. But he never estimated the total size of the Huguenot migration. In contrast, twentieth-century historians have been less cautious and frequently have estimated the size of the migration at between 10,000 and 15,000 refugees, although without documentation. A systematic study suggests that these estimates are at least five times too large.[12]

The approximate size of the Huguenot migration to America can be determined by analyzing the Huguenot population of the colonies between 1695 and 1706. A fortunate historical accident has left censuses and naturalization records that give us a close indication of the Huguenot populations of New York and South Carolina in these years. Reasonable estimates of the Huguenot population also can be made for colonies that received smaller numbers of refugees. Together, they comprise a convenient index of the size of the earlier Huguenot migration.

At least one census for each New York settlement that reportedly received a significant number of Huguenot refugees survives for the years between 1698 and 1706. In New Rochelle a 1698 census counted 98 French adults and 86 children, as well as 43 black slaves. A census for the same year counts 64 adults and 57 children in New Paltz, a few of whom may not have been Walloons. A New York City census of 1703 names 86 households headed by French-surnamed persons containing 155 adults and 162 children. Finally, an undated Staten Island census, probably compiled in 1706, lists the names of 100 French adults and 72 children. In all, these documents record 804 Huguenots—427 adults and 377 children—in New York roughly a decade after the Revocation, some of them born there and, thus, not immigrants.[13]

Two other sources describe the number of Huguenots in South Carolina in 1697 and 1699. One is a census of Huguenots dated March 14, 1699, found in the papers of the peripatetic colonial official Sir Edmund Andros. It counted 438 Huguenots living "this day in Carolina"; 195 in Charlestown and 243 in three country locations: 31 at "Goes Creek," 101 on the "eastern branch [of the] Cooper River," and 111 at the "French Church, Santee River." A second count can be extracted from two lists of French adults and children who had applied for naturalization under a 1697 South Carolina statute. One, entitled "List of French and Swiss refugees in Carolina desiring English naturalization," named applicants throughout the colony. A second, entitled "List of Santee residents," named applicants living along the Santee River.

Some South Carolina Huguenots probably did not appear on either list because they had received denization and its legal privileges in London. Yet the correspondence between the 1699 census and these two 1697 naturalization lists is remarkable. Removing duplicates, the two 1697 lists named 396 Huguenot applicants for naturalization, 235 adults and 161 children, only 42 fewer than the 438 Huguenots counted in the 1699 census. Since a check of all South Carolina land grants between 1680 and 1700 adds the names of only 16 adult males to those already on the two 1697 lists, it seems obvious that the latter named nearly all the male Huguenot household heads then in the colony and may have excluded only a few newly widowed women and orphans.[14]

The number of Huguenots living in other American colonies in 1700 was also small. No more than 75 adults ever were involved with the two New England Huguenot agricultural settlements— 25 at Oxford in Massachusetts and 50 at Narragansett in Rhode Island—and some of these refugees moved to Boston or New York after both settlements collapsed in the 1690s. By 1700 New England probably counted no more than 200 Huguenot children and adults in its population. Certainly no more than 25 then lived in Rhode Island, even fewer lived in Connecticut, and no more than 150 resided in Boston. Indeed, the last estimate probably is overly generous since a 1695 list of Boston residents named only 18 French-surnamed adult males then in the city.[15]

Genealogists have found some Huguenots in Pennsylvania and New Jersey in the colonial period. But many, especially in Pennsylvania, arrived after 1710 as part of the large German emigration to America. Their parents and grandparents first settled in Germany during the time of the Revocation, and it was conditions there that brought them to America in the early eighteenth century. Before 1700 Pennsylvania received fewer than five or six Huguenot families, a generous estimate that includes persons given aid in London to go to "Pennsylvanie" but whose arrival actually is undocumented. New Jersey contained between twenty-five and thirty French-speaking families living near New York City in 1700, many of whom were descended from Walloons who had emigrated to the New Netherlands before its English capture in 1664; only a few New Jersey Huguenots appear to have come to America in the decade surrounding the Revocation.[16]

All the data indicate that the Huguenot migration to America was far smaller than historians have previously believed. Census figures, naturalization lists, and other available seventeenth-century documents suggest that no more than 1,500 Huguenots lived in the American colonies by 1700. Of course, some of these persons were Huguenot childen born in America after the arrival of their parents; conversely, the census could not record emigrating Huguenots who had indeed arrived in America but died before the censuses were taken. Yet it is unlikely that in 1700 the deceased Huguenot immigrants outnumbered the American-born Huguenots. Thus the most reasonable estimate would place the Huguenot migration to the colonies at no more than the size of the Huguenot population in America in 1700, about 1,500 persons and certainly no more than 2,000 persons.[17]

Not all the Huguenots who came to America chose the journey freely. One account of the dangers and difficulties is the remarkable letter Judith Giton wrote in the later 1680s from South Carolina to a brother in Germany.[18] Giton's journey to America began with a simple desire to flee Catholic persecution in France. She lived in the village of la Voulte in Languedoc with her widowed mother and two brothers, Peter and Louis. In 1682 royal troops appeared in the village to enforce the anti-Protestant restrictions Louis XIV had issued before the Revocation. Like other Protestants, Giton "suffered through eight months [of] exactions and quartering ... by the soldiery, for the religion, with much evil," and she resolved "to go out of France by night, and leave the soldiers in bed." With her mother and brothers, she first hid in Romans in Dauphiné for ten days and then traveled to Lyons, Dijon, and Metz. In the last town she sought out a Protestant woman her mother had once known but discovered that the woman was dead. Worse, the woman's son-in-law threatened to denounce Giton, her mother, and brothers if they asked him to aid them. So, they left quickly for Cologne, which had become a major reception place for Huguenot refugees.

Once abroad, mother and daughter argued bitterly with Judith's brother Pierre about their future. They wanted him to visit another brother thirty miles away, but he was obsessed with a desire to go to America, a longing stimulated by one of the several French-language pamphlets South Carolina proprietors already were circulating among Huguenot refugees on the Continent.

Thus Pierre Giton refused to visit his brother, "having nothing but Carolina on his thoughts, for fear of losing any chance of getting there."

Much to her dismay, Pierre never abandoned his scheme. He took Judith and Louis Giton and their mother to Amsterdam and then to London where they booked passage to Charlestown after a three-month wait. The voyage was a disaster. Mother Giton died from scarlet fever. A stop in Bermuda for repairs resulted in the jailing of the ship captain, and the passengers had to hire another captain to take them to South Carolina. Once in America, the price of safety was further hardship and even death. Louis Giton died of a fever eighteen months after landing in South Carolina. Judith survived only after experiencing much "sickness, pestilence, famine, poverty, [and] very hard work. I was in this country a full six months, without tasting bread, ... whilst I worked the ground, like a slave." Despite this, she wrote that "God has had pity on me, and has changed my lot to one more happy. Glory be unto him."

Other refugees also made the decision to come to America only after first leaving France. Certainly this was true of many who settled intially in London. For Judith Giton, the city was little more than a resting place before her brother took her to South Carolina. But for others, London became a place where additional changes in life and circumstances occurred before they departed for America. For example, Jacques Bargeau, Louis Bongrand, Jacques Flandreau, and Jean Tartarin all married in London before they departed for America. Large numbers of later American settlers added children to their families while still in London. These included Auguste Grasset, Jean Melet, and Elie Nezereau who subsequently settled in New York; Jean Aunant, Isaac Baton, Antoine Boureau, Louis Pasquereau, Daniel Perdriau, Isaac Porcher, Louis Thibou, Jacques Varein, and Pierre Videau, who settled in South Carolina; and Pierre Baudouin, Pierre Chaperon, Abraham Sauvage, and André Sigourney, who went to Massachusetts. Many refugees witnessed marriage and baptismal rites for old friends and relatives in one of the London French churches or presented certificates of orthodoxy in the refugee congregations. At least thirty-nine refugees and their families received aid from the Threadneedle Street congregation between 1681 and 1687, after they had arrived in London but before they decided to go to America. Of the thirty-nine, eleven went to New York City, eleven to South Carolina, six to Narragansett, six to New Rochelle, four to Oxford, and one to Boston.[19]

How and when Huguenots settled in America reflected some of the peculiarities of the late seventeenth-century English colonial system. No central imperial agency encouraged, directed, or controlled American colonial immigration. The Lords of Trade, the Privy Council committee that reviewed and implemented colonial policy in America, was far more concerned with what it believed was chaos in government than with the relatively minor problem of immigration. Thus just a year after Louis XIV revoked the Edict of Nantes, the Lords canceled the colonial charters of New York, Massachusetts, Rhode Island, Plymouth Bay Colony, and Connecticut to create a short-lived Dominion of New England to govern the northern colonies. But if the Lords never developed a colonial immigration policy, they also never prevented or discouraged immigration to the colonies. The Huguenot refugees were as free to go to America as their finances, successful planning, and own will allowed.[20]

Certainly some Englishmen wished to see them go. The English committees that aided refugees in London also sent many to Holland. An anonymous petitioner to the bishop of London suggested in the 1680s that the committees send others to Carolina. The refugees were to be shipped out in groups of twenty to thirty persons when the relief committees deemed it impossible to house them in England. Although the committees never implemented the suggestion, they did help refugees who indicated a desire to go to America. In 1688 the London committee claimed that it already had sent 600 Huguenots to the "West Indies." Actually, the available records indicate that it helped about 200 refugee families to settle in America by 1690. The Threadneedle Street accounts list payments to eighteen persons to go to America between 1681 and 1685. The accounts of the London relief committee are lost for the years 1685 and 1686, but those from March 1687 to 1690 list contributions to 148 individuals and several families of unknown size to travel to America—a total of some 160 persons. Among the many Huguenots who indicated a desire to go to South Carolina in 1687, for example, were the minister Elie Prioleau, Jonas Bonhoste, Jean Melet, Mary Sauvageau, Steven Serre, Louis Guion, and Peter and Daniel Guillon. In 1688 and 1689, more refugees received aid to go to Boston, New York, and Virginia.[21]

Occupation and class affected the amount of aid each refugee received. The committee's 1688 published report claimed that the emigrating refugees "had a very large and comfortable Assistance and Relief." But this was not true for everyone. For example, refugees identified in the records as persons of "Middle Quality," like Jérémie Cothonneau, Ambroise Sicard, and Daniel Jouet, received between £25 and £40 to transport themselves and their families to South Carolina. Ministers also fared well. Elie Prioleau received £8 to transport only himself to Charlestown while Pierre Peiret, who would become the French minister in New York City, received £50 to take himself, his wife, two children, and two servants to what the committee believed was "New Jersey." Similarly, Dina and Magdalen de la Rochefoucauld, described by the committee as "Persons of Quality," received £60 "to goe to Boston." But the committee proved less generous with others. Peter Le Sade, "Ploughman," received only £3 to take himself, his wife, and two children to the colonies. Most other refugees received between £2 and £4 for their American passage.[22]

Many of the Huguenots who emigrated to America probably came in response to pamphlets advertising the colonies, especially the new proprietary colonies founded after the 1660 Restoration. Oddly enough that advertising failed to bring them to Pennsylvania, a colony that should have proved attractive to Huguenots. William Penn himself studied with Moise Amyraut at the French Protestant academy at Saumur between 1663 and 1664 and was the only leading English Protestant to observe pre-Revocation French Protestantism so closely. The early stages of the Huguenot exodus from France coincided with Penn's acquisition of Pennsylvania, and Penn wrote the Quaker James Harrison in 1681 that he was "like to have many from fra[nce]" in the colony. Certainly Penn attempted to attract Huguenots. In 1682 he negotiated to bring a group of refugees at Canterbury to Pennsylvania, and in 1684 his agents at The Hague and Rotterdam issued at least three French-language pamphlets advertising the colony to Holland's escalating Huguenot refugee population. Nor was Penn the only

Quaker to take an interest in the refugees. In the 1680s Bristol Friends offered financial aid to Huguenots in the city, and in 1685 George Fox sent French translations of several Quaker tracts to Huguenots recently settled in South Carolina.[23]

Yet all these apparent advantages were not seized, and some mystery surrounds the actual relationship of Penn, Pennsylvania, and the Huguenots. Recent scholars are perplexed by Penn's experiences at Saumur. A thorough lack of documentation makes it impossible to determine what he did and learned there, and the potentially important Huguenot influence on Penn reduces itself to a matter of mere conjecture. Likewise, it is all but impossible to explain why so few Huguenot refugees settled in Pennsylvania before 1700 despite its obvious attractions. Except for Penn's Philadelphia gardener André Doz and perhaps three or four others, the few additional Huguenots who did settle there before 1700 drifted in from other colonies, usually New York. Later eighteenth-century Huguenot settlers there usually came as part of the large German emigration to Pennsylvania, their fathers and grandfathers first having settled in Germany in the 1680s.[24]

The causes of this Huguenot rejection of Pennsylvania remain puzzling. William Penn's friendship with the Catholic Stuarts should not have disturbed them since nearly half the Huguenots who came to America settled in New York, then the personal possession of James, Duke of York. Nor should religious scruples or Pennsylvania's Quaker identity have bothered Huguenots. France's Protestant refugees settled in an astonishing variety of European societies and in American colonies as different as late Puritan Massachusetts and a profoundly secular South Carolina. Indeed, Penn's offers of religious toleration explicitly made to Huguenot refugees in his French-language promotion tracts only deepen the mystery of their absence from the colony.

In contrast, the substantial early Huguenot settlement in South Carolina stimulated a promotion literature that worked. In 1679 the South Carolina proprietors accepted a proposal from two Huguenot refugees, René Petit and Jacob Guerard, to settle eighty refugee families in the colony who were "skilled in the Manufacture of Silkes, oiles, Wines etc." The refugees would expand the infant colony's tiny population and increase its consumption of English commodities, while the proprietors would be doing their part in keeping the Huguenots from having to return "to Babilonn for not being able to find in England such employment as might be agreeable to their skill and industry." The arrival of the Huguenots encouraged the proprietors to print a promotion tract written by the ship captain who brought them to Charlestown, *Carolina, or a Description of the Present State of that Country* (London, 1682), and, like Penn, to print two French-language promotion tracts directed to Huguenots in Holland, *Nouvelle relation de la Caroline* (The Hague, ca. 1685) and *Plan pour former un établissement en Caroline* (The Hague, 1686). These tracts circulated in both Holland and England and stimulated the 1687 and 1688 departure of Huguenot refugees to South Carolina that was funded, in part, by the Huguenot relief committee in London.[25]

Not all Huguenots were happy in South Carolina, however. Judith Gilton's private letter outlined a life of misery there, and an anonymous French pamphlet printed about 1685 claimed that the 1683 tract *Nouvelle Relation de la Caroline* deceived readers about the colony. In fact it described South Carolina as the "least agreeable colony" in America. Rains "cover the country" and drown the cattle. The artificial aristocracy of "Landgraves, Cassiques, Cantons, Manors and Baronies" made a "great show in an empty brain." Sickness induced by the warm climate turned Charlestown into a "great charnelhouse." Prices were high, planting difficult, and profits slim. Yet the anonymous French author did not encourage Huguenots to go elsewhere. Instead, he turned to the problem of religious loyalty. His fellow Protestants should "take great care not to leave their religion behind," he wrote; they should "retain it in such purity and sincerity, that they may render the places to which they may come, better than those whence they came, and be more assured of its permanent enjoyment."[26]

The Huguenot refugees who settled in America in the 1680s resembled the exiles they left behind in England in several important ways. They too originated largely from west and northwest France. Baird traced most of the known Huguenots at Narragansett, Oxford, Boston, New Rochelle, and New York City to Saintonge, Poitou, and Normandy and the remaining number to Bretagne, Picardy, and the Île de France. The South Carolina naturalization lists of 1697 confirm this pattern. Fully 56 percent of the Huguenots who described their home provinces on these lists came from the west of France. Another 16 percent came from northern France, 14.5 percent from central France, and although none came from eastern France, several emigrated from French-speaking Switzerland. A larger percentage of the American exiles came from southern France than was true of those in London, however. Refugees from Languedoc and the Cévennes mountain region of southern France comprised about 6 percent of the members in the London refugee congregations in comparison to 13 percent of the refugees on the 1697 South Carolina naturalization lists, and Baird found surprising numbers of them in the Huguenot settlements of the northern colonies.[27]

Disparities of wealth characterized in the refugee population in America just as they did in London. Some Huguenots carried modest, even significant, wealth to the colonies. Daniel Huger and Pierre Gaillard brought servants to South Carolina and received land allotments from the colony's government for doing so. The DeLanceys, Faneuils, and Droilhets became leading merchants after arriving in New York City and Boston. Most refugees were poor, however. In 1687 and 1689 a few settlers at the Narragansett settlement in Rhode Island contributed as much as thirty-five shillings to Ezéchiel Carré's quarterly ministerial salary. But nearly half the refugees could pay Carré only in crops. Some of their crops were worth only two shillings, and some refugees had harvested so little that they could pay Carré only in labor.[28]

New York City's 1695 tax list (see Table 8 in Chapter 5) reveals an equally striking gap between rich and poor refugees. Although some Huguenots had resided there since 1680, New York still lacked a Huguenot middle class. Huguenots constituted 11 percent of city taxpayers and owned 11 percent of its taxable wealth, but they claimed this seemingly equitable share of the city's wealth in a very peculiar way. Six of the sixty-seven refugees taxed in 1695 owned fully 50 percent of all the wealth ascribed to Huguenots. In contrast, the poorest half of the city's Huguenots owned only 8.5 percent of the group's aggregate wealth. This made poor Huguenots poorer than English or Dutch taxpayers in the bottom half of their tax brackets because each of these groups owned at least 11 percent of the wealth ascribed to their ethnic group.[29]

The occupational spectrum of Huguenot refugees in America reveals the first significant departure from the patterns that characterized London's refugees. The most obvious difference centers on the apparent failure of Huguenot cloth workers to migrate to America. To be sure, some refugees brought these crafts to the colonies. The aid records of the Threadneedle Street Church name several cloth workers who came to the colonies before 1700: Laurant Cornifleau, a chamey dresser; André Doz, a mercer (who became William Penn's gardener); Jean Laurans, a narrow silk weaver; André Naudin, a linen weaver; Antoine Poitevin, a mercer; and Jacques Soulice, a serge maker. But since in the 1690s large numbers of cloth workers still were arriving in London where they comprised half or more of the city's refugees, it is obvious that the predominance of agriculture in the colonies and lack of cloth production facilities there kept most Huguenot cloth workers in England and out of the New World.[30]

Other skilled refugees did not migrate to the New World in proportion to their numbers in London either, despite their potential usefulness to the colonial economy. Again, the aid records of London's Threadneedle Street Church identify several skilled Huguenot craftsmen who came to the colonies: the anchorsmiths Charles Fauchereau and Pierre Poinsett (South Carolina); the shoemakers Noé Royer (South Carolina), Etienne Doucinet (New York), and André Sigourney (Oxford, then Boston): sailmakers François and Jean Vincent (New Rochelle); schoolmasters Auguste Grasset (New York City) and Sanson Gallais (Narragansett); the laborer Jean Doublet (New York City); and seamen Pierre Tillou and Jean Vigneau (New York City). Still, the great numbers of skilled refugees who flooded into London in the 1680s point up their relative paucity in America, where many of them, especially those who settled in South Carolina, ultimately also changed their occupations.[31]

The Huguenots who emigrated to America were drawn from the younger segment of the Huguenot population that left France in the 1680s. The advanced age of many refugees crowding into the exile centers on the Continent and in England is one of the major signs that their migration was involuntary. In proportion to the rest, extraordinary numbers of the refugees in London were over fifty-five years of age when they arrived in the city, and they severely strained London's charity resources. Geneva's city death records also suggest a surprising number of old people entering the city to escape Catholic persecution in eastern and southern France. The median age of death for Huguenot adults in Geneva between 1685 and 1690 was fifty years, and many refugees who died there in the late 1680s were already in their seventies and eighties when they arrived.[32]

Widespread indirect evidence suggests that if old people dominated the Huguenot exodus from France, young people dominated the Huguenot migration to America. If so, this is a major indication that a significant element of choice, rather than force, brought these refugees to America after they successfully escaped from France. One small piece of evidence comes from the Narragansett death records, the only colonial documents that list exact ages of death for deceased Huguenots. In contrast to the pattern at Geneva, adults dying at Narragansett were young. Only five adults died there between 1686 and 1691, but the oldest was only forty-three and the other four were in their twenties and thirties.[33]

The 1698 New Rochelle census also points toward a young Huguenot migration to America. In 1698 most village adults were only forty or fifty years old, and nearly all the village's children were under the age of ten. Of course, the census could not record old adults and young children who died before 1698. But the virtual absence of any adults over fifty or of youths between ten and twenty suggests that, unless they all died from some unrecorded disease or disastrous circumstance before 1698, none of this age group settled in New Rochelle. Instead, in 1688 the new village must have been settled by young adults, most of whom were recently married with either very young children less than two years of age or with no children at all.[34]

The 1697 South Carolina naturalization lists suggest that young refugees also settled that colony. The lists do not name Huguenots who died in South Carolina before 1697 nor do they list exact ages of refugees, as did the New Rochelle census. But by describing the birthplace of all children seeking naturalization they provide a rough guide to the age of their parents at the time of their arrival in the colony. Three characteristics of the population stand out in these lists. First, 68 percent of the married or previously married household heads sought naturalization for dependent children still in their households, indicating that the adults had been relatively young when they arrived nearly two decades earlier in the 1680s. Second, fully 65.8 percent of all children named on the lists were born in South Carolina rather than Europe. Only 18.1 percent of the children were born in France, and only 6.5 percent were born elsewhere in Europe, mainly in England and Holland. As at New Rochelle, this suggests that Huguenots who brought children to South Carolina were young and newly married. They may have had a first or second child in the Old World but most of their children were born in America.[35]

Undoubtedly some of the Huguenot emigrants were middle-aged refugees whose spouses and children sometimes failed to survive their exile in London or their early years in America. According to the records, Antoine Boureau and his wife Jeanne Beraut baptized a son Isaac in London's Threadneedle Street Church on March 11, 1685, but named only a girl, Jeanne, on the 1697 South Carolina naturalization list, Isaac presumably having died in the intervening dozen years. Between 1675 and 1678, the Rouen linen weaver Jacques Varein and his wife Suzanne Horry baptized two little girls named Suzanne (one had died) and a boy named Jacques in London's Threadneedle Street Church. But Suzanne Horry appears on the 1697 naturalization lists as a widow with two children, both born in South Carolina. By 1697 she had lost her husband and her English-born children and lived in South Carolina with only her American-born children.[36]

The youth of the American Huguenots and additional evidence on their London exile experience suggest that the Huguenots came to America in a two-stage process of exile and emigration. In the first stage, French Protestants chose to leave their homes rather than conform to Catholicism or resist the Revocation by force or deception. In the second stage, refugees in exile centers such as London chose their permanent places of residence. In doing so, prospects for material opportunity became as important as freedom from persecution. Certainly this was the understanding of the South Carolina and Pennsylvania proprietors who were attempting to lure Huguenots to settle in their colonies. Of course they promised religious toleration to the Huguenots, but they also filled their pamphlets with exuberant descriptions of the material benefits Huguenots would enjoy when they settled in America.[37]

The dismal experience of the refugees in London made the literature on American colonization attractive to the younger Huguenot exiles. Having fled their native land with few possessions and crowded into a city already teeming with poor Englishmen, the Huguenot refugees faced a bleak future in London. The aid accounts of the Threadneedle Street Church document the frustrations of a surprising number of individuals who finally emigrated to America. Pierre Cante received sixteen grants from the Church's aid committee, one of which took him to Ipswich in an unsuccessful search for work and housing, after which he sailed for Massachusetts. The Rouen linen weaver Jacques Varein received seven grants from the committee and journeyed to Essex before he moved to South Carolina in 1681 and 1682. The committee gave the chamey dresser Laurant Cornifleau twelve grants between 1681 and 1685, including three for "stockings and shoes," before he departed for New York City. Jean Doublet, manual worker, received twenty-nine grants between November 1681 and September 1682 to support his wife and child before he too left for New York. The committee employed the La Rochelle shoemaker Etienne Doucinet to make shoes for poor refugees in 1682, but he subsequently had to ask for thirty-eight grants totaling £12 to support his family and bury a daughter before he left London to settle in New York City. The Soubize anchorsmith Charles Faucheraud apparently spirited some assets out of France because he arrived in London in September 1681 with a wife, three children, and a maid. But lacking work, his assets disappeared, and within a month he had to ask the committee to furnish a straw bed for his sick wife and his children. He worked briefly for the East India Company but soon had to ask the committee for further support. In March 1682 he found another job and repaid £2 of the relief aid he received earlier. But by 1683 he was in South Carolina farming land that the provincial government gave him for migrating to the colony.[38]

The personal history of Auguste Grasset reveals some of the agony that touched refugees long after their flight from France. Grasset, a teacher of mathematics and navigation, arrived in

London in October 1681 with a wife and five young children between one and eight years of age. Within a month two of his children died, and the aid committee at Threadneedle Street Church alloted him ten shillings for their burial. Grasset secured twenty-five grants to support his family in the next two years. Then in March 1683, three days after baptizing a newborn son in the Church, the committee gave Grasset £7 to go to "Nouvelle Angleterre." He traveled instead to New York City. There, the outward circumstances of his life improved substantially and in 1695 the New York City tax collectors assessed his personal property at a value of £20. This placed him above one-third of city residents, although like most New Yorkers he lived in rented rooms. By 1709 Grasset ranked above two-thirds of all city taxpayers despite the fact that he still did not own a house. But if Grasset prospered in New York, he also became a victim of one of the New World's unique institutions—slavery. At that time captive Africans comprised nearly 20 percent of the New York City population, and in 1712 a rebelling slave ran a knife through Grasset's neck killing him in one of the acts that began the city's first slave revolt.[39]

By 1690, young, acquisitive Huguenot refugees had settled in three principal colonial cities, Boston, Charlestown, and New York City, and had organized communities in seven rural settings: Narragansett in Rhode Island, Oxford in Massachusetts, New Rochelle and Staten Island in New York, and "Santee" and "Orange Quarter" in South Carolina. If they fled religious persecution in France and poverty in Britain, they would discover that their individual search for material success would prosper more readily than their collective search for religious stability. By 1696 the rural refugee settlements at Narragansett and Oxford had collapsed, and the New Rochelle settlement had experienced considerable turmoil. Worse, the character of these problems suggested that the bitterness and tension that too frequently afflicted refugee life in London and Amsterdam also crossed the Atlantic to afflict Huguenots in America as well.

The Narragansett settlement collapsed first. It was organized in London in 1685–86, at least in part, by a minister from the isle of Ré named Ezéchiel Carré. Carré and refugees from Saintonge,

Poitou, and Normandy purchased land in Rhode Island's Narragansett country south and east of Providence from London agents of the Atherton Company, a New England firm whose title to the property had been disputed since the 1660s, and they arrived in Boston in the fall of 1686. Just as some English Quakers charged that Friends who emigrated to Pennsylvania were placing material rewards above spiritual ones, some Huguenots in London also apparently criticized Carré and his Narragansett colony for seeking material rewards in the New World. Certainly Carré took considerable care to defend the Narragansett enterprise in the preface to its records. Carré insisted that he and his followers had "come here to seek freedom for our Religion. That is the only reason that has brought us to this place, and the only condition under which we have accepted this new settlement."[40]

Unfortunately the Narragansett refugees soon lost title to their land. In 1688, two years after settling in Narragansett, the Crown voided the Atherton Company's land claim. Since the settlement's land deed was based on the claim, the decision had the effect of turning the refugees into squatters. They remained on the property for three years while they attempted to secure legal title to the land. But neighboring English settlers claimed it for themselves, harassing the refugees, and when the Huguenots proved unable to regain title to their property, they abandoned it in the spring or early summer of 1691.[41]

Severe internal difficulties also ravaged the colony and complicated its legal problems. Many refugees who received land allotments at Narragansett either lacked capital to till their farms or did not manage their lands well. As a result, they scarcely could support themselves, much less contribute to Ezéchiel Carré's salary. In November 1687 Isaac Girard deeply embarrassed settlement leaders by begging in Providence, and in 1688 several settlers claimed that they could no longer pay Carré. Disputes about discipline and morality that were altogether too familiar to Huguenot congregations both in France and in their European exile centers also occurred at Narragansett. In June 1687 the elders reminded residents to kneel and to keep their heads covered during prayer. In November of the same year they warned them against defaming the Sabbath. In January 1688 "packs of cards" were found in the colony. Since cards stimulated blasphemy and trickery—fortune tellers and occult healers used them—the elders voted to bring offenders before the consistory to hear the church discipline on the subject, hoping that "these two strokes falling at the same time will make more impression." But laxity continued. In February 1689 the elders denounced parents who wanted to abandon the use of godmothers and godfathers at baptism, "which is accepted in France," and to sponsor their own children for baptism.[42]

The bickering and the financial problems finally forced Carré to abandon the settlement before its final collapse. In early 1687, only three months after arriving at Narragansett, church elders acknowledged that they could not fulfill their promises regarding Carré's salary They hoped "some day to give him a more creditable support through the incease of private individuals" in the colony, but the settlement's problems made this impossible. Worse, the elders failed to fulfill other promises made to Carré. In July 1687 Carré complained that they failed to build him a house as they had promised, and in January 1688 he argued that his land was so irregularly shaped that it was unsuitable for farming. In the spring of 1688 Carré agreed to preach to Boston's Huguenot congregation to supplement his income and to temporarily relieve the vacancy caused by David de Bonrepos's departure for New Rochelle. This caused further problems at Narragansett. The church elders condemned "ill will and rebellion" in an unidentified group of settlers who now refused to pay the "tax" assessed for the minister's salary. But by March 1689 Carré was complaining about the elders themselves, charging that they had "not maintained peace and concord" in the settlement and still refused to increase his salary. Again he turned to Boston for relief. In May 1689 he announced that he would divide his time between Boston and Narragansett, and in December he moved to Boston permanently, although he agreed to visit the Narragansett refugees six times a year.[43]

In fact Carré's departure was not the first in the colony. In October 1689 Carré himself complained "that several members of the Colony were on the point of leaving it." "Since the church cannot exist without the colony," the minister urged the elders to stop the exodus. But they retorted that it "was impossible to prevent such private persons from leaving this settlement." In any case the Huguenots were gone by the spring of 1691; as the last act of their residence there, they recorded the burial of a twenty-two-month-old child in January of that year. Neighboring English settlers soon occupied their land and the refugees moved to other Huguenot settlements. Most moved to New Rochelle and New York City, and two or three traveled as far as South Carolina. Surprisingly few headed for Boston. It was a sign, perhaps, of their hostility toward the refugees who had stolen their own minister however much they disliked him.[44]

The dispersal of the Huguenots at Oxford in Massachusetts strikes similar themes. By most accounts, the colony's demise is traced to an Indian attack in 1696 that killed the English husband and children of a refugee woman, Susanne Sigourney. But as the Narragansett, this shock came on top of economic difficulties and questionable personal behavior that weakened an already small colony. Although later English settlers thought that thirty French families originally settled there, the available records indicate that no more than fifteen refugee families ever lived there before 1696. Gabriel Bernon, who gathered the colony's settlers among refugees in London and Boston, was a tireless and perhaps overambitious entrepreneur who encouraged the cultivation of grapes for wine and built a grain mill to serve the newly settled area. But some residents turned to less appealing activities for profit. In 1691 the Oxford minister Daniel Bondet reported that they were selling liquor to the nearby Nipmuck Indians. This behavior embarrassed Bondet because the Society for the Propagation of the Gospel in New England was paying Bondet's salary to proselytize among the Nipmucks. According to Bondet, the illict liquor trade already had produced one dangerous incident when "twenty indians [became] so furious by drunkenness that they fought like bears" before they attacked a Christian Nipmuck.[45]

By 1695 the Nipmuck Indians turned their hostility toward Oxford's Huguenots, and the refugees barricaded themselves against an Indian attack. After the murder of Susanne Sigourney's husband and children in 1696, they fled to Boston. Although eight or ten refugee families resettled Oxford in 1699 with Bernon and Jacques Laborie, a new Huguenot minister who had earned a checkered reputation among Huguenots in London, the new colony also failed. Economic difficulties and unceasing Indian turmoil forced the settlers to abandon Oxford again in 1704, with most of the returning refugees settling in Boston. Laborie replaced the recently deceased minister at New York City's French Church for two years until the elders fired him in 1706. Bernon moved his entrepreneurial activities to Rhode Island and later sold his Oxford land to English settlers, who formed a permanent town there in 1713.[46]

Efforts to establish French Protestant congregational life also met with considerable frustration in some of the larger Huguenot communities before 1695. The underlying cause of the problem was the successful Anglican effort to forestall formation of an exile Huguenot denomination in England that also could have ordered affairs in the colonies. The immediate cause was the self-seeking and sometimes scandalous behavior of several early refugee ministers, who knew well that they could not be disciplined effectively by new and weak congregations.

The case of Laurent Van den Bosch demonstrates how thoroughly Huguenots in the colonies needed institutions to guide refugee ministers. A Walloon was was admitted as a ministerial candidate by Amsterdam's Walloon Synod in May 1680, he subsequently moved to England where the bishop of London ordained him in the Church of England in the summer of 1682. He then journeyed to South Carolina where the colony's refugees refused to support him. In 1685 he moved to Boston and formed a congregation among the city's small Huguenot population. He also took his Anglican ordination seriously. He wrote the bishop of London that he intended to sustain the "interests and Liturgy" of the Church of England in Boston even as he ministered to Boston's Huguenots. He did neither successfully. When he married an English couple in August 1685 using the Anglican liturgy, the Suffolk County Court prosecuted him for violating Massachusetts law. Although he promised never to do so again, he married another English couple using Anglican liturgy in September 1686 and then fled to New York City to avoid prosecution in Boston. As a result, a New York City Huguenot minister, Pierre Daillé, had to write Boston's Increase Mather to ask that "the annoyance occasioned by Mr. Van den Bosch may not diminish your favor toward the French who are now in your city."[47]

Van den Bosch scandalized New Yorkers next. In 1687 he used his Amsterdam background to become minister to the Dutch settlement at Kingston on the Hudson River while also preaching occasionally to the Walloon settlement at New Paltz and to the growing Huguenot community on Staten Island. The Kingston and New Paltz settlers soon complained about Van den Bosch's drinking and womanizing. In 1689 they charged that he attempted to strangle his wife after chasing her into the farm fields at Kingston. After a formal hearing, New York's Dutch Reformed ministers defrocked him, and he subsequently exchanged his bruised wife and shocked congregations for an Anglican pulpit at St. Paul's Parish in Cecil County, Maryland, where he served until his death in 1696.[48]

The behavior of David de Bonrepos, who abruptly left two refugee congregations before settling with a third, reveals how the absence of denominational authority exacerbated the religious instability of the colonial refugee communities. De Bonrepos arrived in Boston in 1686 with refugees from the French West Indies colony of St. Christopher where he had been a minister since the early 1680s. His arrival was a fortunate coincidence for Boston's Huguenots because the tempestuous Van den Bosch either had just left Boston or was about to do so. Adding the West Indies refugees to Van den Bosch's abandoned charges, de Bonrepos revived the newly formed Huguenot congregation and secured permission of the Boston Selectmen to hold French Protestant services in one of the city's schoolhouses. But soon after accomplishing this feat, de Bonrepos too left when he was asked to minister in the new and larger Huguenot colony at New Rochelle in New York. His departure left Boston's Huguenots without a minister for the second time in less than a year.[49]

In New Rochelle, de Bonrepos emerged as a prickly man who only further complicated town problems. For their part, the church elders compromised the minister's arrival by placing his glebe on land that one Huguenot already had used to inter his wife and children and then forced de Bonrepos to solve the problem himself. For his part, de Bonrepos carried on a bitter personal dispute with a New York City merchant, Louis Bongrand, who owned land and a house in New Rochelle. The dispute produced a lawsuit, raucous public confrontations in New York City and New Rochelle, and Bongrand's expulsion from the New Rochelle congregation. In September 1693 de Bonrepos himself confronted New Rochelle's church elders. He "warmly" resigned as the town's minister, refused to accept the resignations of the current elders—"they could stay or leave . . . he did not care about it"—and declared that he simply was "no longer in the mood to serve the Church" and left for Staten Island. There, his mood improved. He was the only Huguenot minister who ever lived on the Island, and he ministered to its French residents until he died in 1734.[50]

Despite the lack of denominational guidance, the Huguenot communities in America slowly secured ministers in the mid-1690s. Elie Prioleau of Poitou arrived in South Carolina in 1687 to serve the Charlestown congregation. Two other ministers soon joined him in the colony, probably before 1692. Pierre Robert from St. Imier in French-speaking Switzerland took charge of the Santee congregation, and Laurent Trouillart assisted Prioleau in Charlestown and served the two Huguenot settlements on the Cooper River. Daniel Bondet, formerly at Oxford and Boston, settled in New Rochelle after de Bonrepos moved to Staten Island in 1693, and Pierre Peiret joined Pierre Daillé in New York City in 1688. Even the Boston Huguenots found a clergyman. Laurent Van den Bosch left them in 1686 and they lost three successors in the next decade—de Bonrepos in 1687, Narragansett's Ezéchiel Carré in 1691 or 1692, and Daniel Bondet in 1696. But the congregation finally secured the long term services of the former New York City minister, Pierre Daillé, in 1696.[51]

The arrival of the Huguenot ministers bespoke signs of deepening cohesion among Huguenot refugees in British America. Above all, it demonstrated that the reassertion of a traditional French Protestant religious life was implicit in the Huguenot emigration to America; it simply awaited successful immigration and settlement. At the same time, the Huguenot search for material opportunity stamped the refugees with important social similarities. In the main they were young, often possessed of skills useful in the developing colonies, yet not bound to them in ways that discouraged new occupations and trades. Nearly all the American refugees underwent parallel experiences of unemployment and poverty during their European exile, and their developing social interrelationships, marked by the marriage of many young refugees in London, masked the variety of their regional origins in France.

At the same time, Huguenots encountered societies in America of such astonishing diversity that one could wonder about their common English roots. Boston, South Carolina, and New York—these were the Huguenots' principal places of residence, and they could scarcely have been more different. One was an old Puritan society. Another was a new slave society. The third was a conquered Dutch colony. They offered Huguenots significantly different choices in economics and politics, markedly diverse mixtures of religion and population, even different material cultures. Perhaps all of them—surely one of them—could provide the rich, nurturing New World environment that would sustain the collective life of a people whose exodus from France had already profoundly affected the major Protestant cities of Europe.

PART II

The Disappearance of the Huguenots in America

It is a grave matter that such people who were banished because of the Protestant religion and suffered great hardship can so easily grow indifferent in this country ... there are so many Huguenots here who have grown completely cold and allowed their children and children's children to grow up unbaptized in darkness.

—*The Journals of Henry Melchior Muhlenberg*

3 / If All the World Were Boston

The experience of Huguenots in Boston was a very special and very limited one. Only a small number of them ever settled there, and after the Oxford settlement collapsed in 1691, Boston contained the only Huguenot community in Massachusetts. Unlike the refugees who went to South Carolina and New York, these Huguenots came to an overwhelmingly English city. Boston never burgeoned with the European cosmopolitanism of New York or the racial complexity of South Carolina, and its range of religious institutions proved equally narrow. In 1680 Quakers offered the only major departure from the limited Calvinist orthodoxy of Boston's other churches; not even Anglicans had yet established a congregation there. Clearly, the Huguenots who remained in Boston had chosen to settle in a distinctly unrepresentative colonial American city.[1]

Yet precisely because Boston was more homogeneous, more Puritan, more tightly drawn in its social structure than New York, Charlestown, or the colonies they dominated, Boston's Huguenots provide an important touchstone for the Huguenot experience in the American colonies. On the one hand, Boston's reputation as the capital of New World Protestantism probably encouraged some French Protestants to settle there, just as it probably encouraged some Bostonians to welcome them. On the other hand, Boston's relative homogeneity in religion and nationality may have smothered the small refugee population's cohesion and sustained resistance to conformity. The fate of Boston's French Church might offer a model for understanding the fate of the French churches elsewhere. And if Boston's Huguenots slowly and quietly vanished, the process by which they did so will reveal whether they successfully assimilated into all ranks of city society—top, middle, and bottom—or disappeared from the city to join Huguenots elsewhere.

Uncovering the experience of Boston's Huguenots also offers a convenient opportunity to introduce the major problems of analyzing the Huguenots' fate in America. Tracing their demise admittedly requires a certain tenacity and patience, for several reasons. No dramatic, cataclysmic event, not even the Revocation, shattered their religious and social cohesion. Instead, the Huguenots disappeared as an immigrant group through a subtle, evolutionary process that would be difficult to follow in any group. But it is especially intractable for Huguenots because it was completed so early—by 1748 in Boston, for example, the year the city's French Church disbanded. The Huguenot demise also took place in a sparse early modern society. Early Boston, and early America, simply lacked the fraternal groups, newspapers, book publishers and political parties historians analyze to trace immigrant and ethnic perseverance in nineteenth-century America. The disappearance of the Huguenots also occurred in the often ignored "middle ages" of the colonial period. These years from 1680 to 1750 have only recently begun to receive some of the attention accorded the first decades of colonial settlement or the coming of the American Revolution. Finally, and most obviously, the very result of the Huguenots' disappearance has been to reduce many of the sources useful to understanding how and why it occurred. No French Church records exist for Boston, for example; personal papers from individual Huguenots including letters, diaries, and business accounts are rare; and the principal records of the colonies in which they settled are not as plentiful between 1680 and at least 1730 as is true for subsequent years.

Here the account of the Huguenots in Boston will be used as a preliminary test for reconstructing the Huguenot experience in America. It lays out the principal methods used to recover their history and unfolds many, if not all, of its critical themes. It also briefly illuminates the Huguenots' reception in colonial America's most self-consciously religious city between the twilight of late seventeenth-century Puritanism and the dawn of the American Revolution.

The need of Boston Puritans to remake the world in their own image also shaped Boston's early knowledge of the Huguenot plight. Some Bostonians and other Massachusetts colonists learned about events in France from the older immigrants from the Channel Islands of Guernsey and Jersey who settled in Salem in the 1670s, or from the several Huguenots who settled in Boston. These men—Philip English, John Foy, and John Rawlings—made some mark in Massachusetts commerce and were well known among the colony's elite by 1680. At any rate most New Englanders and certainly most Bostonians knew about "the sore persecution of the Saints in France"—Cotton Mather's phrase— because it served such useful purposes in explaining the failure of the Puritan dream in New England.[2]

Before 1660 a satisfactory Puritan order never emerged in New England, and continuing arguments over religion and politics in the next two decades encouraged the Boston clergy to speculate on Antichrist's destruction of Christ's vineyards. As a result, the Mathers stalked any and all news of the French persecution and shared their findings and interpretations with others. In the 1680s Increase Mather exchanged letters on the accelerating French persecution of Huguenots with numerous New England ministers—Joshua Moody, Samuel Baker, Ichabod Chauncy, Samuel Craddock, Thomas Cobbett, and his son Nathaniel Mather. In a 1682 sermon Cotton Mather warned New Englanders that the Protestant debacle in France was a sign of Protestant disaster elsewhere, including New England. In the late 1680s he cultivated a friendship with the former minister of the Narragansett settlement, Ezéchiel Carré, and in his diary outlined news of the continuing French persecution in the 1690s. In 1698 he translated and published a pious letter from a New York City refugee then imprisoned in Marseilles named Elie Neau. In his preface, Mather bitterly observed that not even support from "persons of the Highest Quality" saved French Protestantism from ruin, a lesson he implored leaders of his own commercial society to remember.[3]

Boston's early Huguenots were as much victims as beneficiaries of the Puritan interest in their exodus. By the mid-1680s Boston had received as many as one hundred refugee Huguenot families. Most emigrated from London, some settling at Narragansett or Oxford, while others came from the French West Indies and South Carolina, Boston being their second American residence. Their arrival coincided with the broadening Puritan attack on

malaise in Massachusetts religion, the abolition of the Mas- ˙
sachusetts charter in 1684, and the installment of the detested
Dominion of New England government in 1686. This was the
context in which a suspicious, anxious General Court ordered
newly arrived refugees from St. Christopher in the West Indies to
take the colony's oath of allegiance if they wished to remain in
Massachusetts. In this way the refugees were made to pledge—
deftly, if unwittingly—to support the old chartered government,
while the General Court satisfied itself that Boston had not
admitted French Catholics in Huguenot disguise sent by the
Antichrist to multiply the colony's woes.[4]

At the same time, religious as well as secular motivations
underwrote a solid Boston record of aid for the refugees. In 1682
the Massachusetts Council proclaimed a fast day to spur collection
of funds to aid the new refugees and urged the colony's churches
to support those Protestants who had "fled hither for shelter by
reason of the present sufferings in their own country." The
refugees received equally positive treatment from Boston's secular authorities despite the town's already well-developed reputation for bitter, insular bigotry. Although many early Boston
Huguenots failed to obtain denization papers that were easily
available in London, Boston's Selectmen regularly admitted
Huguenot refugees to town and allowed them to vote. They did
this for the obscure cloth worker Thomas Mallet in 1685 as well as
for the already wealthy merchant Benjamin Faneuil in 1691. The
only Huguenot refused admittance to the town was the unla-
mented minister Laurent Van den Bosch, whom the Selectmen
rejected because he "hath baptized and Married some persons
here contrarie to Law," not because he was a Huguenot or a
refugee.[5]

The story of Ezéchiel Carré in Boston illustrates Huguenot
interest in pursuing a distinctive French Protestant religious life
as well as their unfortunate dependence on sometimes quixotic
ministerial leadership. Carré was the third Huguenot minister to
serve Boston's small French Church, which Laurent Van den
Bosch organized in 1685 and David de Bonrepos served between
1686 and about 1688. In the case of Carré, a small cache of
materials permits a rare glimpse of a minister's efforts to
strengthen the religious behavior of Huguenots in America. At
Narragansett he demanded adherence to traditional French

Protestant worship and ritual, preached frequently against im-
morality and blasphemy, and railed against trying to eliminate
godparents in Huguenot baptisms. His concern for tradition also
produced the only French Protestant denominational institution
ever created in the colonies, when the refugee congregations of
Boston, Oxford, and Narragansett "resolved to keep up between
them a close communion" by creating a "conference or Synod"
among themselves. This "synod" was to be formed "according to
the usual manner of our Protestant churches in France," despite
the disintegration of the Huguenot ecclesiastical structure after
1660. In fact, this synod would most likely have functioned like a
French colloquy, a meeting of ministers and laymen from
neighboring congregations. The New England representatives
met with some success at their first conference in October 1688,
when they agreed not to offer communion to transients who
lacked certificates from other Huguenot congregations, and to
take up "more exact measures at the next conference or Synod."
But no additional meetings ever occurred because two of the
three New England settlements soon collapsed. Carré moved to
Boston, the Narragansett and Oxford settlement failed, and
by 1696 Boston's French Church remained the only Huguenot
congregation in New England.[6]

Carré's publications in Boston demonstrate that he could
cultivate harmonious relationships with Boston's old Puritan elite
even as he pursued a religious message that fit with at least some
exile Huguenot leaders in Europe. In Boston, Carré satisfied the
anti-Catholic passions of Puritans and Huguenots alike by attack-
ing a Jesuit-Indian catechism published in Canada with his own
small tract, *Echatillon. De la doctrine que les Jesuites enségnent aus
sauvages du Nouveau Monde* (Boston, 1690). Cotton Matter wrote
the preface for Carré's pamphlet, which also became the first
French-language work printed in the British colonies in America.
Not surprisingly, the work frustrated Boston printer Samuel
Green. Green lacked grave accents in his English type and
therefore begged readers to forgive his printing errors. As he put
it, he understood "neither the Language nor the Orthography" of
the French text.[7]

A second publication, a sermon entitled *The Charitable Samaritan*
(Boston, 1689), continues Carré's pursuit of traditional Huguenot
religious practice in America and links him to theological currents

developing among exile Huguenot ministers in Holland. Cotton Mather's friend and fellow minister, Nehemiah Walter of Roxbury, translated the text so that Samuel Green could print it in English. Carré wrote on the subject of charity when he discovered that Boston's Huguenots were not maintaining a poor fund. As at Narragansett, he urged them to uphold this traditional French Protestant practice and also nudged them toward additional practices that would strengthen their piety in this new place of exile. Carré followed a traditional argument of seventeenth-century French Protestant writers when he noted that the "sufferings of the Servants of Jesus Christ . . . strongly confirm the Faithful." But going beyond tradition, Carré's sermon seemed to encourage individual refugees to dwell on their most personal sufferings. They should purge their souls of unrighteousness and cleanse them for the reception of communion: "You must then put your selves into [such] a Condition to receive his grace." Unfortunately Carré raised this issue only briefly, and in the absence of other sermons it is impossible to determine how thoroughly he pursued this theme. Still, in developing links between intensely examined personal suffering and the receipt of God's grace, Carré advanced themes then developing among some ministers and lay Huguenots on the Continent and ones that two New York City Huguenots, the minister Pierre Peiret and the merchant Elie Neau, developed with greater sophistication a decade later.[8]

Carré's sudden departure from Boston revealed the tenuousness of his commitment to the American refugees and their helplessness in the face of restless clerics. Carré disappears from the Boston records by 1691, and previous historians have surmised that he probably died there. In fact he returned to England. In 1688 he had asked the Narragansett congregation for permission to sail for England on business matters, and British Huguenot records reveal that by the summer of 1691 he simply became a reverse migrant. He baptized one child at London's Threadneedle Street Church in July 1691 and another in the Huguenot congregation at Southampton in August 1691. The Southampton clerk described him as "on his way to Guernsey." He apparently settled there. The last record of him is a sermon, *La mort des justes* (London, 1697) preached to commemorate the deaths of forty-four Channel Island sailors in a boating accident. Carré's departure once again left Boston's Huguenots in need of a minister. Daniel Bondet apparently helped them occasionally between 1691 and 1694, and he served them for two years after leaving the Oxford settlement in 1694. But in 1696 Bondet left Boston for New Rochelle, dooming the congregation to yet another search for a minister.[9]

Because of the ministerial crises of the 1690s, a number of Huguenots deserted Boston's French Church to join English congregations. Their defections raise important questions about Huguenot denominational preferences and about the impact of religious change on refugee cohesion in Boston and elsewhere. Robert Kingdon argued that so many Huguenots in the colonies became Anglicans that the historian's principal task is to determine why such a Huguenot-Anglican alliance developed. He suggested that its principal causes were Anglican charity for refugees in London and to congregations in America. Patrice Higonnet has accepted Kingdon's argument and has described the few recalcitrant Calvinist refugees as "more cohesively French, more rural, and less well off then their Anglicanized and assimilated compatriots."[10]

Assessing the significance of defections from Boston's French Church and other Huguenot congregations in the colonies presents a difficult problem. If the refugees had come only to preserve their religious traditions, such defections would be devastating. National loyalty in marriage, business, or politics could not compensate for change in denominational affiliation. But the motives that propelled many refugees to America were sufficiently complex that a shift of denominational allegiance might not undermine refugee cohesion. Numerous nineteenth-century American immigrant groups, especially Scandinavians, underwent substantial religious change without experiencing thorough social disintegration, and the colonial period offers similar models of such occurrences. Scottish immigrants in eighteenth-century New Jersey abandoned many smaller religious groups after settling in America to form a "Scottish" religious order among colonial American Presbyterians. Immigrants in Germantown in eighteenth-century Pennsylvania drifted away from organized religion. Yet both immigrant groups sustained significant national cohesion in marriage, business, and politics.[11]

Although the first Huguenot defections from the French Church were too few to affect refugee cohesion, they reveal a broader dispersal of refugees to Boston congregations than the purely pro-Anglican interpretation would suggest. Boston's first Anglican congregation, King's Chapel, was organized in 1686, and in 1689 the merchants Pierre Bowdoin and Thomas Mallett and the ship captain John Foy contributed funds to construct its new building. None of them apparently joined the congregation, although the absence of the King's Chapel records makes it impossible to determine who did. Several refugees joined Cotton Mather's Second Church, however. In 1690 the congregation admitted Ann LeBlond, wife of James LeBlond. Nine children born to the couple in subsequent years were baptized in Mather's church; there is no record of James LeBlond's membership there. The Second Church also admitted Elizabeth Bowdoin, the daughter of Pierre Bowdoin, in 1693 and the silversmith Solomon Légaré in 1695, on the day he had his infant daughter baptized there.[12]

These early defections of Huguenots from the French Church were offset by a slow rise in the number of Huguenots living in Boston between 1689 and 1696. The collapse of the Narragansett colony in 1691 brought five or six refugee families to Boston, and the Boston tax lists reveal about thirty French families living in the city in 1695. The addition of about a dozen refugee families after the 1696 massacre at Oxford (and just as Daniel Bondet was leaving the Boston congregation for New Rochelle) at least temporarily pushed the number of French families in Boston above forty. Thus, despite the defections to Mather's Second Church, the French Church was better prepared to replace Daniel Bondet in 1696 than it had been for a decade. This time the congregation succeeded. It hired Pierre Daillé, who was born in Poitou about 1650, taught at the famous Protestant academy at Saumur, and came from New York City to Boston in 1696 where he remained until he died in 1715.[13]

On the surface, Daillé brought stability to the Boston refugee community. He assumed a comfortable, if marginal, place at the edge of the Boston ministerial establishment, which may not have been easy. In contrast to New England Puritan practice, the public celebration of Christmas was an important holiday among French Protestants, and the Boston judge Samuel Sewall publicly rebuked one refugee "about his partaking with the French church on the 25. December on account of its being Christmas-day, as they abusively call it." But Sewall and the Boston Calvinist clergy developed an obvious liking for Daillé. The diaries of both Sewall and Cotton Mather describe the presence of "Mr. Dallie" at several Boston funerals including that of Mather's second wife where Daillé acted as a pallbearer. Sewall also visited Daillé before the French minister's death in May 1715, noting sorrowfully that the man was "in a languishing condition."[14]

Daillé's major problem, then, was not his reception by other Bostonians. Rather, weak support from Huguenots vexed his Boston tenure. One problem was paying his salary. In 1700 the Massachusetts Council granted Daillé £12 in aid after French Church elders petitioned it for relief. In 1703 the Council granted Daillé the duty on £300 of European imports but later in the year refused a second request to help him. The Council was understandably surprised, therefore, when the French Church elders submitted a petition in 1704 to construct a building for the French Church. It was to be financed, in part, by a gift of £83 from King William. But since the elders could not pay Daillé's salary and the schoolhouse where they had met since 1686 was "sufficient for a greater number of persons than doth belong to their congregation," their petition was rejected. The hard-pressed Daillé even sought help from Anglicans in London, although certainly not with the knowledge of the Massachusetts Council. In 1703 he petitioned the Society for the Propagation of the Gospel in Foreign Parts to supplement his salary; it was, Daillé told the S.P.G., "only proper that a minister try every resource before forsaking his flock." But because he lacked Anglican ordination and served a nonconformist congregation, the S.P.G. also rejected his plea for aid. In the aftermath of these rejections Daillé probably turned for help to Boston's small coterie of increasingly prominent Huguenot merchants: André Faneuil, James Bowdoin, and Daniel Johonnot, among others. He never left his "flock," and he never again appealed for financial aid from Massachusetts authorities.[15]

During Daillé's tenure, the early assimilation of Huguenots within the economic and political milieu of Boston augured well for their treatment elsewhere and confounded the city's reputation for bigotry. Boston town officials continued to treat the Huguenots without prejudice after 1696, as they had done before. Indeed, some refugees experienced considerable economic success in Boston. The lack of tax lists and the small Huguenot population make it difficult to study Boston's poor refugees systematically between 1695 and the Revolution, but several examples of early Huguenot prosperity are well known. André Faneuil and his brother Benjamin of New York City built one of the largest merchant firms in the mainland colonies in Boston between 1695 and 1715, successfully expanding the trade ventures they first pursued from La Rochelle earlier in the 1670s, while Pierre Bowdoin's estate, valued at £1,344 in 1706, marked him as one of the wealthiest merchants in Boston.[16]

Some refugees ventured into politics, a move that brought them directly into the exercise of government surprisingly early in Boston. Between 1704 and 1711, Boston voters elected four rather well known Huguenots—André Faneuil, John Foy, John Barbour, and James LeBlond—as city constables. In the same years they also elected LeBlond and Barbour as tithingmen to maintain the sanctity of the Sabbath—LeBlond a member of Cotton Mather's Second Church, Barbour apparently a member of the French Church.[17]

The early entry of the Huguenots into the mainstream of Boston political and economic life appears to have had little effect on the refugees' social and religious cohesion. Only two additional refugees joined Boston's English Dissenting congregations between the arrival of Pierre Daillé in 1696 and his death in 1715. Louis Boucher joined Benjamin Colman's Brattle Street Church in 1703, and James Bowdoin joined it in 1711, both at the baptisms of their infant sons. Other Huguenots may have supported the Anglican King's Chapel before 1715, but the congregation's fragmentary financial and business records suggest that the only refugee likely to have done so regularly was the wealthy merchant André Faneuil.[18]

Lurking beneath the veneer of apparent loyalty to the French Church, however, was an early and extraordinary pattern of intermarriage with Boston's English residents—exogamy in sociological terms. Exogamy rates vary widely among modern American immigrant groups, and historians and sociologists have not determined exactly how exogamy promotes assimilation or undermines group loyalty. But most sociologists argue nonetheless that it is a major sign or "indicator" of assimilation because it affects the very composition of the family, whose central role in sustaining immigrant cohesion has long been acknowledged in American ethnic groups. The case of the Huguenots in Boston and in their other colonial residences is especially interesting in this context. To begin with, it tests the rate and effect of exogamy in places where refugees actually were "at risk" to marry non-Huguenots. In Boston as well as in Charlestown and New York City, Huguenots lived in close contact with English and sometimes Dutch colonists with whom they could develop personal relationships that might lead to marriage. This makes their case significantly different from later German, Scottish, and Scotch-Irish immigrants, who frequently resided in isolated rural settlements where they had little contact with different national groups.[19]

The Huguenot case also offers an opportunity to conduct the first systematic study of immigrant intermarriage in colonial America. Historians have long quoted J. Hector St. John de Crèvecoeur, who was himself married by a Huguenot minister in Westchester County, New York, in 1769, that the typical late eighteenth-century American came from a mixed family "whose grandfather was an Englishman, whose wife was Dutch, whose son married a French woman, and whose present four sons have now four wives of different nations." Yet despite criticism from American immigration and ethnic historians that Crèvecoeur was but an early expounder of the seemingly discredited "melting-pot" theory, no one has bothered to demonstrate in any systematic way whether he was right or wrong about early American exogamy. Indeed, a probe of Huguenot intermarriage in Boston suggests that exogamy played a major role in destroying refugee cohesion in the city even as it was a symbol of refugee assimilation.[20]

Huguenot exogamy reached astonishing proportions in Boston as early as Daillé's ministry (Table 2). Between 1700 and 1715,

Daillé himself performed only five weddings in the city; in three of them French grooms took English brides. More significant for Huguenot social cohesion and more ominous for French Church loyalty, thirty-eight marriages involving Huguenots were performed by other Boston ministers, especially Cotton Mather, between 1700 and 1715. In seven cases both spouses were French. This raises the unanswerable question of why Daillé did not marry these persons especially since none of them had joined other Boston churches. The remaining thirty-one marriages all were exogamous ones that represented decay in refugee group loyalty and the assimilation of the refugees into native Boston society. Within the group, men took English spouses more frequently than did the women. Between 1700 and 1715, Boston's male Huguenots married English women at twice the rate that Huguenot women married English men; twenty of the early exogamous marriages involved Huguenot grooms, while eleven involved Huguenot brides.[21]

Activity in the Huguenot community following Pierre Daillé's death in May 1715 suggests that the already high exogamy rate had not yet produced a decline in Huguenot support for the French Church. In fact, the refugee congregation might have appeared to be in extraordinary good health. By summer of 1716

Table 2. Huguenot marriages, Boston, 1700–1749

Nationality						
Groom	Bride	1700–09	1710–19	1720–29	1730–39	1740–49
Performed by Pierre Daillé and Andrew le Mercier						
French	French	2	2	4	3	3
French	English	0	2	2	0	2
English	French	1	1	1	4	1
English	English	1	0	1	3	2
Performed by Congregational, Presbyterian, and Anglican ministers						
French	French	2	6	4	3	2
French	English	12	22	26	31	33
English	French	7	8	18	28	29

Source: Reports of the Record Commissioners of the City of Boston, vol. 28.

a young minister, André le Mercier, arrived in Boston to replace
Daillé. A native of Caen in Normandy, le Mercier enrolled as a
theological candidate at the Protestant academy in Geneva in
1712, where he apparently was ordained; he then moved to
London and was there in 1715, when the merchant André
Faneuil was attempting to secure a replacment for Daillé at the
behest of the French Church elders. The elders agreed to pay le
Mercier a yearly salary of £100 in Massachusetts currency. This
represented a significant commitment to the new minister by
Boston's small Huguenot population. In 1716 the elders also
agreed to construct a small but substantial stone church building
for the congregation on School Street—the French Church's first
private church building. This time the Massachusetts Council did
not object. The Huguenots raised funds among Boston's wealthy
elite—Samuel Sewall's manuscript account book records his gift
of £5 sterling "for his subscription toward building the French
Church"—and rich Huguenot merchants—the Faneuils, Johon-
nots, and Bowdoins—who could have easily underwritten the
costs of constructing such a building themselves.[22]
    Yet the new church building did not symbolize a healthy
congregation, nor did it demonstrate cohesion in the Huguenot
refugee community. Indeed, the construction of the French
Church building and even the hiring of le Mercier were mirages.
Huguenot exogamy only accelerated after 1716, as seen in the
marriage patterns outlined in Table 2. Like Daillé, le Mercier
performed notaby few marriages in Boston; he married only four
Huguenot couples between 1716 and 1719, three of whom
entered exogamous unions. Boston's remaining Huguenots were
married by New England ministers, and they took English
spouses. Between 1720 and 1729, Boston's Congregational,
Presbyterian, and Anglican ministers performed no less than
forty-eight weddings involving Huguenots. In four cases both
spouses were French, but in forty-four cases the unions were
exogamous. This rush to exogamy, already fervid in the 1720s,
never slowed. Between 1740 and 1749 Boston's English ministers
performed sixty-four marriages involving Huguenots (le Mercier
performed six) of which sixty-two were exogamous. The only
difference in the pattern after 1716 is that Huguenot women
overcame their initial reluctance to take non-Huguenot spouses.

Whereas twice as many Huguenot men took English spouses as did Huguenot women between 1700 and 1720, after 1730 the ratio became very nearly equal. In the decades between 1730–39 and 1740–49, Huguenot men took English spouses only slightly more often than did Huguenot women.[23]

The movement of Huguenots into Boston politics also accelerated after 1716. Huguenot political participation in Boston scarcely could depend on their large numbers in the city. Nor did Huguenots control small election districts as did some ethnic groups in America's nineteenth- and twentieth-century cities. Rather, their small numbers meant that they were thoroughly dependent on Boston's native English voters for success at city polls. This they clearly achieved. Through the early and mid-eighteenth century, Boston was a commercial city governed and managed by unpaid office-holders and ever multiplying committees, elected to supervise a complex web of preindustrial urban services. By 1750 Boston voters had elected Huguenots as city constables twenty-eight times and as clerks of the market four times. Voters also elected James Bowdoin numerous times to the committee that inspected town defenses; Stephen and James Boutineau, Pierre Chardon, William Foy, and André Sigourney to the school committee; and Sigourney, Thomas Boucher, Isaac Dupeu, and James LeBlond to the scavenger committee that managed town waste.[24]

As Huguenots joined other Boston congregations after 1715, they simply assimilated into the local denominational structure of the city without demonstrating any special affinity for Anglicanism. One refugee family and perhaps others maintained a dual religious affiliation that obviously eased their adoption of new church loyalties. The merchant André Faneuil was a French Church elder, and fulfilled his duties there, but in 1707 he contributed £12 sterling to construct a new building for the Anglican King's Chapel in Boston, and in 1715 his son Peter contributed £16 sterling to construct an Anglican church in Marblehead. These gifts reflected the Faneuils' growing Anglican sympathies. Fragmentary records at King's Chapel suggest that the Faneuils supported the congregation regularly after 1720. In 1741 Peter Faneuil managed the campaign to enlarge the church. He raised £25,000 in Massachusetts currency and contributed the largest gift to the campaign, £200 sterling. Yet throughout this period the Faneuils helped maintain the building that the French Church owned and contributed to André le Mercier's salary.[25]

Certainly other Huguenots joined the Faneuils at King's Chapel to become Anglicans in a Dissenter city. Unfortunately, the loss of the King's Chapel baptismal records for most of the colonial period makes it impossible to follow any but the more prestigious Huguenots who affiliated with the congregation, including members of the Johonnot, Chardon, and Cazneau families as well as the Faneuils. Other Boston Huguenots affiliated with its older New England congregations, however. The First Church admitted Elie Depeu in 1721—his father had been a French Church elder. It also baptized André le Mercier's slave woman in 1743 although it would not allow her to "come to full Communion." The Brattle Street Church baptized infants from seven Huguenot families between 1714 and 1750, including children born to Pierre Chardon and James Bowdoin, the future governor of revolutionary Massachusetts. Like Dupeu, the fathers of both Chardon and Bowdoin had been French Church elders. The Second Church baptized children and admitted members from five Huguenot families—Angier, Boucher, De la Place, Favriéres, and Pellow—between 1716 and 1750.[26]

Finally, some Huguenots, like many Bostonians, lagged or drifted into erratic patterns of church affiliation. In mid-eighteenth century Boston less than a third of the city's adults were church members, and many of the Huguenots who were married by clergymen do not appear in subsequent membership and baptism records. Although some probably affiliated with King's Chapel, others who were married by Dissenting ministers probably did not. Instead, they apparently exhibited one of the more peculiar signs of assimilation in Boston by drifting off into the ambivalent, erratic relationships with organized religious groups that characterized enormous numbers of eighteenth-century American colonists even in New England.[27]

Boston's Huguenots as a group probably experienced reasonable economic success in the city although the lack of tax lists makes it impossible to investigate their status thoroughly. Between 1740 and 1760, only four Huguenots appear on the city's extensive list of poor persons bound out to apprenticeships, in part because of the city's serious economic decline in these years. Other Boston Huguenots achieved at least modest economic success. Boston's best known "French" silversmith, Paul Revere, actually had no significant connection with the city's old Huguenot community. His father, Apollos, only arrived in Boston in 1715 bearing a checkered Protestant background (his own parents probably had reconverted to Catholicism in France in the 1690s), and Apollos learned his silver crafts not from one of the great Huguenot silversmiths of the diaspora who worked in London, Amsterdam, Geneva, and Berlin but from Boston's own John Coney. Still, two other Huguenots—René Grignon, who worked in Boston from 1691 to 1713, and Peter Feurt, who worked there from 1727 to 1737—achieved at least modest success with their Huguenot silver and gold crafts before Revere's rise to prominence in the city.[28]

Other Huguenots became well known as merchants. James Bowdoin's merchant success underwrote his later political career in the revolutionary era. Earlier, the Faneuils enjoyed extraordinary success as shipowners and traders. They capped that success with their gift to Boston of a magnificent building in 1742, Faneuil Hall. However, Peter Faneuil's unexpected death in 1743 offered an unusual perspective on the assimilation of this refugee family. The sermon that the Boston minister John Lovell preached at Peter Faneuil's death failed to mention his Huguenot heritage in even the most oblique fashion.[29]

Accelerating assimilation and sometimes spectacular economic success did not, however, thoroughly shatter all ethnic cohesion among the Huguenots before 1740. Between 1697 and 1714 André Faneuil formed shipping partnerships with several Boston Huguenots, including James LeBlond and John Mariette, and with Clement Lempriere of Jersey in the Channel Islands. Louis Boucher's trading partners were friends of his brother Paul in London, most of them Huguenots. However, the surviving Faneuil account books suggest that the older Huguenot business connections faded by the mid-1720s, and they reveal no special Huguenot merchant or investment links in either Boston or London. Smaller signs of ethnic cohesion appear in different records. When Judith Grazilier's husband died in 1735 leaving her a "poor Widow, with young children to bring up," Boston's

Huguenot elite rallied to help her. André Faneuil, James Bowdoin, Stephen Boutineau, and Daniel Johonnot petitioned the Boston Selectmen to give her a license to "Retail Liquors, etc." so she could make a living. Sometimes Boston authorities sought out Huguenots to perform special tasks. In 1746 the Massachusetts governor Sir William Pepperell asked Stephen Boutineau and André le Mercier to catechize a Catholic woman who had arrived in Boston from French Canada. They lectured her extensively on the subject of transubstantiation and promised Pepperell they would continue their discussions with her, but whether they converted her to Protestantism remains unknown.[30]

The story of Anne Faneuil is a sad tale of ethnic empathy and of the ability of wealth and position to transcend serious personal problems. In 1719 André Faneuil's brother Benjamin died unexpectedly in New York City at the age of fifty-one. As a result, the Faneuils' New York business and Benjamin Faneuil's widow and six children—Peter, Benjamin, Mary, Anne, Susanne, and Mary Anne—all moved to Boston. Sometime around 1725, however, Anne Faneuil, then fifteen, returned to New York City. There she lived in a house that the city assessor valued at only £5, a figure that reflected her poverty and her estrangement from her family. In February 1726 she gave birth to an illegitimate child. Its father was a twenty-two year old New York City Huguenot named Jean Garreau. Four years later, on April 27, 1730, the New York City French Church minister Louis Rou baptized the child with the name Jean and noted that it was born "without the benefit of marriage." Despite the importance of the baptismal rite among French Protestants, no member of the Faneuil family took part in the ceremony, which was unusual enough in that it occurred four years after the child's birth. Garreau's mother acted as the child's godmother, and an otherwise obscure city Huguenot, Elie Pipon, became its godfather.[31]

What happened to Anne Faneuil's child, Jean, and to his father remain unknown. But what happened to Anne Faneuil demonstrates that wealth triumphed over adversity for many colonial Americans. Sometime after 1730 she returned to Boston, presumably without her child, and became reconciled with her uncle André and with her brothers and sisters. She also began attending King's Chapel with the Faneuil family, and in 1740 she married Addington Davenport, the assistant minister at King's Chapel who became the minister of Boston's third Anglican congregation, Trinity Church, in the same year. Certainly Anne Faneuil's path to exogamy reflected the benefits of extraordinary family wealth, even as it also demonstrated how persistently Boston Huguenots sought and gained membership in mainstream Boston society.[32]

The French Church minister André le Mercier also turned toward mainsteam New England Protestantism and away from his isolated French Church. In 1729 he became one of fourteen ministers to form the Presbytery of Londonderry. This was the first presbytery in New England and the only colonial presbytery that ever attracted a Huguenot minister, whatever the earlier seventeenth-century links between Huguenots and English and Scottish Dissenters. For some ministers le Mercier offered an important bridge between Old and New World religious traditions. In 1732 le Mercier published a two-volume work, *The Church History of Geneva,* dedicated to all of New England's ministers, which he wrote to answer their incessant questions about Geneva church affairs and church government. He was, after all, the only minister in all of New England with any direct knowledge of ecclesiastical and church practice in Calvin's home city, and he took special care to explain Geneva's parish system to his New England colleagues for whom formal parishes were becoming increasingly important in the eighteenth century. On the other hand, the only work he dedicated to his listeners at Boston's French Church was entitled *A Treatise Against Detraction* (Boston, 1733). In it he testily thanked his church elders for their support—"You have since excused my Infirmities, . . . as I did the same in respect to yours"—and inveighed against rising detractions from true piety and true religion.[33]

The combination of assimilation and social disintegration among Boston's Huguenots made the collapse of the French Church inevitable and stimulated a bitter fight that revealed accelerating tension among the few remaining French Church members. In 1748 only seven subscribers remained to pay French Church expenses. Therefore, on March 7, 1748, the French Church elders sold their building for £3000 in Massachusetts currency to the expanding New Congregational Society formed in the aftermath of George Whitefield's revivals in Boston. A week later the Massachusetts General Court granted le Mercier's petition to allow his Huguenots to worship in the South Grammar School "as they are deprived of a place to meet in at present." But by November 1748 this symbolic collapse of the French Church led to the cessation of worship services and to a bitter, vindictive argument between le Mercier and the Church elders that only further exposed the shallowness of their earlier cohesion. The elders refused to give le Mercier even part of the money they received from the sale of the church building. Le Mercier therefore petitioned the General Court to place the deed in his hands and backed his demand by blaming everyone but himself for the demise of the congregation. He claimed that its members never paid the salary agreed to in 1715, suggested that André Faneuil tricked him into thinking that he was to receive a yearly salary of £100 sterling, not £100 in inflated Massachusetts currency, lamented that death removed his oldest and best supporters from his subscription list, and complained that assimilation removed the younger Huguenots from the congregation because they were "altogether Educated in the English Tongue, [and] frequent[ed] and belong[ed] to the English Churches."[34]

The elders rejected le Mercier's charges. They claimed that although he was "in exceeding low circumstances" when he arrived in 1715, through their support he had "maintained his Family in a handsome manner and purchased a considerable Estate" that included a farm at Roxbury and an island off the Nova Scotia coast. They claimed that they paid le Mercier's salary regularly, that they gave him money from the congregation's poor fund, and that some of the Church's wealthy supporters, such as André Faneuil, James Bowdoin, and Daniel Johonnot, regularly gave him cash gifts or left him legacies in their wills. The elders denied any responsibility for the Church's collapse. They scarcely could be "answerable for the Death of any of our People," and they insisted that le Mercier himself, not assimilation, had "driven all our Young People to other Churches." Still they wished him well and now offered to give him half the proceeds from their sale of the church building.[35]

The dispute revealed the complete disintegration of refugee cohesion among Boston's Huguenots. Le Mercier died at his

Roxbury farm in 1764 but was interred in Boston. His congregation disbanded in 1748 and never sought another minister. The French Church building that passed into the hands of the mid-eighteenth century revivalist congregation was sold in 1788 to a group of Irish laymen who used it as Boston's first Catholic chapel, an event that was as ironic for the Huguenots who built it as it was for the old Puritan city that surrounded it.[36]

Thus through intermarriage, political achievement, apparent economic success, and shifts in church membership, Huguenot refugees assimilated in a city as renowned for its Puritan past as for its Yankee future. All the bonds that could have united the refugees shattered, some as early as the 1720s, and the sale of the French Church building in 1748 marked only a delayed finale to a long-accomplished fact: Boston's Huguenot refugees had disappeared as a separate people. But elsewhere—in South Carolina where more Huguenots would settle in both urban and rural environments and in New York where they would settle in a multiethnic society—the Huguenots entered astonishingly different New World societies. If they were going to assimilate in these other societies as well, they would emulate social and religious patterns quite unlike those of either Puritan or Yankee Boston.

4 / South Carolina: Refugees in Slavery's Elysium

Early travelers between Massachusetts and South Carolina in the 1680s and 1690s must have wondered how the British colonies in America could have been so different from each other. While New England had entered its post-Puritan age by 1680, the farm villages of Massachusetts and the expanding port of Boston still felt the impress of that imperfect, crabbed society, if only as a legacy. But South Carolina was a new colony with no concern for old reformers and would-be Saints. Here, Royalists and wealthy Barbadian planters scrambled for simple commercial success and brought over West Indian slavery to reap profits from the new colonization then reinvigorating British settlement on the North American mainland.

The early, sharp contrasts between South Carolina and Massachusetts in the 1680s only increased in the next half-century. As Huguenots were entering both societies, Boston emerged as a comfortable, even ornate commercial capital whose momentum had slowed down in an erratic, stagnating economy, though with little noticeable effect on its tiny Huguenot population. But South Carolina emerged as a lush and rich planter society where, by 1720, African slaves comprised two-thirds of the population and as much as 85 percent of the population in some rural parishes. If Charlestown was provincial, it never was sedate or even merely comfortable. Rich planters jammed it with opulent houses, fine furniture, magnificent church buildings, paintings and silver, and, of course, their ubiquitous slaves. Before mid-century some observers had already characterized this materialism as a decadence and sensuality unique in Western culture. John Martin Bolzius offered a particularly critical description of the city and society in 1742. Each day closed with a ceremonial stroll in the damp ocean air. Women teasingly shaded their faces with black masks, while "whites and Negroes of both sexes act most shamefully and make much noise late into the night." "Anyone who has lived in London may have seen and heard [of these] abominations," Bolzius wrote, "but here they have reached the highest peak."[1]

Despite South Carolina's early attachment to slavery and lack of any specific religious purposes, the colony proved an attractive residence for French Protestants just escaped from Catholic persecution. In widely distributed French-language pamphlets, its proprietors advertised firm commitments to religious toleration and freedom and described material opportunities available to Huguenots in opulent terms. In response, Huguenots arrived in the still infant colony as early as 1679 and continued emigrating to it through the 1690s. Once there they never merely followed established patterns, as happened inevitably in Boston. Rather, they took a subtle and sometimes direct role in the shaping of South Carolina. They also began very quickly to assimilate within this newly evolving society. Despite early English resentment of the speed with which Huguenots began to participate in colony politics and despite some Huguenot resistance to the demise of independent French Protestant congregations in the colony, refugee cohesion had suffered serious erosion as early as 1710 and had thoroughly shattered by 1750. By mid-century these Huguenots simply were South Carolinians; aside from their surnames they were indistinguishable from all other settlers in the colony except, of course, slaves.[2]

The seeds of Huguenot assimilation in South Carolina lay in the colony's character as a new, rapidly expanding agricultural settlement. Despite the Huguenots' reputation as bourgeois merchants and artisans, the South Carolina proprietors always emphasized agricultural opportunities in their French-language colonization literature. Certainly the Huguenots responded to these attractions. The list of promises about land, crops, and religious freedom in South Carolina very early obsessed Judith Giton's brother and drove his sister and mother from London to a disastrous New World voyage in 1681 or 1682. The Gitons, like most other Huguenots who came to the colony before 1700, settled in rural, agricultural environments. The largest settlement was in Craven County on the Santee River forty miles north of Charlestown. By the mid-1690s it probably contained about sixty families, and it remained a relatively isolated settlement until sometime after 1700. The second major settlement, variously called Orange Quarter, Poitevin, or St. Denis Parish after 1706, was reached by rowing west and north up the Cooper River past English farmers near Charlestown to the east branch of the Cooper River in Berkeley County. Here, some forty to fifty families lived by the mid-1690s. Two smaller rural Huguenot settlements probably contained no more than ten to fifteen families by the mid-1690s. One was on the west branch of the Cooper River in St. John's Parish in Berkeley County west of the Orange Quarter settlement, and the other was located in St. James Goose Creek Parish in lower Berkeley County just across the bay from Charlestown. Together with the refugees who remained in Charlestown, still an agricultural and trading village in the 1690s, these Huguenots scarcely could have removed themselves further from the ever rising persecution of Protestants in France or from the depressing circumstances of the exile centers of Europe.[3]

The material prospects that attracted the first Huguenots to South Carolina brought laymen rather than ministers to lead the early refugee settlements there. René Petit and Jacob Guerard arranged the settlement of the Santee refugee community after they arrived in South Carolina in 1680. Antoine Poitevin probably performed similar functions for the Orange Quarter settlement, since several documents refer to the settlement simply as "Poitevin." In fact, the South Carolina refugees lacked a permanent Huguenot minister until the mid-1680s. A clergyman named "Fourestier," perhaps Pierre Forestier of Cozes who died in Holland in 1713, was scheduled to sail with Petit and Guerard in 1679 but appears in no South Carolina records. He may have returned to Europe as Boston's Ezéchiel Carré did later, or he may never have embarked for America. Laurent Van den Bosch arrived in Charlestown in 1684 but won no support from the Huguenot community, perhaps because he behaved as outrageously there as he did later in Boston and New York. In any case, he left for Boston in 1685.[4]

However, by at least 1690 and perhaps earlier, three Huguenot ministers served the Huguenot congregations already established by the lay refugees in the colony. Elie Prioleau of Pons in Poitou probably was the first to arrive and is the most visible of the three early ministers. He succeeded his late father as the Protestant minister at Pons and several nearby congregations in 1683 only to watch royal troops destroy the Pons church building in April 1686. Prioleau then fled to London. A year later he received his denization papers, and in May he obtained £8 from the Thread-needle Street Church for a voyage to South Carolina. He probably arrived there in the fall of 1687, joining several refugees from Pons and its neighboring communities who preceeded him to South Carolina.[5]

Prioleau offered South Carolina's early refugees steady, ex-perienced, and committed religious leadership. A seven-page manuscript fragment outlines Prioleau's defense of the Huguenot order in Poitou between 1677 and 1680. He delivered injunctions to new deacons and elders, explained the Lord's Supper, warned against Catholic exhorters who accompanied royal troops, and upheld the need to support poor Protestants. Prioleau's quick departure from Pons and his short stay in London suggest a minister eager to serve French Protestants in the New World, but no surviving manuscripts document his work or success in South Carolina.[6]

In the next several years the South Carolina Huguenots settled two more ministers in their communities, which gave them a ministerial contingent as large as that serving the colony's English-speaking population. Pierre Robert, born in French-speaking Switzerland in 1656 and a minister there until about 1685, served the Santee settlement when he applied for naturalization in 1697. He probably had arrived by 1692 although the exact date remains uncertain. Laurent Trouillart, born about 1646 and a minister at Guines near Calais between 1673 and 1685, was in Charlestown by at least 1693. He shared the French Church pulpit there with Elie Prioleau and preached to the Huguenot farmers at Orange Quarter, St. James Goose Creek, and St. John's Parish in Berkeley County; he settled among the latter in 1700 and died about 1712. In 1695 South Carolina's three Huguenot ministers equalled the number of English ministers in the colony—two Dissenting

Congregationalists at Charlestown and Dorchester and a Church of England minister at Charlestown best known as a drunk who baptized bears.[7]

The Huguenot laity brought diverse skills to their rural settlements, ignoring the strong emphasis the proprietors put in their advertisements for settlers who would take up farmlands. A 1683 letter from the merchant Louis Thibou to a London Huguenot, Gabriel Bontefoy, explains their reasoning. South Carolina needed skilled craftsmen precisely because it was an agricultural colony, and Huguenots "who have a trade [should] come and settle here rather than stay in England." While they languished in London, South Carolina needed them as "carpenters, cobblers, tailors, and other craftsmen necessary for building." It even needed weavers and cloth workers to make clothes, and Thibou told Bontefoy that at least one linen weaver, Jacques Varein of Rouen, was "making lots of money at his trade" in South Carolina.[8]

The 1697 South Carolina Naturalization Act reveals how thoroughly Huguenot males still identified with the occupations in which they had been trained and how diverse those occupations were. The act listed fifty-eight Huguenots by name and occupation. Only twelve (20.7 percent) described themselves as planters. Surprisingly, fourteen (24.1 percent) referred to themselves as workers in the cloth trades (eleven as weavers, two as chamey dressers, and one as a throwster), while only seven (12.1 percent) called themselves merchants. The remaining twenty-five Huguenots plied fifteen skilled trades that included a wheelwright, saddler, brazier, sailmaker, clockmaker, gardener, doctor, watchmaker, apothecary, two goldsmiths, two gunsmiths, two joiners, three blacksmiths, three coopers, and four shipwrights.[9]

Yet even Huguenots who identified themselves with their traditional occupations had already begun farming. Judith Giton's letter of the 1680s describing the miseries of farm labor was particularly significant because it makes the point that so many refugees then were turning to agriculture despite their previous training. On the surface, this transformation may seem surprising. Protestantism in France was closely linked to the bourgeois merchants and artisan and craft classes that furnished many of the Huguenot immigrants in the colony. Nonetheless, the transformation of South Carolina Huguenots from skilled craftsmen and even merchants into farmers fitted the nature of early modern society as well as the peculiarities of the Huguenot migration to America. First, the relative youth of the South Carolina immigrant meant that many refugees had not invested long years of training and experience in their crafts or trades. Second, small farmers always comprised a significant portion of the Huguenot laity in western and southern France, the areas from which most American refugees originated. Third, the narrow occupational specialization characteristic of nineteenth-century industrial society in Europe and America was not applicable to seventeenth-century France. In the face-to-face intimacy of this still overwhelmingly agrarian society, craftsmen, merchants, tradesmen, government officials, and common laborers all possessed useful knowledge about farming methods, animal husbandry, and markets. Even if this knowledge remained incomplete, the men and women of early modern France constantly used it to make basic decisions about their own economic activity.[10]

Although Huguenots were identifying themselves with special skilled occupations in the 1697 Naturalization Act, they began to follow English settlers in buying and farming ever expanding tracts of land. At least twenty-five of the forty-six Huguenots described as merchants and skilled tradesmen in the 1697 Naturalization Act received grants of land from the South Carolina government by 1700, while they and others bought and sold lands through private purchases not recorded in the colony's land grant records. In fact, between 1680 and 1711, at least 147 Huguenot males received land grants from the provincial government. Some were small and unique. Isaac Remich for example, received only a single grant of 100 acres in 1696, and Isaac Varry, who arrived as an indentured servant in 1686, received fifty acres when he completed his indenture in 1694. Neither man received any more from the South Carolina government.[11]

Other refugees received much larger single grants. Adam Carlie moved to New York by the mid-1690s but had received a grant for 360 acres from the South Carolina government in 1687; Peter Dubartee received 200 acres in 1696; and Gideon Faucheraud received 160 acres in 1708. Far more Huguenots received several large grants, and some refugees acquired enormous amounts of land in their lifetimes. James De Bourdeaux received three grants of unknown size in 1692 and 1693, acquired 400 additional acres in 1697, 100 acres in 1698, and 240 acres in 1711 for a total of over 740 acres in twenty years. Other refugees acquired even more land. John Gaillard received 300 acres in 1696, 100 acres in 1698, 200 acres in 1708, 1,900 acres in 1709, and two grants of 640 acres each in 1710 for a total of 3,780 acres in fourteen years. Philippe Gendron received 650 acres in three separate grants made in 1697, 300 acres in 1703, 1,420 acres in two grants in 1709, and 1,980 acres in three grants in 1710, thus totaling 4,350 acres of land in thirteen years—all of this exclusive of any private purchases.

The magnitude of lands held by early Huguenot settlers in South Carolina and of the colony's generosity to the refugees stands out when their record is compared to that of English settlers in seventeenth-century New England. Most farmers in New England towns acquired about 150 acres of land, much of which was given out in fifty or sixty-acre allotments in the course of their lifetime. The largest New England farmers received as much as 300 or 350 acres. In contrast, between 1680 and 1700 South Carolina Huguenots acquired at least 36,000 acres of land from the government, and between 1701 and 1711 they nearly doubled that figure to more than 68,000 acres. Thus between 1690 and 1711 South Carolina's colonial government gave and sold them well over 104,000 acres of land, or an average of 710 acres per farmer, twice as much as even the largest farmers received in seventeenth-century New England.[12]

South Carolina's Huguenot refugees also began assimilating when they lost interest in agricultural products traditionally associated with them: wine and silk. Both appeared in South Carolina, but wine-making only briefly, and silk production only in the context of other farming activities. Viticulture and its accompanying wine-making process occupied the attention of at least some refugees in the 1690s. In 1694, for example, the South Carolina Council awarded Jean Boyd, a member of the South Carolina Assembly, 3,000 acres to encourage planting a vineyard. The effort failed, however, and all reliable evidence shows that wine-making remained a casual enterprise among South Carolina

Huguenots until the 1760s when the government made new efforts to encourage a profitable viticulture in the colony.[13]

More refugees attempted silk production, especially before 1710. The enterprise was a subtle blend of agriculture and industry. Silkworms imported from Europe fed on the leaves of native mulberry trees and produced a raw silk that throwsters spun into thread. The thread then could be woven into a pure silk cloth that brought high prices or into a coarser cloth, a mixture of silk and wool called drugget, that was less expensive. In Europe, French Protestants had dominated the silk industry, and they did so in South Carolina as well. Some produced the raw silk; others spun both silk and drugget. And some raw silk went to London where throwsters, most of them also Huguenots, turned it into cloth, probably raw silk, and thereby realized the mercantilist conception of the colonies as purveyors of raw goods for Old World industries.[14]

The Huguenot silk industry played an important but short-term role in the Carolina refugee economy. Although it never dominated Huguenot agricultural enterprises, some thought it would. The *Richmond* carried silkworm eggs with it on the voyage to South Carolina in 1679, but when the voyage took longer than anticipated, the worms hatched at sea and died for lack of food. Despite this setback the refugees who pursued the industry met with some success in the next decade. In the late 1690s Governor John Archdale presented the colony's proprietors with a sample of raw silk to demonstrate the increasing importance of the product, and in the next decade, he told the proprietors that the industry had made "great improvement, some families making 40 lb. or 50lbs. a Year and their plantations not neglected."[15]

Yet this was probably the zenith of Huguenot silk production in the 1710s. Twenty years later, only estate inventories of the wealthiest Huguenot planters mention materials associated with the silk industry. When South Carolina authorities turned to Huguenots to reinvigorate the industry in the 1730s, they had to restudy the industry. A 1738 legislative commission headed by Isaac Mazyck hired John Lewis Poyas to launch a subsidized six-year experiment to renew silk production, but the effort apparently failed. Authorities launched another such attempt in 1764, engaging the wealthy Gabriel Manigault to manage the project.

But so few South Carolinians, including the head of the project, knew anything about the industry that Manigault had to hire several of the new Swiss immigrants from the backcountry settlement of New Bordeaux "to wind and teach the winding of silk," and he put silkworms on display in the main room of the Charlestown Library Society to familiarize even Huguenot planters with an 'industry they had long since forgotten.[16]

In fact, Huguenots soon turned from silk production to the diversified agriculture that characterized South Carolina's evolving agrarian economy. Louis Thibou's 1683 letter to Gabriel Bontefoy of London only slightly romanticized the multiple crops harvested in early South Carolina. Food could be gotten from "fine rivers full of fish." The soil produced "bountiful crops of peas, wheat, and garden-melons." The cherries "become as red as wine inside." Domestic pigs, bulls, and cows fed in the woods, and "the only trouble they are is to milk them." Madeira grapes produced fruit that was "sweet, winey and full of juice." Thibou wished he could get vines from "Champagne, Suresne and Argenteuil"; perhaps others did too.[17]

The cornucopia described in Thibou's letter was less glowing in reality, and in the early colony Huguenot and English farmers both squeezed livings out of nature and necessity together. In this agricultural context Huguenot farmers never concentrated exclusively on viticulture or silk production. They cultivated numerous crops, harvested wild fruits, and slaughtered both wild and domestic animals just as their English neighbors did. Their silk production and, perhaps, their viticulture provided additional income in a diversified economy that welcomed and needed such goods. When English settlers intensified their animal production after 1695, Huguenots also followed suit. In just two years between 1696 and 1698, the colony's secretary recorded cattle marks for fourteen Huguenots in the settlements at Santee, Orange Quarter, and in St. John's Parish in Berkeley County. In registering his mark, Isaac Mazyck demonstrated that the refugees had not yet forgotten their persecution in France. Even Mazyck's cattle maligned the Sun King as they wallowed in the Carolina mud since, as the colony secretary wrote, Mazyck "recorded his Brand Mark for Cattle etc. which is a Flower-de-Luis upon the Right Buttock."[18]

In its own strange way, it is the career of a silversmith, Nicolas de Longemare, Jr., that demonstrates how versatile the refugees could be in teasing a living out of a young and rapidly expanding society. Together with his father and the former Boston refugee Solomon Légaré, de Longemare is best known as one of South Carolina's first silversmiths and goldsmiths. His account books for 1703–1710 demonstrate an extraordinary, clever, and wide-ranging involvement with the trades. De Longemare made silver and brass seals, shoe buckles, brass weights, spoons and forks, mourning and wedding rings, eyeglasses, and various types of seals for the South Carolina government and its officials. But his Charlestown shop sold more than silver. He also traded in rum, olive oil, linseed oil, lamp oil, and hoes. He purchased 100 acres of land at the Santee settlement in 1685 and owned land at the Cooper River settlement as well. He registered marks for cattle and swine with the South Carolina secretary in 1696. According to his account books, de Longemare lived on his Santee farm for several months during the year where he bought and sold raw silk, silkworm eggs, and drugget, rented cattle pens to other farmers, and sold wheat, cotton, beef, and mutton.[19]

As the South Carolina Huguenots turned increasingly to farming, they also turned ever more steadily into slave-holders, and neither their religion nor their own experience of persecution led them to oppose this developing colonial institution. In the earlier seventeenth century, Huguenots sometimes expressed dismay over slavery but never prohibited the ownership or trade in slaves. In 1637 the Huguenot Synod at Rouen criticized the slave trade but failed to ban French Protestant involvement in it. After the Revocation, refugees in Holland sometimes lashed out at slavery as antithetical to Christian ethics. Pierre Jurieu argued that slavery contradicted nature, and another refugee, Jacques Bernard, argued that it violated the "golden rule." But neither spoke with any institutional authority, and they addressed their comments to European refugees for whom slavery was an obscure, abstract issue.[20]

In South Carolina Huguenots acquired slaves very early and used them, as did English colonists, to furnish the labor demanded by their ever expanding farms. The French refugees arrived in America in the very decade that many mainland

colonists first began importing slaves in massive numbers. South
Carolina's Huguenots quickly joined this accelerating trend. Even
as early as 1683, Louis Thibou observed in a letter that "several
good Negroes and other good servants" would quickly increase
one's wealth in the colony. Some refugees had indeed arrived with
indentured servants. In 1680 Thibou himself brought two, a
Monsieur De Russerie arrived with one, and Jacob Guerard came
with six. But in the 1690s Huguenots and Englishmen alike
increasingly turned to slaves for laborers. Two of three surviving
South Carolina Huguenot estate inventories before 1700 list
slaves—Pierre Perdriau's (1693) with one adult male and Arnaud
Bruneau's (1695) with four men, two women, and one child—and
other refugees received government land grants for importing
slaves.[21]

Material describing early Huguenot interaction with slaves is
very limited. The Revolutionary War General Peter Horry
recalled that his Parisian grandfather worked long saws with
African slaves at the Santee settlement in the 1690s. In 1710 the
minister James Gignilliat observed that many Santee Huguenots
owned slaves and that they were as reluctant to baptize them as
were their English neighbors. The refugees believed that once
baptized, slaves became poor workers, in part because newly
arrived slaves ridiculed them. In his reconstruction of the South
Carolina population, the historian Peter Wood demonstrates that
in 1720 Craven County's St. James Santee Parish, still largely
French, was nearly three-fourths African, with 584 slaves (73.6
percent) living among only 210 whites. Only two of the colony's
eleven parishes, St. John's and St. James Goose Creek, both in
Berkeley County, contained larger percentages of slaves (74.4
percent and 79.1 percent).[22]

Despite the Huguenots' already deep accommodation to the
South Carolina economy, the refugees found themselves effectively disenfranchised and all but thoroughly excluded from the
South Carolina Assembly between 1695 and 1710. This English
bigotry and manipulation of national hostility might have forged
new links of unity among the refugees in the colony. But that did
not happen, perhaps because those who acted against the Huguenots in good part confined their discrimination carefully to
certain formal aspects of the colony's political life and never

allowed popular anti-Huguenot sentiment to shape broad public
policy toward the refugees.

The political problems that Huguenots experienced in South
Carolina stemmed from their inability to avoid entanglement in
the bitter political struggles that divided the colony's English
settlers between 1690 and the overthrow of the proprietary
government in 1719. After 1680 the political climate in the colony
vibrated with factional tension. These factions included settlers
who backed the proprietors, the "Goose Creek" faction that was
against them, an ill-defined "Dissenter" group ostensibly linked to
Presbyterian interests, and an equally ill-defined "Church party"
informally linked to Church of England interests. These factions
complicated South Carolina's political maturation, and they
prospered through shifting personal alliances rather than
through clear ideological and religious principles.[23]

Huguenots could not escape becoming involved in the colony's
byzantine political struggles. For one thing, the multiplicity of
political factions increased the potential importance of the refugees. Huguenots constituted between 10 and 15 percent of the
colony's adult white population, a group as large as some of the
English factions. Secondly, the use of single-county election
districts, combined with the government's willingness to allow
Huguenot voting and office-holding before 1695, exaggerated
Huguenot political strength. Since the Santee community remained the only significant settlement in Craven County, Huguenots won election to all six county seats in the first South
Carolina Assembly of 1692–4. This gave Huguenots a third of the
assembly's twenty seats. Before 1691, tangential evidence suggests
that some of these budding Huguenot politicians supported the
anti-proprietary Goose Creek faction. By 1692 this relationship
apparently soured and the Goose Creek men who dominated the
South Carolina Council retaliated by peevishly restricting Sabbath
worship at Charlestown's French Church to 9 A.M. or 2 P.M. At the
very least, the order was inconvenient. The French Church
frequently changed its hours of worship to accommodate rural
members who could only row to Charlestown at high tide. When
the congregation's assistant minister, Laurent Trouillart, pro-
tested the council's action, the London proprietors used the
occasion to chastise Huguenots for earlier supporting the anti-

proprietary faction. "When you have tried all," the proprietors wrote, "you will find the Lords Proprietors themselves the best Friends you have . . . and the only persons that will protect you against the Envy and Injurys of the People there."[24]

Unfortunately, during the next decade the proprietors defended the Huguenots no better than they governed the colony. Some English colonists claimed that Huguenot children might not be able to inherit property if their parents' naturalization or denization papers were not in order. Others taunted the refugees with claims that marriages performed by Huguenot ministers who lacked Anglican ordination were unlawful and that the "Children that are begotten in such Marriages are Bastards." Although the proprietors denied the truth of the claims, they could not keep South Carolinians from making them. Nor could they keep these prejudices from affecting colony politics. In 1695 some 100 English settlers petitioned the council to "have an Assembly of Purely English & Elected onely by English." According to the council, the petitioners asserted "their priviledge of English men and think it very hard that the French who are refugees and ought to be Subject to our Lawes are permitted to be Law Maker[s] and to Serve on Juryes." In agreement, Governor John Archdale, a Quaker, ordered assembly elections in 1695 for Colleton and Berkeley counties but refused to issue election writs for Craven County, "there being not above Thirty Inhabitants and those all French." For several subsequent elections, the Council combined Craven County with Berkeley County to dilute Huguenot voting strength. The technique worked. In five elections held between 1696 and 1705, only six Huguenots won seats in the assembly—two in 1696 and one each in 1698, 1702 and 1703—although voters chose thirty assemblymen in each election.[25]

The exclusion of the Huguenots from the assembly proved to be a narrow, specific effort to keep the colony's bitter factionalism within English bounds. It never signaled persecution of the refugees and failed to stimulate long-term cohesion among them. In fact the 1696 election reveals how easily Huguenots had voted before 1695, and how some English voters still elected Huguenots to the assembly after 1695. When the Berkeley County sheriff demanded letters of naturalization before allowing Isaac Cailleboeuf, James Le Sade, and James Bonhoste to vote in 1696, the refugees "answered that they had not any [letters] but had lived in the county several years, and never before had been denied to vote for members of the assembly." Despite this intimidation, the largely English voters of Berkeley County sent two Huguenots to the 1696–7 Assembly. In turn, the assembly in which they sat passed an act that naturalized the Huguenot refugees. This far-reaching legislation offered "foreign aliens" all liberties accorded English residents in South Carolina including those of owning and inheriting property, voting, and jury service. The act mentioned fifty-eight French males by name and also included four Sephardic Jews then trading in Charlestown. All of them would receive South Carolina naturalization as would other aliens who registered with the colony's secretary within three months of the final passage of the act.[26]

From an English perspective, the 1697 Naturalization Act simply legalized liberties the refugees had in fact enjoyed since their arrival in the 1680s. Thus, even as some South Carolinians ridiculed Huguenot political activity and the council restricted Huguenot worship in Charlestown, the refugees continued to receive land grants from the government. But the 1697 Naturalization Act carried special importance for the Huguenots, who drew a crucial distinction between *de facto* and *de jure* liberties. Memory of the misuse of law in France and the recent, if limited, outbreak of anti-Huguenot sentiment in South Carolina led them to seek all the legal devices they might claim to protect the property and position they had obtained in the colony since 1680. Thus, South Carolina's Huguenot family heads registered themselves and some 350 others for naturalization after passage of the act, even though about a fifth of the family heads already had been endenized in London. South Carolina naturalization gave the sanction of law to the property and voting privileges they already acquired in the colony but which the London denization did not actually protect.[27]

The 1697 Naturalization Act eliminated an important formal bar to further Huguenot assimilation in South Carolina. However, it could not eliminate continuing English prejudice against Huguenots in the colony. Such hostility apparently forestalled the move of some Huguenots to an area near Port Royal south of

Charlestown in 1699. In the same year, Governor Joseph Morton complained that a Huguenot ship captain from New York as well as other "foreigners" frequently belittled British officials in America, although records of these slights seem not to have survived. In 1702 the so-called Dissenter party in the assembly cited some thirty Huguenots for illegal voting but prosecuted none of them, and in 1704 the Dissenter party grouped Huguenots with other despised minorities who opposed their faction and demanded dissolution of the 1704 assembly on grounds that it had been elected by "Jews, strangers, sailors, servants, negroes and almost every Frenchman in Berkeley and Craven Counties."[28]

However, the response of the assembly to an incident in 1707 revealed that anti-Huguenot prejudice often masked partisan political maneuvering in South Carolina and lacked deeper cultural roots. In June 1707 Peter Maillett attempted to reinforce Huguenot support in the upcoming assembly elections for the badly weakened Church party by charging that the Dissenter party intended to abrogate the privileges of voting and inheriting property granted to Huguenots by the 1697 Naturalization Act. In a letter to Antoine Poitevin, leader of the Orange Quarter settlement, Maillett claimed that these "Gentlemen presbiterians would bring Tyranny upon us as pharoh did upon the Children of Israel." But if Poitevin came to Maillett's home, Maillett would show him the "true lists [of] those [you should] vote for" and thereby would "not only oblige me but also the Governor," who backed the Church party, "and the Rest of the french."[29]

The 1707 Assembly adamantly repudiated Maillett's charges. The new assembly ordered officials to prosecute Maillett "for the words written in the said Letter" and passed a declaration "for the Quieting and Appeasing the minds of the french Inhabitants". The new assembly denied that it or its predecessor intended to discriminate against the Huguenots. Instead, it would do its "utmost To Confirm and Strengthen their Interest and Inheritance To Them and There Posterity, whatever the mallice of Selfe Intresed people may Suggest To them To the Contrary."[30]

Later outbursts of anti-Huguenot sentiment in South Carolina expressed personal sentiment or prejudice rather than any dangerous government policy. In the early 1710s the Anglican

Commissary Gideon Johnston belittled religious disputes then plaguing the Huguenots at Orange Quarter and Santee as stemming from the "levity and fickleness of the French Nation." A decade later, charges of illegal Huguenot voting again surfaced in the assembly during a bitter debate over paper currency. Yet neither produced long-term consequences. Johnston's comments were only personal observations made in private letters to London Anglicans, and the assembly ignored the illegal voting charges. Rather, both demonstrate that even the limited anti-Huguenot sentiment of the 1690s receded significantly after 1710.[31]

To the contrary, there is substantial evidence of Huguenot entrance into South Carolina elite society by as early as 1710. Jack P. Greene's analysis of committee assignments in the South Carolina Assembly demonstrates that the Huguenot Jean Boyd was a second rank assemblyman in the 1692–94 Assembly and that Benjamin Godin, John Guerard, Henry Le Noble, John Motte, and Louis Pasquereau were first or second rank assemblymen between 1706 and 1720. Henry Le Noble carved out a distinguished political career from the mid-1690s through 1712 despite the attempt to restrict early Huguenot political activity. He was one of the two Huguenots elected to the assembly from Berkeley County in 1696, and he served on several important committees in that assembly to audit public accounts and rewrite the Jury Duty Act. Le Noble then moved on to serve on South's Carolina's Grand Council in the next decade, after which he returned to the assembly between 1708 and 1712. Huguenot efforts to cultivate political influence can sometimes be seen in personal affairs. The merchant Isaac Mazyck, for example, invited Governor Edward Tynte to be godfather to his infant daughter Penelope at her baptism in January 1710 even though Tynte had no known Huguenot background and had only arrived in the colony in 1709.[32]

The Huguenot presence in South Carolina's high society is even recorded in the art of Henrietta Johnston, South Carolina's first known portraitist. While her husband, Anglican Commissary Gideon Johnston, guided the fortunes of the Church of England in the colony, Henrietta recorded the faces of its elite in oil and pastel portraits painted between her arrival in 1707 and her death in 1728. She was not a great artist, alas, and the faces of the men and women she painted lack depth and individuality. But she provided a touch of refinement that early Charlestown residents both desired and lacked. Huguenots are the subjects of a full third of her forty surviving portraits, and she became well acquainted with many of the refugees, especially Paul L'Escot, Charlestown's Huguenot minister between 1700 and 1719, who developed a close relationship with her husband. Her portraits of the Charlestown silversmith Samuel Prioleau and his wife Mary Magdalen Gendron, the son and daughter-in-law of the early minister Elie Prioleau, underscore the position these and other Huguenots reached in South Carolina in the three decades after their arrival in the 1680s.[33]

Whether this entry of Huguenots into South Carolina's elite also signaled their early simultaneous turn to exogamy is impossible to tell. The colonial records of Charlestown's French Church have been lost, and only fragmentary records of the colony's English churches have survived for the years before 1720. Still, at least a few exogamous unions involving Huguenots appear in the remaining early records: the marriages of the widow Elizabeth Gaillard and Jonathan Skrine in 1719; Susanne Poitevin, daughter of the Orange Quarter Huguenot Antoine Poitevin, and John Snow in 1720; Isaac Lesesne and Frances Netherton in 1722; Anne DuBose, a Huguenot painted by Henrietta Johnston, and a German, Job Rothmahler, in 1722; Francis Le Jau, son of a Dublin-educated Huguenot minister who served the English parish of St. James Goose Creek, and Mary Ashby, a resident of that parish, in 1726. Clearly, at least by the early 1720s a few Huguenots were finding spouses outside their national and religious group. But it is impossible to determine the pace and depth of this early Huguenot exogamy without additional records.[34]

The substantial deterioration of French Protestant church life in the critical years between 1700 and 1710 gave special meaning to the secular assimilation Huguenots had already experienced and profoundly shaped their future in South Carolina. By the early 1690s the settlers had formed French Protestant congregations in each settlement and hired three French Protestant ministers to serve them. But between 1700 and 1715 much of this

1. Portrait of Samuel Prioleau, by Henrietta Johnston, c. 1720

2. Portrait of Mary Magdalen Gendron, wife of Samuel Prioleau, by Henrietta
Johnston, c. 1720

early work was undone. The important rural congregations at Santee and Orange Quarter conformed to the Church of England, the small Huguenot congregations in Berkeley County in St. John's Parish and St. James Goose Creek Parish disbanded, and Charlestown's independent French Church struggled with a minister who came to be much disliked by his congregation because, in part, he advocated conformity to the Church of England.

None of these difficulties originated in a social vacuum. The apparently easy adoption of English ways in farming, the rapid turn to slave-holding, the passage of the 1697 Naturalization Act, and the acceptance of Huguenots by the colony's social and political elite all promoted fragmentation of South Carolina's French Protestant church order, the church being the main agency of refugee cohesion. Yet neither the secular causes nor the social effects of that fragmentation fully explain its occurrence. Other causes, some religious, some linked directly to South Carolina's political milieu, proved equally important. The lack of a larger denominational structure uniting refugees in Europe and America, an affinity for Anglicanism among Huguenot ministers if not the laity, poor finances in the congregations, and the immediate pressure of South Carolina factionalism also played important roles in shattering Huguenot religious institutions in South Carolina between 1700 and 1710.

There are also important signs of cooperation among South Carolina's French congregations and evidence of help extended to the Charlestown congregation by London's Threadneedle Street Church in the 1690s even though all formal records of the colony's French Huguenot congregations were lost. A 1699 letter to the Threadneedle Street Church and government land grants to Laurent Trouillart between 1704 and 1711 suggest that Trouillart served the congregations in Charlestown and in St. John's Parish in Berkeley County in the 1690s and subsequently ministered to the congregations in St. John's Parish and Orange Quarter between 1700 and at least 1706, when the latter conformed to the Church of England. Additional evidence, admittedly oblique, suggests that the congregations maintained a common burial ground in Charlestown as early as 1694. Family records kept by the merchant Isaac Mazyck refer to interments of infants in 1694 and 1712 in the cemetery of "lesglises [sic] francoise De Charlestown" and to the interment of another infant in "le Simetiere de Notre Esglises" in 1714—the use of the plural *églises* suggesting that all the colony's French congregations maintained the Charlestown burial ground. This cooperation may have reflected a broader unity among the early refugee congregations, perhaps even a "colloquy" of the kind Ezechiel Carré attempted to organize in New England. But, again, it is impossible to establish the point in the absence of church records.[35]

Participation of South Carolina's refugees in the exile community formed by the international Huguenot diaspora is more available from London sources than from South Carolina materials. The death of Elie Prioleau in 1699 and the subsequent decision of Laurent Trouillart to move to the small Huguenot settlement in St. John's Parish in Berkeley County forced Charlestown's French Church elders to look beyond the colony for a new minister. They found help at London's Threadneedle Street Church. In May 1700 the London congregation received two letters from Charlestown offering a prospective minister a yearly salary of £60 for five years plus £30 for ship passage to America. The Threadneedle Street officers acted swiftly to help Charlestown's French Church fill its vacancy. Through their contacts on the Continent they secured Paul L'Escot from Geneva, and L'Escot was preaching in Charlestown by Christmas 1700.[36]

L'Escot could have strengthened Charlestown's French Church and the other Huguenot congregations in South Carolina. Instead, the new minister's sophistication and international connections weakened his commitment to a distinctive French Protestant church order, strained relations with his Charlestown congregation, and finally led him to denounce attempts to preserve traditional French Protestant worship in the rural congregations. Letters to the Genevan theologian Jean Alphonse Turrettini reveal something of L'Escot's intellectual interests. L'Escot conducted an international correspondence with Turrettini, with the well-known Neuchâtel theologian Jean Frederic Ostervald, and with exiled Huguenot ministers in England and Berlin. In 1713 he sent Turrettini a manuscript on South Carolina (now lost) and a set of dried rattlesnake skins to satisfy Turrettini's interests as a naturalist.[37]

Paul L'Escot's links to Turrettini and Ostervald probably encouraged his sympathy for the Church of England. Turrettini and Ostervald both were corresponding members of the Anglican-sponsored S.P.G. and S.P.C.K. (Society for the Propagation of the Gospel in Foreign Parts, and Society for Promoting Christian Knowledge). They promoted ecumenical union among European Protestants to combat the Catholic menace dramatically evidenced in the Revocation and Huguenot diaspora. In Charlestown L'Escot at first developed close links to the dissenting minister of the small New England-style Calvinist congregation. But as early as 1710, the Anglican Commissary Gideon Johnston reported that L'Escot had severed these ties and "would most willingly receive Episcopal Ordination, could he conveniently go for South Britain."[38]

L'Escot's Anglican sympathies stimulated a decade of tension within the Charlestown French Church. L'Escot asked his elders in 1710 if they would permit his Anglican ordination, but they refused. His Huguenot ordination was legitimate, and they claimed that they did not want to "be without him for so long a time, as a Voyage to S. Britain would require." Between 1713 and 1715 L'Escot compromised his position among many of his fellow Huguenots when he warned laity and ministers alike against resisting Anglican conformity in South Carolina's rural French churches. Finally, sometime after 1717, L'Escot's disagreement with his congregation came to a head over money. L'Escot reported that when he and his wife built "a rather lovely little brick house" in Charlestown and "bought two black slaves for our service," the French Church elders refused to raise his salary although L'Escot believed they had "more than enough means to support him." Rather than sell house and slaves just to preach in Charlestown, L'Escot left the congregation in 1719 to settle in England.[39]

The other ministers either shared L'Escot's Anglican sympathies or refused to oppose Anglican conformity when the issue was first raised in 1706 and when Huguenot laymen rebelled against it after 1712. Laurent Trouillart's brother Pierre was the Anglican-ordained minister of the conformist Huguenot congregation at Canterbury in England, and it is possible, but not at all certain, that Laurent received Anglican ordination before coming to South Carolina. Certainly neither of the English ministers at St. John's Parish where he lived after 1700 recorded any expressions of hostility on his part to the issue of Anglican conformity at Orange Quarter in 1706, and in 1710 the Anglican Commissary Gideon Johnston described him as distinctly favorable to the Anglican cause. Very little is known about Pierre Robert, minister at Santee from the early 1690s until 1709, except for one important fact: when the Anglican-ordained Huguenot minister James Gignilliat assumed the ministerial duties at St. James Santee Parish in 1709, he recorded no opposition from Robert. The Dublin-educated and Anglican-ordained Huguenot minister Francis Le Jau arrived in the colony a year after the Santee and Orange Quarter settlements conformed to the Church of England, but he was able to aid the Anglican cause later. His ministry for the English settlers of St. James Goose Creek Parish encouraged refugees in the parish's small Huguenot settlement to join his Anglican congregation. Later he preached at Orange Quarter and Santee and rebuffed lay Huguenots who opposed Anglican conformity.[40]

Conditions within the South Carolina Huguenot congregations in the countryside further encouraged Anglican conformity and weakened the Huguenot commitment to independent French churches. The Santee settlement probably contained some forty families by 1705 but reputedly found it difficult to support its minister. Whether the problem was purely financial or stemmed from a disagreement with Pierre Robert remains unknown. The Orange Quarter settlement was larger but never had a minister of its own. Instead, its settlers shared the services of Paul L'Escot, Laurent Trouillart, or Pierre Robert. In quite different ways, Anglican conformity solved the problems of both parishes. In exchange for recognizing Anglican ecclesiastical authority and for using the Anglican liturgy, the Orange Quarter settlement finally received its own minister, and the salaries of the ministers of both settlements were paid by the South Carolina government.[41]

The real catalyst for the sudden Anglican conformity of South Carolina's rural Huguenot congregations in 1706 was the tumultuous political skirmishing in the colony. The specific political cause was the protracted dispute over the establishment of the Church of England that began in the 1690s. This dispute was a

largely three-sided affair. It involved Dissenters who opposed
Anglican establishment altogether, moderate Anglicans who supported the establishment but without a commissary representing
the bishop of London, and more traditional Anglicans who
believed a strong Church of England needed a commissary with
strong disciplinary powers. In 1704 an assembly dominated by the
latter group narrowly passed a church act that, for the first time,
established the Church of England in the colony, authorized a
commissary and a board of lay church commissioners (a sop to
critics of the commissary), and disqualified all non-Anglicans and
Dissenters from the assembly. However, the act said nothing
about Huguenots or their conformity. The political disen-
franchisement of Dissenters and the establishment of the church
commission of laymen angered both Dissenters and Anglicans in
London, so the Privy Council vetoed the act and thereby left the
colony once again without a government-supported church.[42]

The South Carolina Church Act of 1706 established the ecclesiastical system that shaped much of the colony's religious life
down to the Revolution and brought most rural Huguenots
within the Anglican fold. Huguenots played a fascinating role in
passing this act. While the 1704 act failed to mention the
Huguenots at all, the 1706 Church Act established Huguenot
parishes at Orange Quarter (St. Denis) and Santee (St. James
Santee). Although only a single Huguenot sat in the thirty-
member 1704 Assembly and only three Huguenots sat in the
1706 Assembly, their votes may have been important in the
closely divided assembly. The first church legislation passed by
that assembly was a peculiar bill that established a government-
supported parish at the Santee settlement but failed to link it to
any larger church-establishment plan for the colony. This may
have been done to test Huguenot support for conformity and to
probe assembly support for subsequent full Anglican establishment. Failure to secure the conformity of the rural Huguenots
would have excluded major portions of the South Carolina low
country from the traditional system of territorial parishes Anglicans hoped to establish in the colony. However, Huguenot
conformity at Santee and Orange Quarter gave the newly
established church significant territorial breadth even as it sub-

stantially increased the number of Anglican adherents in the colony.

It probably was no accident, then, that in April 1706, seven months before passage of the 1706 Church Act, the assembly received a petition from an unknown number of Huguenots at Santee, where Pierre Robert was the minister, asking the legislature to incorporate the settlement as an Anglican parish. The assembly granted the request quickly. It named the parish St. James Santee, authorized an Anglican-ordained minister to be paid a yearly salary of £100 in South Carolina currency, and obliged the parishioners to use a French translation of the *Book of Common Prayer,* meaning John Durel's *La Liturgie* which Anglican printers in London had just issued in yet another edition.[43]

Passage of the more comprehensive 1706 Church Act in November completed the legal process of Huguenot conformity of Santee and Orange Quarter. The new act included all the details of the legislation passed earlier incorporating St. James Santee Parish. But it also created a second conformist Huguenot parish at Orange Quarter called St. Denis Parish. Here, Huguenots and Anglicans solved a difficult legal problem in a strikingly creative way. Because Huguenots at Orange Quarter never were thoroughly separated from other English settlers along the Cooper River, the 1706 Church Act defined St. Denis parish by language rather than by geography. The 1706 Church Act simply defined St. Denis as containing all the French-speaking Anglicans within the larger English parish of St. Thomas that encompassed much of central Berkeley County. This made St. Denis the first and only linguistically defined Anglican parish ever created in the American colonies. The 1706 Church Act also stipulated that St. Denis Parish would cease to exist when its French-speaking adherents died and that any church building constructed for French use (one was built in 1708) would become a "chapel of ease" for the larger St. Thomas Parish. Finally, the act named three Huguenots to the twenty-one member church commission empowered to assist the commissary in governing the colony's new church establishment. Although the commission possessed little effective authority, its inclusion of Huguenots as much bespoke their special role in establishing the Church of

England in South Carolina as it uncovered their eagerness to dismantle the independent French Protestant congregations in the South Carolina countryside.[44]

However, not all Huguenots were willing to surrender the independent congregations, whatever the benefits of Anglican conformity. About 1712 discontented Huguenot laymen in St. Denis Parish (old Orange Quarter) forced their minister to abandon Anglican-style worship. By 1720, when the colony's authorities suppressed this revolt, they faced a more bizzare, if less widespread, challenge to the Anglican hegemony from several St. Denis families in what became known as the "Dutartre affair." These challenges to the establishment suggest that many lay Huguenots carried deep commitments to traditional French Protestant worship and believed that they had been betrayed by their Huguenot ministers and some Huguenot laymen.

Even before the St. Denis revolt, the Huguenot laity often balked at using the new Anglican ritual. The Anglican-ordained James Gignilliat arrived at St. James Santee in 1709 and promptly wrote the S.P.G. in London that his parishioners viewed John Durel's *La Liturgie* as "strange." He warned that they probably would reject it despite his assurances that its rituals and prayers "derive[d] from the primitive church." Yet an equally severe obstacle to "anglicanizing" the St. James Santee Huguenots proved to be Gignilliat himself. In 1715 he embarrassed both the Santee Huguenots and his Anglican superiors by leaving the ministry to marry a rich, childless Huguenot widow whom he soon abandoned after acquiring all her lands. His successor, Philippe de Richebourg, compromised the Anglican cause again when he too slighted Durel's *La Liturgie* and returned to traditional French Calvinist services. The South Carolina Anglican Commissary Gideon Johnston charged that de Richebourg "wholly made use of the 'Geneva Way'" despite his receipt of a government salary. After many threats from Johnston, de Richebourg finally reintroduced Durel's liturgy in the parish sometime around 1720. By 1723, however, de Richebourg's successor, Albert Pouderous, told the S.P.G. that Anglican conformity was no longer an issue. St. James Santee possessed "a Parish Church and a fine Chappell [and] a fine parsonage for the minister" and was "exactly served according to the Cannons of the Church of England."[45]

In the St. Denis revolt of 1713–1720, transatlantic links to the larger refugee communities of Europe transformed local anti-Anglican sentiment into a potentially dangerous religious radicalism at the edges of the American wilderness. As at St. James Santee, lay Huguenots objected to Durel's *La Liturgie*, and the new St. Denis minister, John La Pierre, departed from it so frequently that Commissary Gideon Johnston threatened to suspend his salary and dismiss him from the parish. When La Pierre resumed use of the Anglican liturgy, his parishioners secured the aid of St. James Santee's Philippe de Richebourg in performing traditional Calvinist services. Again Commissary Gideon Johnston objected and ordered de Richebourg to return to his own parish. Significantly, however, the St. Denis Huguenots claimed that when the 1706 Church Act was passed, Governor Nathaniel Johnson assured them that they could receive the Lord's Supper "in the Genevan Posture." Otherwise, as Governor Johnson reportedly acknowledged, there "would be no Purpose" to send an Anglican-ordained minister to the Huguenot parish.[46]

What made the St. Denis revolt dangerous was that it drew on the radical views of London's so-called French Prophets. These Huguenot exiles from France's War of the Cévennes fled to London in 1705. There, they promoted spiritual enthusiasm, spoke in tongues, preached millennialism, and believed in the performance of miracles including the raising of the dead. They alarmed refugee Huguenot ministers from both conformist and nonconformist Huguenot congregations, all of whom expended enormous energy combating the Prophets' influence among the Huguenot laity.[47]

The Huguenot laity at St. Denis used London's French Prophets as inspiration and a general model for an eclectic protest that revealed enormous spiritual vitality and deep religious convictions. They knew of the Prophets through correspondence with refugees in London, and some of the South Carolina Huguenots owned literature on the French Prophets. These included works that attacked them—*An Account of the French Prophets and Their Pretended Inspirations* (London, 1708)—and others that defended them—*Plainte, et censure des colomneuses accusations publiees par le Sr. Claude Grosteste de la [Mothe]* (London, 1708—referring to "the calumnies of de la Mothe," one of London's leading conformist Huguenot clergymen and an active S.P.G. member. Indeed, the St. Denis minister John La Pierre wrote de la Mothe himself to complain that his parishioners, especially the poor, had adopted the principles of the "false prophets of London" and had left the St. Denis congregation.[48]

La Pierre's letter to de la Mothe, written in 1714, illustrates the spiritual range of the St. Denis dissidents. The Parish had witnessed protests "of a furious manner against Anglican ministers" and against Durel's *La Liturgie*. La Pierre traced these protests to "Maître Bochet," probably either Nicholas or Abel Bochet, who appear on the 1697 South Carolina naturalization lists, but failed to name Bochet's other supporters. La Pierre claimed that the dissidents believed "that the French Prophets who made such an uproar in London were the true prophets" and that the "Scripture of both Testaments are but a dead letter," meaning that revelation had superseded them. But La Pierre claimed that the dissidents also imbibed Antinomian and Sabbatarian principles. They believed that "in general Men must not be obeyed" and "that the Jewish Sabbath ought to be kept instead of the Lord's Day." Yet London's French Prophets only hinted at Antinomianism and never adopted Sabbatarian views. Clearly, the Huguenot dissidents were weaving a unique religious revolt in South Carolina's low country, not merely following pamphlets sent from England.[49]

However inventive they were, the St. Denis dissidents could not withstand unending pressure from South Carolina's religious and secular authorities. Commissary Gideon Johnston forced Philippe de Richebourg to return to St. James Santee and to end his Calvinist services at St. Denis. He also pressed John La Pierre to attack the St. Denis dissidents directly. La Pierre wrote a tract, "The Vindication of the Christian Sabbath," now lost, to refute their Sabbatarian views, then invoked the authority of the government against the dissidents. According to Gideon Johnston, La Pierre forced the dissidents to appear before a South Carolina magistrate, on unknown charges. Charlestown's Paul L'Escot also thundered against the dissidents, ridiculed them, and, according to Johnston, "remonstrated . . . that not Conscience, but Malice, or at least groundless Prejudice, made them Quarrel at so good a Church." Despite this intense opposition, the St. Denis revolt persisted for nearly a decade. As late as 1720 the English minister at St. Thomas parish reported that the Huguenots there still used Calvinist services and repudiated the 1706 Church Act. But by 1722 the dispute had been settled. Lacking any clerical support and facing continued pressure from South Carolina officials, most of the St. Denis Huguenots finally abandoned their protest, allowing the St. Thomas minister to write the S.P.G., with some relief, that "all the French [are] now Conformist and make a large Congregation."[50]

Not everyone conformed, however. Between 1723 and 1724 a small group of St. Denis Huguenots pursued a religious radicalism that led to murder and then execution. In this episode, collective Huguenot dissent shaded off into individual eccentricity. But it demonstrated that religious radicalism might stalk the edges of the French Protestant refugee community in America just as it did in London or Amsterdam. This revolt, since called the "Dutartre affair," involved the St. Denis refugee John Dutartre, his children, his son-in-law Peter Rombert, a friend named Michael Bonneau, and several other friends whose activities bore significant signs of familiarity with the work of the London Prophets. According to the colony's new Anglican Commissary, Alexander Garden, Dutartre was encouraged to pursue religious speculations by a Pietist and "strolling Moravian, Christian George," and soon thereafter proclaimed Peter Rombert a prophet. The new prophet, Rombert, announced that the Dutartres were "the only family on earth who had the knowledge of the true God." He "put aside" his wife, John Dutartre's previously widowed daughter, revealed that God would raise her first husband from the dead (a familiar theme among London's French Prophets), and married Dutartre's younger daughter. In this way the Dutartre family was "restored entire, and the holy seed preserved pure and undefiled in it."[51]

South Carolina authorities were first angered by the two men's refusal, on unspecified religious grounds, to serve in the militia or even repair roads. But they did not order the arrest of Dutartre and Rombert until they learned that Rombert's new "wife" was

pregnant. When the local magistrate, an English settler married
to a Huguenot woman, approached the Dutartre farm accompanied by members of the militia, God instructed Rombert to
abandon his pacifism, and Rombert killed the magistrate before
he could be subdued. In September 1724, the courts convicted
Dutartre, Rombert, two Dutartre sons, and their friend, Michael
Bonneau, of murder. Governor Francis Nicholson reprieved the
sentences of the sons but ordered the execution of the others. At
their hangings, the trio reiterated their claims to prophecy in
language again reminiscent of London's French Prophets. They
insisted that the "Spirit of God" spoke "inwardly to their souls,"
and they assured their friends that "they should soon see them
again, for they were certain they should rise from the dead in the
third day."[52]

The execution signaled the end of significant Huguenot protest
against Anglican conformity in rural South Carolina. The Anglican ministers at St. Denis and St. James Santee reported no
further disturbances in those parishes in the next decade. In 1724
the English minister at St. John's Parish in Berkeley County
reported that although a few Huguenots there still refused
Anglican communion, they nonetheless attended Anglican
church services, and three Huguenots served as vestrymen at the
parish as early as 1721. Six Huguenots who moved to St. Andrews
Parish, just west of the Santee settlement, signed a petition to
support a new minister for the parish there in 1723. Nor did the
protests undermine Francis Le Jau's efforts to incorporate Huguenots into the largely English St. James Goose Creek Parish.
Although few refugees lived in the parish, two Huguenots served
as vestrymen in 1707, the year Le Jau arrived; later, in 1719, the
wealthy merchant Benjamin Godin gave the parish sixteen acres
of land for a church yard; by 1721 Le Jau's English successor
continued to record baptisms of Huguenot children, one being a
granddaughter of Charlestown's early Huguenot minister Elie
Prioleau.[53]

The Anglican victory in South Carolina's rural Huguenot
settlements ushered in the final stages of full Huguenot assimilation in South Carolina between 1720 and 1750. This assimilation
never was a passive phenomenon. Huguenots became important

energizers of a new society in the eighteenth-century British colonies. They did not blend quietly into an already existing society undergoing little change; rather, they helped create its major social patterns. In a colony where slave-holding was extraordinarily widespread among whites, Huguenots outstripped their English neighbors in acquiring slaves through about 1745. In the wealthiest mainland colony, Huguenots amassed larger estates than their English neighbors through about 1745. In a colony notable for erecting a harmonious political elite in the aftermath of the overthrow of the South Carolina proprietors in 1719, Huguenots quickly became experienced politicians. They won frequent election to the South Carolina Assembly and claimed membership in the colony's great landed and merchant aristocracy. Huguenots did not achieve these distinctions by pursuing the tight group discipline characteristic of some nineteenth- and twentieth-century immigrant groups. Quite the opposite. Between 1720 and 1750 Huguenot cohesion in secular affairs, especially marriage, disappeared altogether, and Huguenot cohesion in religion, already badly weakened, unraveled even in Charlestown, where the French Church became an institution supported by the legacies of the dead rather than by the attendance of the living.

The final stages of Huguenot assimilation in South Carolina between 1720 and 1750 are especially evident in Huguenot agricultural activity and in their role in encouraging the growth of slavery in the colony. The estate inventories available after 1730 reveal that Huguenot decedents derived their income from agriculture as fully as did the colony's English settlers and farmed in ways that linked them firmly to the larger South Carolina agrarian economy. Huguenots produced all the major crops and products for which South Carolina became well known; Huguenot inventories are thus choked with references to rice, naval stores, corn, livestock, and, after 1740, to indigo. Small estates naturally contained a narrow range of goods—pigs but no horses, rice but little corn—while larger estates bespoke a sophisticated and surprisingly self-sufficient plantation economy in mid-eighteenth century South Carolina.[54]

The South Carolina estate inventories also reveal that Huguenots turned to slave-holding in astonishing numbers and with great enthusiasm. Rather than return to the nuclear family farming they had known or practiced in France, Huguenots rushed to purchase slaves to labor on the large farms they began acquiring in the 1690s. According to the estate inventories, between 1736 and 1745 Huguenot planters owned an average of 25.5 slaves at their deaths; this average rose to 33.3 slaves in the estates inventoried between 1746 and 1755, then fell to 19.2 slaves between 1756 and 1765.[55]

A few Huguenots owned a great many slaves. For example, two of the estates inventoried between 1746 and 1755 contained a total of no less than 722 slaves—353 in the estate of Benjamin Godin (1749) and 369 in the estate of Daniel Huger (1755). But a more important guide is the pattern established by relatively modest Huguenots. Even excluding estates with more than 100 slaves, the average Huguenot estate inventoried between 1746 and 1755 still contained 19.5 slaves. Other measurements give an equally dramatic picture of Huguenot slave-holding. Between 1736 and 1766, fully half of all Huguenot estates contained between five and twenty-five slaves, and at no time did more than 18 percent of the inventories contain only 0–4 slaves. In fact, between 1736 and 1766 less than 10 percent of the Huguenot inventories described estates with no slaves at all.

Like other South Carolinians, Huguenots also profited from the slave trade. John Guerard became one of Charlestown's leading slave merchants in the eighteenth century. He imported eleven cargoes of slaves between 1736 and 1744 and brought in fourteen more slave cargoes between 1752 and 1761. Gabriel Manigault, Solomon Légaré, Jr., and David and John Deas also traded in slaves with some frequency between 1740 and 1770, although on a smaller scale than Guerard. But again, it is the many Huguenots making small investments in the slave trade who illustrate the deep involvement of the community in this lucrative business. John and George Bedon, John Boyer, the firm of Bonny and Poyas, John Dart, the merchants Daniel Huger, Samuel Légaré, and Peter Manigault, and the silversmith Samuel Prioleau, Jr., all occasionally invested in slave cargoes.[56]

The sparse surviving material reveals only the strongest similarities in the way Huguenots and English settlers treated their slaves in South Carolina. The South Carolina *Gazette* regularly carried advertisements from Huguenots for runaway slaves, and, like other settlers, Huguenots branded slaves to mark them as their property. Alexander Godin advertised in 1738 for three runaways "branded BG on the right or left Breast"—the initials of his father, Benjamin Godin—so other whites might return them. And, of course, slaves did more than run away from their masters. A slave on Daniel Huger's massive plantation at St. John's Parish in Berkeley County spoiled the 1739 Stono Rebellion when he revealed the plot to South Carolina authorities, but not before other slaves burned the house of Alexander Hext and killed Hext's overseer and the overseer's wife.[57]

The Huguenot slave-owning pattern also provides dramatic evidence of Huguenot economic success in the colony. Since slaves usually constituted 70 percent to 80 percent of the total value of South Carolina's inventoried estates, comparing the number of slaves in Huguenot and English estates provides a reasonable guide to the refugees' economic achievement. Table 3 digests the comparative slave-holding record of English and Huguenot settlers in the colony between 1736 and 1766 and demonstrates that most Huguenots did extremely well in South Carolina. Having arrived at the earliest stages of South Carolina's development, they acquired a remarkable amount of land and turned quickly to slaves as their major source of agricultural laborers. As a result, at no time between 1736 and 1765 did Huguenots trail English settlers in amassing slaves and wealth in the colony. In fact, between 1736 and 1745, Huguenots outstripped English settlers in owning slaves. More than twice the percentage of Huguenot estates (12.2 percent) held 61 or more slaves that did English estates (4.7 percent). Nearly 60 percent of all Huguenot estates but only 40 percent of English estates contained 11–60 slaves. Conversely, only a third of Huguenot estates, but over half of the English estates, contained only 1–10 slaves.[58]

A partial tax list from St. James Goose Creek Parish in 1745—the only significant colony tax list to survive from the pre-Revolutionary period—reveals how Huguenots fared in a larger English parish and suggests a leveling off of Huguenot economic achievement by the middle of the eighteenth century. A small number of Huguenots lived in the parish since the 1690s, and the 1745 tax list named eleven Huguenots among fifty-nine taxpay-

Table 3. Slave-holding in South Carolina, 1736–1765 (number and percent)

Number of slaves	1736–1745		1746–1755		1756–1765	
	Huguenots	Others	Huguenots	Others	Huguenots	Others
1–10	12 (29.3)	212 (54.8)	22 (37.3)	370 (48.4)	29 (48.3)	377 (46.7)
11–60	24 (58.5)	157 (40.6)	30 (50.8)	339 (44.3)	25 (41.7)	365 (45.2)
61+	5 (12.2)	18 (4.7)	7 (11.9)	56 (7.3)	6 (10.0)	65 (8.1)
Total	41	387	59	765	60	807

Source: Richard Waterhouse, "South Carolina's Colonial Elite: A Study in the Social Structure of a Southern colony, 1670–1760" (Ph.D. diss., The Johns Hopkins University, 1973), 170–182; Estate Inventories, 1736–1765, South Carolina Archives, Columbia, S.C.

ing households. Four of the eleven held over fifty slaves, the largest Huguenot slaveowner being Paul Mazyck with seventy-nine slaves. Thirteen of the forty-eight English households held over fifty slaves, and three contained more than 200 slaves. These large English plantations pushed the average size of the slave contingent owned by English settlers above that in the Huguenot households—443 slaves in the English households, 355 slaves in the Huguenot households. On the other hand, no Huguenot households but six English households lacked slaves. Yet six of the eleven Huguenot households but only thirteen of the forty-eight English households (including the six with no slaves) contained fewer than fifteen slaves.[59]

The leveling off of the early Huguenot economic achievement suggested by the St. James Goose Creek tax return at mid-century is borne out in the colony's estate inventories. As the century progressed, Huguenots lost the initial advantages gained from their early arrival, massive land grants, and quick turn to slavery, and they began to record more modest economic gains. Nevertheless, their early advantages secured them a substantial place in South Carolina society. A comparison of Huguenot and English estate records between 1746–1755 and 1756–1765 (Table 3), shows that the percentage of Huguenot estates with only 1–10 slaves increased from 29.3 percent to 37.3 percent in these decades, while the percentage of Huguenot estates that contained 11–60 slaves declined from 58.5 percent to 50.8 percent. By the decade 1756–1765 Huguenots and English settlers held slaves at about the same levels. A slightly higher proportion of Huguenot estates (10 percent) contained 61 or more slaves than did English estates (8.1 percent). But now more English estates contained 11–60 slaves (45.2 percent) than did Huguenot estates (41.7 percent), and for the first time a slightly higher percentage of Huguenot estates (48.3 percent) contained only 1–10 slaves than was true of English estates (46.7 percent).

The human dimensions of the Huguenot assimilation in South Carolina are well measured by their extremes. The experiences of Pierre Manigault and his wife, Judith Giton, suggest how fully some refugees achieved prosperity and security in South Carolina's expansive slave-owning economy. Pierre and Gabriel Manigault arrived in South Carolina in the 1680s as young, single men from La Rochelle. They developed a modest merchant business and pursued farming and slavery, and Gabriel Manigault received 100 acres of land from the South Carolina government for importing "Negro Sam" in 1695. In 1699 Pierre Manigault and Judith Giton were married. Certainly Judith's earlier life had not been happy. Her brother had forced her to migrate to South Carolina where her mother and another brother died. Her first husband, the shoemaker Noé Royer, died shortly after they applied for naturalization in 1697; they had no children. She and Pierre Manigault had two children, a son Gabriel born in 1704 and a daughter whose birthdate is not known. Judith Giton died in 1711, having lived more comfortably in the last decade of her life than in the first three or four, and her second husband died in 1729 leaving a modestly successful merchant business to their son Gabriel.[60]

In the next half-century, Pierre Manigault's successors emerged as extraordinarily influential planters and politicians and their phenomenal wealth placed them in the ranks of the richest eighteenth-century American colonists. In the 1730s Gabriel Manigault diversified the family's merchant business and expanded its land holdings and plantations. His wealth and social prestige won him the post of public treasurer of the colony at the age of thirty-one in 1735, and in 1743 he moved into the South Carolina Assembly where he served for a decade as an important legislator. When he left the assembly in 1754 he arranged the election of his twenty-three year old son Peter to one of the seats he previously held himself. Peter Manigault remained in the assembly for nearly two decades becoming a major assembly leader and assuming the prestigious speaker's post in 1765. When he died in 1773, at the young age of forty-two, Peter left his children the largest estate probated in the mainland colonies on the eve of the American Revolution; its personal property amounted to £32,700 sterling and included nearly 300 slaves. His father, Gabriel Manigault, left an even larger estate when he died in 1781 at the age of seventy-seven; he owned 490 slaves, much additional property including mansions, houses, and buildings, and 47,532 acres of land.[61]

Assimilation also meant that some Huguenots remained or became poor. Although historians have outlined a rise in poverty in the northern port cities of Boston, New York City, and Philadelphia and even in rural New England in the pre-Revolutionary period, we lack general studies of poverty in the southern colonies including South Carolina. Yet poor people obviously inhabited even this lush, expanding society. Charles-town's vestrymen dealt with them regularly from the 1730s on through public relief and a workhouse, and the colony's estate inventories record quite a number of persons who were poor not only by comparison with their neighbors but by absolute stan-dards as well. While most South Carolina Huguenots succeeded in commerce and agriculture, some never did. John You left an estate valued at only £13 in inflated South Carolina currency in 1749, and Peter Desseline and John Bonnet left estates valued at only £85 and £242 in South Carolina currency in 1758, ranking their estates at the very bottom of the recorded inventories. Other Huguenots fell into deeper poverty. As was true of poor English settlers, the extremely poor Huguenots were often women with needy children. Their numbers are impossible to determine because the relief records of the Charlestown vestry are so fragmentary, but a pathetic sample emerges from the lists of persons granted relief in the early 1750s. The St. Philip's vestry of Charlestown authorized poor relief to Susannah Trezevant in 1751 because she was "frequently afflicted with illness" and because her children were "almost naked and in want of neces-sities"; Hannah Hext had come from the country "in distress" in 1752 and "received £5 to help her home"; and Mary Lesueur and her child received clothes and blankets worth £5 in 1752 to ease her poverty.[62]

Between 1720 and 1750, Huguenots moved deeply into South Carolina electoral politics. The style and extent of their political success testified to their full assimilation in the colony and revealed yet another facet of their disintegration as a cohesive refugee group. Unfortunately, office-holding is difficult to follow for any bodies other than the South Carolina Assembly. The colony's unique political centralization smothered development of the numerous committees and elected local offices found in Boston, for example. Especially before 1720, the assembly disbursed nearly all funds and levied nearly all taxes in the colony. As a result, many local units of government common to other colonies, except vestries, became superfluous. After 1720 scarce local records make it difficult to follow office-holding patterns in the local parish and county institutions that did develop in advance of the Revolution. Fortunately, the comparatively rich assembly records provide a superb profile of Huguenot participation in the colony's most important political institution.[63]

Throughout the eighteenth century, the appearance of Huguenots in the assembly matches their economic success. As Table 4 suggests, Huguenot assembly membership rose dramatically after 1706 when passage of the Church Act settled a major political problem in the colony. Between 1707 and the end of the proprietary assemblies in 1721, Huguenots regularly held three seats in the thirty-member assembly. Between 1725 and 1736, Huguenot representation increased to an average of five seats in a thirty-eight seat assembly. Huguenot representation then escalated dramatically in the next two decades. Between 1736 and 1757, Huguenots held an average of 13.9 seats in the assembly, which contained between forty-two and forty-five seats. After 1757, Huguenots held an average of nine seats in an assembly of between forty-five and fifty-one members. This represented a decline from the unusually high rate of membership in earlier years but still gave Huguenots more than twice the number of assembly seats than was justified by their proportions in the colony's white population.[64]

Within the assembly, Huguenots exercised leadership roles that fit their numbers and class. Like lawmakers in other colonies and in South Carolina, Huguenot assemblymen came from the upper

Table 4. Huguenots in the South Carolina Assembly, 1691–1776

Assembly number	Years	Election districts	Election districts with Huguenots	Total number of assembly seats	Total number Huguenots elected
		Proprietary assemblies			
1	1692–94	3	1	20	7
2	1695	—	—	19[a]	2
3	1696–97	2	1	30	2
4	1698–99	2	1	30	1
5	1700–02	2	0	30	1
6	1702–03	2	1	30	1
7	1703–05	2	1	30	1
8	1706–07	2	2	30	3
9	1707	—	—	28	0[a]
10	1707–08	2	0	30	0
11	1708–09	—	—	34	3
12	1710–11	2	1	30	3
13	1711–12	2	1	30	2
14	1713–15	2	2	30	3
15	1716–17	2	1	30	2
16	1717	10	4	30	4
17	1720–21	—	—	35	3
		Royal assemblies			
1	1721–24	—	—	49[a]	2
2	1725–27	12	3	38	5
3	1728	12	3	38	4
4	1728	12	2	38	3
5	1728	12	2	38	2
6	1729	12	4	38	5
7	1729	12	2	38	2
8	1730	12	4	38	6
9	1731–33	12	4	38	8
10	1733–36	12	5	38	8
11	1736–39	14	9	42	14
12	1739–42	14	7	42	17
13	1742–45	14	8	42	19
14	1745–46	15	9	43	12
15	1746–47	15	7	43	13
16	1747	15	7	40[a]	11[b]
17	1748	16	9	44	11
18	1749	—	—	—[a]	—
19	1749–51	16	8	44	14

Table 4. (continued).

Assembly number	Years	Election districts	Election districts with Huguenots	Total number of assembly seats	Total number of Huguenots elected
20	1751–54	16	10	44	16
21	1754–57	17	10	45	12
22	1757–60	18	7	45	7
23	1760–61	18	4	47	5
24	1761	19	8	48	11
25	1762	19	6	48	8
26	1762–65	19	4	48	4
27	1765–68	20	9	50	11
28	1768	22	8	50	9
29	1769–71	23	8	51	11
30	1772	21	6	46	8
31	1772	21	6	48	8
32	1773	21	8	48	11
33	1773–75	21	11	48	15
Provincial congresses					
1	1775	27	14	207	33
2	1775–76	27	14	204	29
General assemblies					
1	1776	27	13	202	29

Source: Biographical Directory of the South Carolina House of Representatives, ed. Walter B. Edgar, 2 vols. (Columbia, S.C., 1974).
  a. The numbers for these assemblies are uncertain.
  b. This assembly never met.

ranks of colonial society. Of the twenty-three Huguenot assembly-men before 1770 whose estate inventories have been preserved, all but two owned twenty or more slaves at their deaths. Half of these owned sixty or more slaves when they died; paradoxically, the Charlestown Assemblyman John Guerard, long the colony's leading slave merchant, owned only fourteen slaves at his death. The wealth and prestige of these Huguenots led them to positions of authority within the assembly in the pre-Revolutionary period. Jack P. Greene's study of the eighteenth-century southern as-semblies reveals that South Carolina Huguenots deepened the leadership roles they began to develop around 1710. Huguenots comprised about 10 percent of the first and second rank leaders Greene has identified in his study of the assembly, and Peter Manigault's elevation to the speaker's position in 1765 simply capped the rise of Huguenots to political power in the colony.[65]

Assimilation rather than ethnic cohesion accounted for the Huguenots' political success in South Carolina. For later American immigrant groups public office-holding usually reflected and reinforced ethnic cohesion. Eighteenth-century Pennsylvania German and Scotch-Irish assemblymen came from counties with dominant German and Scotch-Irish populations. Similarly, nineteenth- and twentieth-century black and Catholic lawmakers have nearly always represented districts where their own racial, religious, and ethnic groups held large voting majorities. But the South Carolina Assembly election patterns reflect a startlingly different relationship between Huguenots and the society in which they lived—they had assimilated into and become a virtually indistinguishable part of that society by at least 1750, perhaps as early as 1720.[66]

Oddly enough, one of the two South Carolina Assembly districts where Huguenots comprised as much as a third of the eligible voters was one of the last districts to begin sending Huguenots to the assembly regularly. In nine assembly elections in Berkeley County's St. Thomas-St. Denis district, which included the area of St. Denis's anti-Anglican revolt of 1713–1720, only one of twenty-seven assemblymen elected between 1717 and 1730 was a Huguenot. But voters in the colony's other election districts sent Huguenots to the assembly with increasing frequency between 1710 and 1750 and with no apparent regard for their religion or national background. The remarkable Huguenot record of land acquisition made Huguenots eligible for election to many districts since Carolinians could represent any district in which they owned land. Some assemblymen ignored this advantage; Gabriel and Peter Manigault represented only two parishes in their political careers—St. Philip's in Charlestown and the St. Thomas-St. Denis district in Berkeley County. But other Huguenots changed districts frequently. David Hext, for example, represented four districts between 1736 and 1751, while Isaac Mazyck represented six different districts between 1736 and

1757. Even stronger assimilation patterns emerge in the broad distribution of Huguenot assemblymen among different election districts. By 1735 voters in half the colony's election districts customarily elected Huguenot assemblymen. The eleventh Royal Assembly of 1736–39 exemplifies the breadth of Huguenot penetration of South Carolina politics. In that assembly voters elected Huguenots in ten of the fourteen election districts: St. Andrews, St. George Dorchester, St. James Goose Creek, St. Paul, and St. Thomas-St. Denis each elected one Huguenot; St. Helena, St. James Santee, St. James Berkeley, and St. Philip (Charlestown) each elected two Huguenots; and St. John Colleton elected three Huguenots. Obviously, Huguenot ancestry no longer barred anybody's election to the assembly.

The Huguenot penetration of South Carolina's political and economic elite between 1720 and 1750 also gave them access to other offices and occupations. When the South Carolina *Gazette* printed the names of the colony's justices of the peace in 1734, Huguenots comprised no less than fifteen of the eighty-eight men named as magistrates (17.0 percent), and the list formed a convenient and comprehensive guide to South Carolina's elite and its Huguenot members. Ranking below this elite was a far less wealthy but nonetheless sophisticated coterie of refugees who pursued specialized trades and crafts in Charlestown. Certainly not all Huguenots became farmers and planters. South Carolinians could obtain everything from raisins to books from a host of Huguenot merchants in Charlestown. Huguenots taught French, Latin, Greek, German, arithmetic, geometry, and history. They made candies, sugar confections, razors, swords, and knives. They brewed beer and provided "good Stabling, and Entertainment for Horses." They sold medicines, including "a Plaster for all sorts of Women's Hysteri[a] Vapours."[67]

For much of the colonial period Huguenots also dominated the Charlestown silversmith trade. The first silversmiths in the colony included Nicolas de Longemare, his son Nicolas, Solomon Légaré, and Samuel Prioleau. Between 1710 and 1770 at least thirteen Huguenots plied their silversmith trade in the colony. Some, like Lewis Janviere and James Courteonne, were trained by the great silversmiths in London and did not arrive in Charlestown until mid-century. But others, like Andrew Dupuy, Benjamin Motteux, Isaac Peronneau, and Daniel Trezevant, were trained in Charlestown by local masters like de Longemare and Samuel Prioleau. However, other than small spoons, virtually none of their work has survived.[68]

The marriage patterns of the South Carolina Huguenots after 1720 trace the full extent of their assimilation in the larger society and of the internal disintegration of a cohesive Huguenot community. The colony's capital of Charlestown offers a superb focus for the study of Huguenot exogamy. As in Boston, Huguenots mixed easily with English settlers there so that intermarriage was a real possibility for individuals from both groups. Although the city's French Church records were lost, the marriage records of the city's major Anglican congregation, St. Philip's Parish, provide a graphic view of rapidly accelerating exogamy among the city's Huguenot population. Indeed, the church records also point out indirectly the problems of Huguenot religious loyalty in the city after 1720: Even the refugees who took Huguenot spouses were being married at St. Philip's. Table 5 demonstrates that between 1721 and 1730 endogamous marriages accounted for no less than 14 of 36 (38.9 percent) of Huguenot marriages performed there, and even in the 1750s endogamous marriages accounted for 10 out of 38 (26.3 percent) of Huguenot marriages performed there.[69]

At the same time, the St. Philip's records demonstrate that after 1720 a large percentage of Charlestown Huguenots took English spouses when they married. Exogamous unions among Huguenots marrying at St. Philip's ranged from a low of 61.1 percent in the 1720s to a high of 90.7 percent in the 1760s. Men and women rushed toward exogamy with nearly equal speed, a pattern that was somewhat different from that among Boston's Huguenots. Between 1731 and 1760 Huguenot women accounted for slightly more exogamous marriages at St. Philip's than did Huguenot men, and in the 1720s and 1760s they accounted for most such unions— 16 of 22 (72.7 percent) in the 1720s and 25 of 39 (64.1 percent) in the 1760s.

In South Carolina, this extraordinary record of exogamous Huguenot marriages transcended the relatively cosmopolitan milieu of Charlestown and affected even rural Huguenots. The records of St. Thomas Parish, which, after about 1730, began to

Table 5. Huguenot marriages, South Carolina, 1701–1770

Nationality								
Groom	Bride	1701–10	1711–20	1721–30	1731–40	1741–50	1751–60	1761–70
				St. Thomas and St. Denis Parish[a]				
French	French	2	1	1	2	5	8	2
French	English	0	3	2	2	9	8	2
English	French	3	3	3	0	6	8	8
				St. Philip's Parish, Charlestown				
French	French	—[b]	—	14	13	12	10	4
French	English	—	—	6	20	24	13	14
English	French	—	—	16	21	26	15	25

Source: The Annals and Parish Register of St. Thomas and St. Denis Parish, in South Carolina, from 1680 to 1884, ed. Robert F. Clute (Baltimore, Md., 1974); *Register of St. Philip's Parish, 1720–1758,* eds. D. E. Huger Smith and A. S. Salley, Jr. (Columbia, S.C., 1971); *Register of St. Philip's Parish, 1754–1810,* eds. Smith and Salley, Jr. (Columbia, S.C., 1971). The decline in Hugenot marriages at St. Philip's Parish after 1750 matched the decline in all marriages performed there and was due to the establishment in 1751 of a second Anglican parish in the city, St. Michael's, a parish with which many Huguenots were connected, including the wealthy Manigaults.

a. These records appear to be largely those kept by the British ministers at St. Thomas Parish, and they probably exclude marriages performed by the French ministers at St. Denis.

b. No sources available for these years.

include numerous families formerly belonging to the French-speaking St. Denis Parish congregation, reveal high exogamy rates among Huguenots of both sexes: fifteen of twenty-one (71.4 percent) marriages contracted in the 1740s and sixteen of twenty-four (66.7 percent) of those contracted in the 1750s. Although female Huguenots accounted for only six of the fifteen (40 percent) exogamous unions in the 1740s, they accounted for half of all such marriages in the 1750s and for eight of ten in the 1760s.[70]

Social class and wealth did little to affect Huguenot exogamy in South Carolina. We cannot assess these effects systematically because the South Carolina estate records can only rarely be linked to Huguenot genealogies. Even if we know a father's economic standing at his death, it is rare to have a complete record of his children's marriages. But a reasonable reading of the marriage records leads to some general observations. First, so many South Carolina Huguenots from such diverse backgrounds took English spouses after 1720, that their numbers preclude assigning any critical importance to wealth in stimulating exogamy. In consequence, the family ceased to be a major source of refugee cohesion for all Huguenots. Second, even the South Carolina aristocracy presents at best a confused record on exogamy. Certainly enough Huguenots entered the upper ranks of South Carolina society so that wealthy Huguenots easily could have found French spouses for their children within the elite had they wished to do so. While five of the six children of Isaac Mazyck, a prominent merchant and assembly leader, took Huguenot spouses when they married in the 1730s, eight of the ten children of Jacob Motte, also a prominent merchant and the South Carolina treasurer between 1743 and 1770, took English spouses when they married in the 1760s.[71]

Finally, the colony's Huguenot churches, whether independent or Anglican, could not withstand the dual onslaught of social assimilation and cultural disintegration. The Huguenot congregations might have compensated for secular assimilation by promoting a self-conscious Huguenot religious life among the refugees. Instead, the strong conformist Anglican trend reinforced the secular assimilation occurring within the congregations, while Charlestown's independent French Church proved no more capable of providing vigorous religious leadership after 1720 than before.

The rural congregations at St. James Santee and St. Denis, which conformed to the Church of England in 1706, could neither preserve traditional French Protestant worship nor promote any Huguenot identity within their new Anglican home. Even for those who favored it, Anglican conformity did not easily fit the French form. In 1708 two Huguenots at St. James Santee unconsciously used traditional French Protestant titles when they signed church documents as *anciens* rather than as vestrymen in the parish. Both vestrymen and *anciens* in South Carolina and France were respected older men who guided the affairs of their congregations. But in South Carolina the Anglican vestryman also was a government functionary whose legally prescribed duties involved, among other things, disbursement of government funds and the obligation to administer the parish in a way that upheld the general authority of the Crown. In addition, the finally successful implementation of John Durel's *La Liturgie* in the conformist parishes indelibly changed Huguenot services because they became far more liturgical than traditional Huguenot services used to be. In everything except language they duplicated the worship of English settlers in the colony's other Anglican parishes.[72]

Anglican authorities in London and even in Charlestown might have fostered some special Huguenot features in the conformist congregations, as they did later for the natives in nineteenth-century British colonies. Instead, Anglicans essentially ignored the special character of the Huguenots after they secured their conformity. They furnished the refugees with no special religious literature. Beyond publishing John Durel's *La Liturgie* in numerous editions, neither the S.P.C.K. nor the S.P.G. issued any significant religious works in French. The only major French-language work issued by the S.P.G. after 1700 promoted Anglican ecumenical activity among prestigious continental divines, such as Jean Alphonse Turrettini and Jean Frederic Ostervald, with whom Charlestown's Paul L'Escot had corresponded. This work, Claude Grosteste de la Mothe's *Relation de la société établie pour la propagation de l'Evangile dans les pays etrangers* (Rotterdam, 1708), noted that the S.P.G. had given the St. Denis and St. James Santee refugees considerable financial aid. By the 1720s the S.P.G. abandoned that support and stopped the salary payments to the conformist ministers in those parishes on grounds that the 1706 Church Act authorized a yearly salary for their ministers to be paid from government funds. And since the S.P.G. was chartered to work only in places where the government did not underwrite salaries of Anglican ministers, the Huguenot clerics lost their S.P.G. support.[73]

Worse, at St. Denis the congregation dwindled as the assimilating refugees began to lose the use of the French language This was a special problem because the 1706 Church Act defined the parish linguistically and authorized its disestablishment when the language disappeared. In 1720 the minister John La Pierre reported that nearly all his parishioners understood English except some "ancient persons who Humanely speaking cannot Live very long." Three years later the English minister of St. Thomas Parish, which encompassed St. Denis, asked the S.P.G. to send English tracts so he could distribute them among the numerous young Huguenots who already attended services at St. Thomas. Although a French-speaking minister officiated at St. Denis through the next two decades, the congregation declined steadily, and in 1758 it quietly merged with the St. Thomas congregation although the South Carolina Assembly did not formally acknowledge its collapse until 1768.[74]

St. James Santee suvived as a parish because it was defined in traditional geographical terms. Yet it finally became as English as St. Thomas. In the 1720s its minister, Albert Pouderous, pleaded for return of S.P.G. aid because floods along the Santee River destroyed his crops, and he was being ruined by travelers who regularly "ate [at] my table, there being no taverns nor Ens in the parish." He offered English-language services to please his English-speaking parishioners, some of whom were French. After his death in 1730, however, tension developed between older Huguenots who wished to retain French in their worship and younger Huguenots who, together with the parish's growing English population, wanted additional English services. The dispute cost the new parish minister, Joseph Bugnion, his position but was short-lived and stimulated no return to Calvinist services as happened in the 1710s. By 1741 so few French-speaking residents lived in St. James Santee that the vestry very nearly hired an English minister, and by mid-century St. James Santee simply was one of many Church of England parishes that dotted the South Carolina low country, with its major Huguenot feature being the predominance of French surnames among its parishioners.[75]

After 1720 Charlestown's independent French Church lost significant active lay support. The congregation drifted without a minister between 1724 and 1732, but Huguenots joined other Charlestown churches even after a minister had been hired, and when the French Church closed in 1774, it was as much the victim of internal disintegration as of Huguenot secular assimilation. Paul L'Escot's departure in 1719 brought a decade of turmoil to the congregation. The French Church elders and heads of families signed a statement praising their former minister, but after arriving in England, L'Escot complained widely to friends in London and Geneva about his treatment in Charlestown. Despite his carping, in 1720 the French Church found Pierre Stoupe of Geneva to replace him, apparently with the help of London's Threadneedle Street Church. But Stoupe too developed Anglican sympathies that undercut his loyalty to Charlestown's independent Huguenot congregation. Although he had not received Anglican ordination, Stoupe assisted John La Pierre at St. Denis in 1722. After learning of the death of New Rochelle's Anglican minister, Daniet Bondet, in 1724, Stoupe sailed for England, was ordained by the bishop of London, then traveled to New York to assume Bondet's position.[76]

The eight years that elapsed before François Guichard was hired in 1732 left Charlestown with a badly weakened Huguenot congregation. Two now lost letters written by Isaac Mazyck in 1724 and 1725 despaired of finding a replacement for Stoupe and worried that the congregation would conform to the Church of England as the rural Huguenot congregations had done. The new minister worked to sustain the congregation by securing help from the old Huguenot elite, many of whom had joined other congregations. When Charlestown's disastrous fire of 1741 gutted the French Church building, Guichard arranged to rebuild it with contributions from Huguenots like Gabriel Manigault, who was by then a vestryman at St. Philip's Parish. Guichard quietly performed the special functions that accrued to the head of the city's only French institution such as caring temporarily for the indigent, although in 1752 he refused to house the "lunatic" Peter Calvet. Calvet's presence would obstruct "his Ministerial Function as Pastor of the French Church." Guichard also accepted the Anglican hegemony in the colony and never challenged the Anglican ministers at the conformist rural congregations or the laity that supported them. His tolerance was politically motivated; when Commissary Alexander Garden complained that Guichard allowed the Anglican revivalist George Whitefield to preach in the French Church building in 1740, Guichard dropped any appearance of support for Whitefield.[77]

The instability at the French Church after 1720, the earlier Anglican conformity of the rural Huguenot settlements, and the

broad secular assimilation of the Huguenots in the colony all
drove Huguenots out of Charlestown's French Church. The
breadth of the Huguenots' dispersion to different South Carolina
congregations belies any deep lay preference for Anglicanism.
Indeed, considering the Anglican conformity of the rural Huguenots and the dominance of the Church of England elsewhere
in the colony, a surprising number of Huguenots patronized
Dissenting congregations. Until 1780 only one apparent Huguenot appears in the records of Charlestown's Quaker meeting;
Thomas Bedon, who signed a Quaker marriage certificate in
1731. More Huguenots moved to Charlestown's Circular Church,
a New England Calvinist congregation formed in the 1690s.
Solomon Légaré had joined it by 1697, and after 1720 it won the
allegiance of Charles and Henry Peronneau, John Dart and
Benjamin D'Harriette, who had patronized the Dutch Reformed
Church in New York City before he moved to Charlestown. A few
other South Carolina refugees became Baptists. Anne Bonneau
helped organize a General or Arminian Baptist congregation in
Charlestown in 1736, and Mathurin Guérin was a trustee in a
Baptist congregation at Stono in 1746.[78]

The wealthy Gabriel Manigault signed the deed for the
property on which Charlestown's French Church built a new
building in 1744 and the following year gave the Church a gold
communion service. Yet he married Ann Ashby in an Anglican
ceremony in St. Thomas parish in 1730, baptized their son Peter
at St. Philip's in Charlestown in 1731, and was an elder there by at
least 1732. Records connected with the 1706 Church Act reveal
even more striking instances of dual denominational affiliation.
The first surviving minute book of the colony's church commissioners lists three Huguenot commissioners in 1717: Benjamin de
la Conseilliere, Benjamin Godin, and Jacob Satur. Although the
Church Act required them to be Anglican communicants, de la
Conseilliere signed the 1719 testimonial for Paul L'Escot as an
elder in the Charlestown French Church and Godin signed it as a
member. In 1731, more than a decade later, Satur pledged to
support a minister for the French Church if London's Threadneedle Street Church would send one. The signatures under that
request include many Charlestown Huguenots with ritual links to
other congregations. Of the eleven men who signed it, Satur had

served as a South Carolina church commissioner, James le Chantre
and Etienne Mounier had baptized children at St. Philip's in
Charlestown, Anthony Bonneau would baptize a son at St.
Thomas a year later in 1732, and Andrew Deveaux, who married
at St. Andrews in 1723, would baptize children at St. Helena
between 1736 and 1740.[79]

Despite the efforts made to revitalize the French Church,
devastating numbers of Huguenots moved directly into St.
Philip's Church, Charlestown's major Anglican congregation
through the 1750s. Table 6 traces the rise in ritual events
performed for Huguenots at the congregation between 1721 and
1760. The number of marriages rose from thirty-six in the 1720s
to sixty-two in the 1740s. Death brought even more Huguenots to
St. Philip's. The parish ministers performed burial ceremonies for
thirty-four Huguenots in the 1720s, when the French Church
often lacked a minister, and for 148 Huguenots between 1731
and 1750, during the tenure of François Guichard. A small
number of these Huguenots expressed a preference for some
things French in death if not in life, however. They directed that
after their funerals had been conducted under an Anglican ritual,
their bodies be interred in the French Yard, the Huguenot burial
ground that surrounded Charlestown's French Church. Thus,
five of thirty-four Huguenots whose funerals were conducted at
St. Philip's in the 1720s were interred at the French Church, three
of fifty-eight in the 1730s, and ten of ninety in the 1740s.[80]

As the French Church withered after the 1720s, some Huguenots apparently fell away from organized religion, as happened in Boston. Although the number of Huguenot marriages

Table 6. Huguenot ceremonies performed in St. Philip's Parish, Charlestown,
1721–1760

Ceremonies	1721–30	1731–40	1741–50	1751–60
Marriages	36	54	62	38
Baptisms	33	33	44	11
Burials	34	58	90	14

Source: *Register of St. Philip's Parish, 1720–1758*, eds. D. E. Huger Smith and
A. S. Salley, Jr. (Columbia, S.C., 1971), and *Register of St. Philip's Parish, 1754–
1810*, eds. Smith and Salley (Columbia, S.C., 1971).

and funerals doubled at St. Philip's Church between 1720 and 1770, Huguenot baptisms increased by only a third. By the 1730s Huguenot marriages even outnumbered baptisms there, although the ratio should have been quite different if Huguenot couples were having children at the normal eighteenth-century rate of about one child every two to three years. Since few of these couples can be traced to other colony churches, they were very likely following the patterns of indifference to organized religion, which Anglican ministers criticized in other colony residents, and using religious ritual to solemnize marriages without baptizing children or supporting churches.[81]

After 1720—actually after 1700—South Carolina Huguenots also eschewed the legacies to the poor and to church institutions that were a traditional part of French Protestant wills. In the 1690s four of six Huguenots whose wills survive offered these traditional gifts to the poor or to Huguenot congregations in the colony. But between 1700 and 1720 only one in twelve followed the tradition, and between 1721 and 1740, nine of thirty-nine. In Charlestown itself, the gifts of a few wealthy families compensated for the general loss of support from the laymen. Gabriel Manigault contributed greatly to the congregation while he was a vestryman at St. Philip's, and Isaac Mazyck left the congregation £50 for its poor fund and £700 to support the French Church minister when he died in 1736; thus, the Anglican minister Charles Woodmason could report in 1766 that the French Church was small "but is rich and well endowed." But the trend toward secularization of wills became astonishingly common among eighteenth-century South Carolina Huguenots. In contrast to traditional practice, they simply used their wills to convey property to family and friends and ignored all other possible public ends such as contributions to the poor or to churches, either English or French.[82]

The eighteenth-century Huguenots also stopped purchasing French Protestant religious publications. Sometime in the 1690s Isaac Porcher acquired copies of Jean Claude's *Les plaintes des protestants cruellement opprimez dans le royaume de France* (Cologne, 1686) and *Histoire et apologie de la retraite des pasteurs à cause de la persecution de France* (Frankfurt, 1687) in which he inscribed his name—copies that are now in the library of the Huguenot Society of South Carolina—and other South Carolina Huguenots obviously purchased publications relating to the French Prophet controversy in the 1710s. But there is no evidence of a sustained interest in buying these distinctively Huguenot publications. Some estate inventories, like those of Peter Porcher (1754), Isaac Porcher (1743), and Philip Combe (1757) mention "old books" or "old French books" without listing their titles. Only James le Chantre's inventory of 1732 lists relatively recent French publications, namely Jean Frederic Ostervald's French version of the Bible (in seven copies) and the sermons of Jacques Saurin. The 1750 catalogue of the Charlestown Library Society, supported by Gabriel Manigault and many other Huguenots, contained no French language works. The 1770 catalogue of the library suggests that, by then, some Huguenots had donated older French Protestant works owned by their ancestors. In 1770 Huguenot religious works included a 1619 Geneva edition of *Histoire des martyrs,* a 1693 edition of the Geneva Bible, one work by Jean Alphonse Turrettini, and two works by Turrettini's Geneva colleague Benedict Pictet. But the library contained many more books that reflected the influence of the secular French Enlightenment. These included the complete works of Voltaire, Rabelais, and Rousseau, the poems of Racine, the novels of Cervantes, and Montesquieu's *Esprit des loix.*[83]

South Carolina Huguenots also failed to transfer their religious fervor to the revivals of George Whitefield or other evangelists. To be sure, Peter Porcher owned Whitefield's *Journals,* Whitefield preached in Charlestown's French Church on his first visit there in 1740, and a Huguenot woman named Anne Le Brasseur committed suicide in 1742 after dwelling on Whitefield's printed sermons for two years. But Porcher owned many kinds of religious books; Whitefield did not preach to a specifically Huguenot audience but only used the French Church building to preach to anyone who would listen; and not even contemporaries linked Anne Le Brasseur's spiritual depression and suicide to her Huguenot ancestry.[84]

All the evidence supports the conclusion that the collapse of Charlestown's French Church was, indeed, inevitable after 1750. Following François Guichard's death in 1752, the French Church employed Jean Pierre Têtard as its minister until 1758, then hired

Barthelemi Henri Himeli of Geneva until he left for a visit home in 1772. Like Guichard, both ministers appear to have been supported through legacies and yearly gifts from wealthy Huguenots such as the Mazycks and the Manigaults. In its delicate condition, the French Church scarcely could withstand controversy. But controversy followed Himeli's departure. Perhaps even before Himeli left, a disputatious, venal Huguenot minister named Pierre Levrier landed in Charlestown. He had served an unsuccessful colony of French-speaking Swiss Protestants in British Florida in the 1760s, and after its collapse he attempted to replace Himeli at Charlestown's French Church. Like Charlestown's first Huguenot minister, Laurent Van den Bosch, Levrier won little support from the congregation's already tiny laity. In 1774 he announced in the South Carolina *Gazette* that the French Church suffered from such "great decay and almost utter Dissolution" that he would have to tutor students in the French language to make a living. He also attempted to shame South Carolina's Huguenots. He wrote that his effort to rescue the French language in Charlestown ought to meet with special favor from "those whose Ancestors bravely encountered all the hardships of flight into a Wilderness to serve their God." If Levrier succeeded he would "preserve . . . a Church created by their pious Fathers" and might, thereby, "perpetuate this Monument of their Fortitude and Zeal."[85]

Levrier's ploy failed. Rather than endure his ministry, the Charlestown Huguenots kept the French Church closed until Himeli returned from Switzerland in 1780. When Himeli died in 1785, another Swiss Protestant, John Paul Coste, replaced him, but the congregation apparently closed the church within a year. It remained closed for a decade until April 1796 when the French Church elders secured Peter Daniel Bourdillon of Geneva as their minister. Then fate conspired against both the French Church and its minister. In July 1796, during the city's third major fire of the eighteenth century, municipal authorities dynamited the French Church building to keep the flames away from Charlestown's wharfs. A month later Bourdillon died from a fever he neglected as he labored to keep the congregation functioning. Ironically, and quite unlike other Huguenots of the previous half-century, Bourdillon had to be interred in the Anglican burying ground at St. Philip's Church because debris from the Charles-town fire still covered the French Yard.[86]

In 1805 and again in 1845, the remaining elders of Charles-town's French Church constructed new buildings in which to worship. But, as in the years after 1740, they found few Huguenots willing to make the congregation the center of their religious life. Their major financial supporters belonged to other Charlestown congregations, and the French Church simply failed to reestablish itself as a major religious institution in the city even in decades when the elders succeeded in hiring a full-time minister. Instead, the congregation began to function as a memorial church whose "members" gathered each October to commemorate the 1685 Revocation of the Edict of Nantes, something still done in the city in the building dating from 1845.[87]

5 / New York: Refugees in an Ethnic Caldron

Colonial New York presented a third face of early American society to Huguenots arriving from London and the Continent in the 1680s that was quite unlike Boston or South Carolina. Here Huguenots entered an old Dutch colony which the English had conquered twice, in 1664 and 1673. New York never was homogeneous. Under Dutch rule it developed a polyglot population of Dutch, Walloon, Swedish, and Finnish settlers, and on the eve of the Huguenot emigration, Englishmen, Sephardic Jews, and African slaves were appearing in the mixture. New York's religious diversity reflected this population heterogeneity. Governor Thomas Dongan described it in 1687 as a spiritual cornucopia of Dutch Calvinists, Dutch Lutherans, Anglicans, Roman Catholics, orthodox Quakers, "Singing Quakers, Ranting Quakers, Sabbatarians, Antisabbatarians, some Anabaptists, some Independents, some Jews; in short of all sorts of opinions there are some, [while] the most part [are] of none at all."[1]

New York's economy also differed from that of South Carolina or New England. Its farms produced grains and livestock rather than the rice and indigo crops of South Carolina, and although New York City manifested the astonishing occupational diversity that characterized all the northern port cities between 1690 and 1730, its economy stood up to the eighteenth-century colonial wars that devastated Boston. Unlike New England, New York also emerged as the most important northern slave colony of the eighteenth century. Slaves not only worked on the New York City wharfs, in merchant firms, and in homes, but they labored extensively on farms on Staten Island, Long Island, and in Westchester County. While Africans comprised only 1–2 percent of the Massachusetts population after 1690, they comprised 15 percent of the New York population between about 1710 and

1760 and as much as 20 percent of the population in the city and the rural counties surrounding it at several periods before 1760.[2]

Huguenots should have found colonial New York's environment to be especially supportive. The colony attracted a significant number of refugees to both rural and urban settlements. The diversified economy offered opportunities for the pursuit of both skilled trades and farming. The population diversity meant that Huguenots would form only one of many foreign-speaking non-English minorities in the colony. New York's religious community included numerous groups that, like the Huguenots, wished to sustain a unique religious life. The colony certainly offered the Huguenot refugees a political, social, and cultural milieu dramatically different from that of either Boston or South Carolina and seemingly well suited to the preservation of refugee cohesion.

Yet Huguenot cohesion slipped away in New York as surely as it did in Boston and South Carolina. It was already badly shattered by 1710, when assimilation in politics, social life, and the economy already was remarkable. By 1750 Huguenot assimilation and internal disintegration were virtually complete and awaited only the collapse of New York City's French Church in 1776. Both processes are exemplified in the story of an otherwise obscure New York City tailor, John Laboyteaux. Laboyteaux followed the exogamous marriage patterns exhibited by most other New York refugees when he married an English woman, Hannah Smith, in 1762. Their children were baptized in the city's Presbyterian Church in the course of the next decade, rather than in its French Church. His career as a tailor exhibited the vagaries of social mobility in the colony. His merchant grandfather Gabriel Laboyteaux ranked in the top 10 percent of all city taxpayers on the 1695 and 1699 city tax lists. But John Laboyteaux was only a tailor. Like a number of other descendants of the original refugees, he survived in New York. But he never became rich and never held public office. Indeed, his one notable political act is hidden within the baptismal records of the New York City Presbyterian Church. On September 17, 1775, Laboyteaux and his English wife named their seventh child George Washington Laboyteaux, becoming the first known parents in the American colonies to name a child after the man who in June had been

designated to command the military forces of the Continental
Congress then meeting in Philadelphia.[3]

In the 1680s the New York Huguenots exhibited the same
pattern of initially secular migration, residential clustering, and
subsequent formation of religious institutions apparent in South
Carolina. Huguenots who settled outside the city did not scatter
randomly across the countryside but huddled together on contig-
uous farms to form distinctive Huguenot communities. Huguenots who settled on Staten Island apparently purchased lands
individually from the colonial government or from local farmers.
By the mid-1680s their numbers were sufficient to form a
separate French congregation and to end joint services with the
Dutch Reformed congregation. A decade later one observer
counted thirty-six French families amidst forty English and forty-
four Dutch families on the Island, and he noted that the
Huguenots were supporting a minister of their own, David de
Bonrepos, formerly of New Rochelle.[4]

New Rochelle emerged as a major refugee settlement north of
the city in Westchester County when a number of Huguenots
bought land there in 1686 or 1687. In 1688, de Bonrepos moved
from Boston to become their minister. In 1689, in the thick of the
Leisler Rebellion, Jacob Leisler acted as their agent in purchasing
3,000 acres of land from the Pell family to sell to other refugees.
By the early 1690s the town had put up a wooden building for
Huguenot church services and claimed a population that was,
except for slaves, entirely French. Huguenot refugees clustered
together even in New York City, beginning with the first arrivals
in the mid-1670s and continuing in a migration that increased
steadily through the 1680s, then dropped off in the 1690s.
Although the city was still only a "walking" town with no more
than 5,000 persons in 1698, the 1695 and 1699 tax lists reveal
significant Huguenot segregation in its five wards: the Dutch-
dominated West and North Wards each housed a tenth of the
refugees; the Dock and South Wards each housed a fifth of the
refugees; and fully a third of the refugees lived in the East Ward.[5]

New York City's refugees gained a minister by 1682. Pierre
Daillé, who later moved to Boston, arrived in that year after
French authorities closed the Protestant academy at Saumur

where he had taught. He formed a congregation of city refugees that worshipped in the Anglican chapel at Fort George, preached on Staten Island, and became the first French minister to preach to the Walloons at New Paltz. In 1686 or 1687 Pierre Peiret arrived in New York City from Foix in southern France. Daillé continued his services at the chapel in Fort George, and Peiret led a group that erected a church building on Petticoat Lane in the city proper in 1688. By 1692 the new French Church constructed a gallery to accommodate increased numbers of worshippers. Three years later the former Anglican chaplain at Fort George counted 200 families patronizing the French Church. This made it the city's second largest congregation, half the size of the Dutch Reformed Church with its 450 families but twice as large as the Anglican congregation of 90 families, which still lacked a church building outside Fort George.[6]

The New York government very early brought Huguenots into the colony's political process and gave them legal privileges (including voting) through naturalization, denization, and freemanship, thereby fostering assimilation. The first New York Naturalization Act of 1683 authorized the Assembly to naturalize petitioners through private acts passed in the next decades. New York's governors used their executive powers to naturalize additional Huguenots and other foreigners, while the New York City Council regularly granted freemanship privileges to foreign-born settlers including Huguenots. The record of freemanship grants was especially impressive. Refugees sometimes paid a fee to receive freemanship and sometimes won it without cost. However they received it, a large number of Huguenots qualified to enter the mainstream of New York City economic and political life very early. Eighty-four Huguenots became freemen between 1687 and 1700; fifty-nine between 1701 and 1710; thirty-one in the 1710s; thirty-eight in the 1720s; and fifty-six in the 1730s.[7]

Liberal New York officials also ignored problems that could have plagued refugees who lacked naturalization or denization. These Huguenots could have been prevented from owning and inheriting property, voting, and holding public office. Instead, New York officials treated the refugees as though they had been naturalized or endenized and, in effect, granted Huguenots *de facto* naturalization. As in South Carolina, it was the refugees who worried most about naturalization and denization. Some New York Huguenots naturalized under a 1715 bill had already been endenized in London, and others had lived and worked in New York for more than twenty years. Other New York City Huguenots who received freemanship in the 1690s did not bother to qualify for New York naturalization until 1715, and many New Rochelle residents who qualified under the 1715 act had already held town office although their lack of naturalization should have made them ineligible to do so.[8]

The New York government, obviously receptive to the refugees, allowed them self-government in their rural settlements. The provincial government never prevented New Rochelle Huguenots from managing their own town affairs and never diluted Huguenot voting strength in the town by incorporating nearby English settlers within its boundaries as the South Carolina government did with assembly districts in 1696. Nor did the government intervene in any special way when personal disputes afflicted the village. The disputes displeased the minister, David de Bonrepos, who moved to Staten Island in 1694, and they grew more violent toward the end of the decade, culminating with the murder of the refugee David Bourguet in 1700. The Westchester County grand jury indicted Pierre Villeponteux for the crime, but the Court of Sessions subsequently quashed the indictment. Villeponteux never faced trial on the charges and, instead, began disputing with town residents, including the new minister, Daniel Bondet. New York authorities preferred to ignore these problems, as they had done with the matters of naturalization and office-holding in New Rochelle. In Staten Island New York officials showed their liberality in a different fashion. The Island was governed as a county, and through much of the colonial period the governor appointed all local officials except the county supervisor. Even before 1700, the governors appointed an array of public officials that usually reflected the distribution of Dutch, English, and French residents on the Island, and they continued the pattern into the 1770s[9]

New York City voters drew Huguenots directly into city politics by electing some of the Huguenot freemen to public office. The voters elected a Huguenot as assistant alderman in 1691—assistants voted in city council proceedings but did not act as magistrates—and by 1700 had elected Huguenots as constables three times and tax assessors and collectors fourteen times. Like most English and Dutch office-holders, the first Huguenot assistant alderman, Stephen DeLancey, was rich. The other Huguenot office-holders were modest merchants. Their election reflected the importance of class in a polyglot city as well as Huguenot residential cohesion, since DeLancey and most of the Huguenot constables, assessors, and collectors came from the voting districts where most Huguenots lived: the South, East and Dock Wards. The early elevation of Huguenots to city offices was not always in tune with some realities of refugee life. Although New Yorkers voted Huguenots into public office, language problems and age made it difficult for some Huguenots to serve. In 1696 the city Council heard requests from Louis Bongrand and Jean Hastier to be relieved of their constable duties because they did not understand English, were poor, or were old. The Council approved Bongrand's request but rejected Hastier's perhaps because Hastier's residence in the South Ward at least alleviated the language problem.[10]

Evidence of deeper Huguenot assimilation in New York may be derived from early patterns of occupations and slave-holding before 1700. Again, here as in South Carolina, striking numbers of refugees farmed. The New York censuses of 1698 and 1706 suggest that by 1700 roughly half of the colony's Huguenot refugees lived in the rural settlements of New Rochelle and Staten Island. Their remarkably diversified agriculture fitted the early development of New York much in the way South Carolina's Huguenot refugees fitted into that colony's early economy. Although the lack of records makes it impossible to follow land acquisition as closely in New York as in South Carolina, the evidence suggests that New York's rural Huguenots owned small farms as did most of the colony's Dutch and English farmers. A map of New Rochelle, undated but probably drawn before 1710, lists the largest farm in the village at 776 acres, the smallest at 20 acres, and nearly two-thirds of the farms at between 30 and 90 acres.[11]

The rural Huguenots earned their living in many different ways. New Rochelle developed dock facilities, and some Huguenots fished. Guillaume Cothonneau and his wife both farmed and buried the dead. Her 1699 estate contained "two cows, three heifers, one bull, two mares, three colts, two sows, and thirteen pigs," and fourteen funeral shrouds. The 1695 and 1697 inventories of two Staten Island Huguenots are likewise dominated by farm tools, unsold crops, cattle, and sheep—100 in the 1695 inventory of John Bodin.[12]

These Huguenot farmers also followed the slave-owning pattern already emerging in the colony. Slavery must have had a wide appeal to Europeans in the northern colonies, because the practice first appeared under Dutch rule and persisted in the state until 1827, scarcely three decades before the Civil War. In New York as in South Carolina, Huguenots acquired slaves early. Four Staten Island estate inventories of the 1690s describing small estates of less than £500 in New York currency still include slaves used for farming: two men and a woman in one, a man, woman, and child in two others, and a man in the fourth.[13]

The 1698 New Rochelle census provides dramatic evidence of the Huguenot penchant for slavery. Refugees there owned greater proportions of slaves than did other white New Yorkers; in 1698 slaves comprised fully of 18.9 percent of New Rochelle's inhabitants. Forty-three slaves lived amidst 184 French men, women, and children—in short, one slave for every 2.3 adult Huguenots. Some refugees owned only one or two slaves, usually males in their early twenties. But others owned whole families; typically, a male in his late twenties, a female in her late teens or early twenties, and one or two children under the age of four.[14]

New York City Huguenots owned slaves in equally astonishing numbers. In fact, Huguenot household heads more often owned slaves than did all but one other group of white householders in the city. According to Joyce Goodfriend, slave-owing households of Dutch, English, French, and Jewish residents all contained about 2.2 slaves in 1703. But whereas 37 percent of Dutch households and 44 percent of English households contained slaves, slaves could be found in half of the city's French households. The Huguenots lagged behind only the city's Jews, most of whom were prosperous merchants and three-quarters of whose households contained slaves.[15]

While many Huguenots became farmers and fitted into the colony's dominant agricultural economy, other refugees became part of the emerging and complex urban society of New York City. The arrival and settlement of refugees in the city itself became a measure and cause of its development as an urban center. Their migration fed the population growth that helped turn town into city, and their arrival deepened the occupational specialization that characterized developing urban economies in early modern culture.

Fortunately, the value of Huguenots to the New York City economy as well as their assimilation in city society did not depend on their matching precisely the occupational structure of the entire city. Joyce Goodfriend has linked New York City's 1695 tax list with occupational identifications in the freemanship records to discover that Huguenots comprised about 11 percent of city taxpayers in 1695 (Table 7). This matched their proportion of professionals (10 percent), employees in the service trades (13 percent), workers in the cloth and leather trades (13 percent). They comprised a slightly larger than expected share of city merchants (17 percent) and of persons in the maritime trades (19.5 percent) and a smaller than expected share of those employed in the wood, metal, and stone trades (7 percent).[16]

Imbalances also emerge in comparing the Huguenot occupational spectrum with that of the city's English and Dutch population. A larger percentage of Huguenot freemen were merchants (31 percent) than were English (26.4 percent) and Dutch residents (18 percent); a smaller percentage of Huguenots were laborers (1.7 percent) than were English (4.7 percent) and Dutch (5.2 percent) residents. Huguenots held a middle ground between English and Dutch residents in other occupations, however. For example, 6.9 percent of the Huguenots were professionals compared with the Dutch (6.4 percent) and the English (16.3 percent), and 10.3 percent of Huguenots were cloth and leather workers compared to 15.1 percent of the Dutch and 2.3 percent of the English.[17]

The differences in occupations among Huguenots, Dutch, and English residents never isolated New York City Huguenots or made them odd, peculiar, or difficult to assimilate because the occupational differences were minor. It was the English, for example, who veered most severely from the city's occupational norms. In contrast, the Huguenot exceptions probably proved

Table 7. Occupations of male taxpayers by ethnic group, New York City, 1695 and 1703

Occupation	Nationality					
	Dutch	English	French	Jews	Unknown	Total
1695						
Professionals	16	21	4	0	—	41
Merchants, retailers	46	34	18	7	—	105
Service trades	31	16	7	1	—	55
Maritime trades	32	30	15	0	—	77
Cloth, leather trades	38	3	6	0	—	47
Wood, metal, stone trades	75	19	7	0	—	101
Laborers	13	6	1	0	—	20
1703						
Professionals	10	4	4	0	1	19
Merchants, retailers	36	29	31	8	6	110
Service trades	40	20	4	1	6	51
Maritime trades	39	38	12	0	18	107
Cloth, leather trades	38	6	3	0	1	48
Wood, metal, stone trades	75	17	6	0	17	115
Laborers	11	1	0	0	1	13

Source: Joyce D. Goodfriend, "'Too Great a Mixture of Nations': The Development of New York City Society in the Seventeenth Century" (Ph.D. diss. University of California at Los Angeles, 1975), 146–147, and Thomas J. Archdeacon, *New York City, 1664–1710: Conquest and Change,* 52. Copyright © 1976 by Cornell University; used by permission of the publisher, Cornell University Press). In the main, both authors have used the freemanship records in *The Burghers of New Amsterdam and the Freemen of New York, 1675–1866,* New York Historical Society *Collections,* 18 (1885) to provide occupational identifications for persons appearing on the 1695 and 1703 New York City tax lists. I have standardized this data where necessary using the classifications in Jacob M. Price, "Economic Function and the Growth of American Port towns in the Eighteenth Century," *Perspectives in American History,* 8 (1974): 123–186.

important to their assimilation within the city's economic structure. Their distribution across the full spectrum of city occupations kept them from a narrow occupational isolation. Most important, Huguenots added significantly to craft and trade diversification in the city. Between 1694 and 1700, sixty-seven successful Huguenot freemanship applicants pursued more than twenty different occupations. In 1695 alone, for example, they included two victuallers, two merchants, a shopkeeper, weaver, tailor, ship carpenter, joiner, cordwainer, and surgeon. This occupational diversity of the Huguenots continued into the next century. Between 1701 and 1710, fifty-nine Huguenot freeman-ship applicants pursued twenty trades that included a bolter, armorer, surgeon, cordwainer, confectioner, schoolmaster, sail-maker, apothecary, shopkeeper, lawyer, farmer, gentleman, and several shipwrights, tailors, periwigmakers, carpenters, coopers, victuallers, mariners, and merchants.[18]

Signs of group loyalty in business appeared only erratically among Huguenots in the city although, in part, this conclusion may be faulty owing to vagaries of the evidence. The New York City merchants Stephen DeLancey, Benjamin Faneuil, and Gab-riel Laboyteaux engaged in international trading in France before the Revocation, and other Huguenots came to New York with significant experience in all aspects of the maritime trades. The New York customs records list no fewer than twenty Huguenots engaged as masters of ships sailing from New York City between 1700 and 1709 and list at least eighty-seven Huguenot merchants active in the city in the same period. Some of these merchants clearly utilized nationality and kinship connections in pursuing their businesses. Thomas Bayeux maintained business relation-ships with his brother John in London in the 1690s, and Gabriel Laboyteaux appears to have maintained ties with relatives in Amsterdam in the same years, and, in the 1720s, at least, the Jays maintained business ties with their affines, the Peloquins of Bristol. These relationships testify to the importance of kinship among these merchants, but they say little about the specific influence of religion in business matters and no records survive that could reveal it.[19]

Ethnic loyalty seems to have affected the hiring of apprentices by New York City's Huguenot businessmen. Many refugees still understood English poorly, and it was more convenient for Huguenot masters to teach trades and skills to French-speaking children rather than to English or Dutch youths. Between 1697 and 1707, eleven of twelve Huguenot businessmen who regis-tered apprenticeship contracts with the city took Huguenot youths as their apprentices. Other Huguenot parents reacted in different ways, however. Faced with the reality of preparing children for a changing, heterogeneous society, a significant minority of refugee parents looked beyond Huguenot traders and merchants. Thus seven of the eighteen Huguenot youths apprenticed in the city between 1697 and 1707 acquired non-Huguenot masters, and five of these seven found themselves bound out to a merchant or craftsman from the politically dominant English minority in the city.[20]

Alongside the significant early economic and political assimilation of the New York Huguenots in the 1690s, three signs of real and potential tension also emerged among the refugees. The first, the Huguenot role in the Leisler Rebellion, produced temporary effects. The second, a continuing disparity between rich and poor refugees, may have eased after 1700 and was familiar to Huguenots in France and Europe as well as to English colonists. The third, an astonishingly high rate of exogamy among Huguenots marrying in the 1690s, posed significant dangers to cohesion among the refugee families.

New York's Leisler Rebellion of 1689–90 divided the Huguenot refugees, although their role in the affair was minor. The rebellion itself has stirred significant debate among historians. Recent analysts generally agree that its leading figure, the Dutch-German merchant Jacob Leisler, represented the frustrated political and economic aspirations of modest Dutch city merchants and that he used the opportunity of the Glorious Revolution of 1688, which removed the Catholic James II from the British throne, in an effort to increase their political power in New York. Class and religion also were important to the revolt although historians disagree about the extent of their influence. The colony's richest merchants and politicians, including leading Dutch merchants and the leaders of the Dutch Reformed Church, all opposed the rebellion, and Leisler utilized much evangelical, anti-Catholic, and anti-aristocratic—if not democratic—rhetoric in the revolt.[21]

Most modern historians describe the city's recently arrived Huguenots as anti-Leislerians. Jerome Reich, for example, notes that Leisler publicly humiliated the minister Pierre Daillé, cursing him with the words "The Devil take you!" after Daillé rejected Leisler's demand for an extra sermon on the Sabbath, and that several Huguenots requested compensation for damages after

Leisler fell from power in 1691. Thomas Archdeacon also argues—incorrectly—that Huguenots who contracted exogamous marriages in the 1690s took only English spouses and that this pattern reflected an English-Huguenot alliance that undercut potential Huguenot support for Leisler.[22]

In fact Huguenots divided over Leisler and his rebellion along the lines of wealth, if not class. Certainly the Huguenot "establishment" in the city opposed him. The Huguenot minister Pierre Peiret and four wealthy merchants, including Stephen DeLancey, who identified themselves as "ancien[s] de l'eglise de refugiez," signed a petition in May 1689 demanding Leisler's ouster from the New York government. The physician Giles Gaudineau refused to surrender his lieutenant's commission in the militia to Leisler and found himself under arrest. Elie Boudinot, who signed the anti-Leisler petition, turned his opposition into a public spectacle. In June 1689 a woman alleged that Boudinot "affronted the Lieutenant Governor Leisler by putting his finger in his nose and then pointing at the said Lieutenant Governor." When Leisler asked Boudinot "why he mocked him," Boudinot answered, "may I not clean my nose, and is not my nose my own?"[23]

Other refugees did support Leisler, probably for personal as well as religious reasons. Paradoxically, one of them was the minister Pierre Daillé, who was then preaching to the Huguenots worshiping at Fort George. Leisler's public outburst at Daillé probably reflected a certain familiarity. According to a 1698 letter, Daillé was "accustomed to go to Commander Leisler, and exhort him to moderation." After Leisler's overthrow, Daillé reportedly "exerted his good office with Governor Sloughter to prevent his execution." Leisler also won support in New Rochelle because he acted as the agent for the town's Huguenots in purchasing land from the Pell family in May 1689, and Daillé circulated a petition in the town in 1690 to protest Leisler's death sentence. When the anti-Leislerian assembly of 1691 demanded that Daillé surrender the petition, Daillé refused, and the assembly censured and fined him.[24]

Leisler also won the support of several Staten Island Huguenots, especially for his well-advertised hatred of Roman Catholics. The Staten Island refugee Jacques Pouillon served on

Leisler's Committee of Safety and accepted Leisler's commissions as a Justice of the Peace and a militia captain. In the company of the refugee John Bedine, Pouillon confiscated personal property of a Staten Island customs inspector on the ground that the inspector and the man who appointed him, former Governor Thomas Dongan, were Catholics. The action fit the anti-Catholicism of both Leisler and the colony's Huguenots. But whether it reflected deeper Huguenot support for Leisler remains uncertain; Pierre Daillé burned a pro-Leisler petition he had earlier circulated at Staten Island, and no other sources provide any additional evidence of Leisler's Huguenot support.[25]

Disparities of wealth created additional grounds for potential divisions among New York Huguenots. In 1695 the Anglican chaplain at Fort George described the colony's Huguenots as "poor, and therefore forced to be penurious." But most evidence suggests that the refugee community's major economic feature was a gulf between rich and poor that did not begin to fill until after 1700. New Rochelle's land distribution and slave-owning records suggest that only a small number of settlers owned land, goods, and slaves in large quantities while most others owned very modest amounts of property. However, only the New York City tax lists allow a precise analysis of Huguenot wealth stratification. Three lists from 1695, 1699, and 1703 in Table 8 point toward significant gaps between rich and poor refugees in the city. Between 1695 and 1703, roughly 40 percent of the Huguenot taxpayers occupied the bottom three brackets in the city's tax assessments, while the percentage of Huguenots in the top three brackets rose rather sharply from 22.4 percent in 1695 to 35.1 percent in 1699. At the same time the percentage of refugees in the four middle brackets (where an even distribution would have placed 40 percent of the refugees) shrank from 35.8 percent in 1695 to 24.3 percent in 1699, then rose again to 32.6 percent in 1703.[26]

In fact, the economic disparities within the New York City refugee community probably were greater than the early tax lists suggest because, like most such lists, they excluded the poorest people in the city. City assessors recorded valuations for everyone able to pay a minimum tax, or more, but usually failed to record the names of the abject poor. In 1695, for example, many more

Table 8. Tax categories of Huguenot taxpayers, New York City, 1694–1735 (number and percent in each decile group).

Year	Poor, 0–30	Middle, 31–70	Rich, 71–100	Total
1695	28(41.8)	24(35.8)	15(22.4)	67
1699	30(40.5)	18(24.3)	26(35.1)	74
1703	36(39.1)	30(32.6)	26(28.3)	92
1709	12(18.5)	15(23.1)	38(58.5)	65
1725	22(21.6)	50(49.0)	30(29.4)	102
1730	16(17.8)	40(44.4)	34(37.8)	90
1735	24(23.7)	48(47.5)	29(28.7)	101

Source: New York City Tax Lists, 1694–1735, Klapper Library, Queens College.

Huguenots lived in the city than the twenty-eight refugees recorded in the lowest three brackets. None of the regular pensioners of the city's French Church in the 1690s appear on the tax lists nor do any of the poor persons temporarily given aid by the French Church between 1693 and 1699. During the same years, however, the number of Huguenots with substantial wealth increased while the number of middling refugees remained the same or actually fell. Thus the city's richest Huguenots—Stephen and Abraham DeLancey, Jean and François Vincent, Isaac Deschamps, Elie Boudinot, Anthony Lispenard, Gabriel Laboyteaux, Jean Pelletreau, Jean Papin, and Paul Droilhet—competed for business with the city's richest Dutch and English merchants, while poor refugees—the widows Geoffroy and Paillet, Madame Prou, Michel Belin, M. Massiot and Jean Hain—took charity to survive. The New York City Huguenot elite contributed regularly to the poor fund of the French Church and perhaps eased some of the potential tension introduced by the disparity of wealth among the refugees. But how well their aid defused social tension and how long the contributors would remain loyal to the French Church were questions unanswered by their previous or current behavior.[27]

Exogamous marriages posed an immediate threat to Huguenot cohesion in New York. Exogamy did not preclude refugee loyalty to the French Church or refugee cohesion in politics and business. But the early incorporation of Huguenots in the colony's economy and politics made exogamy a serious matter because it reduced potential sources of refugee cohesion. In Boston few Huguenot marriages were recorded in the 1690s, and in South Carolina no significant marriage records exist before 1720. But New York City offers a superb opportunity to view Huguenot marriage loyalty; as in Boston and Charlestown the city's heterogeneous population allowed Huguenots to exercise real choices among ethnic groups when taking spouses.

New York City's French Church remained a bastion of endogamy and, hence, of refugee loyalty in family composition between 1690 and 1710. Only the marriage of the merchant Jean Barberie to the Dutch widow Françoise Brinqueman in 1694 marred the nearly perfect record of endogamous marriages in the city's French Church—forty-four of them between 1689 and 1700. Yet exogamy claimed an early place inside the French Church even before 1700. Despite the congregation's obvious disapproval of exogamous marriages, 21.2 percent of all baptisms performed there in the 1690s were performed for children born to refugees who had taken non-French spouses. This meant that Huguenots were, indeed, marrying Dutch and English New Yorkers but were doing it outside the French Church. Looking at all known Huguenot marriages in the surviving New York records—the records of the French Church and the Dutch Reformed Church as well as the New York colonial marriage licenses—reveals that fully 40.8 percent of all the known Huguenot marriages of the 1690s involved exogamous unions between Huguenots and English or Dutch spouses.

Clearly, in New York City, exogamy was not delayed until the second generation of refugees but was common among the city's early European-born refugees. Moreover, contrary to expectations, these Huguenots demonstrated considerable catholicity in their choice of spouses. Although the percentage of French-Dutch marriages is exaggerated by the loss of the records of Trinity Church where Englishmen might have married Huguenots, Huguenots married Dutch residents in impressive numbers particularly because it is difficult to find any notable Huguenot-Walloon affinity in the records. Between 1690 and 1699, 20 of the 76 (26.3 percent) total recorded Huguenot

Table 9. Huguenot marriages, New York City, 1690–1719

| Nationality | | French Church marriages | | | All Huguenot marriages[a] | | |
Groom	Bride	1690–99	1700–09	1710–19	1690–99	1700–09	1710–19
French	French	31	14	1	45	37	8
French	English	0	0	0	9	6	3
English	French	0	0	0	2	13	1
French	Dutch	1	0	0	16	9	6
Dutch	French	0	0	0	4	2	0
Total		32	14	1	76	67	18

Source: Registers of the Births, Marriages, and Deaths, of the "Eglise Française à la Nouvelle York," from 1688 to 1804, ed. Alfred V. Wittmeyer (Baltimore, Md., 1968); *Marriages from 1639 to 1801 in the Reformed Dutch Church,* in *Collections,* New York Genealogical and Biographical Society, 9 (1940); and *New York Marriages Previous to 1784* (Baltimore, Md., 1968). The last source contains records of licenses for marriages issued by the colonial government.

a. Includes marriages performed in the French Church, the Dutch Reformed Church, and marriages performed in other unknown churches under licenses granted by the New York colonial authorities. Duplicates have been removed in the few cases in which a record of both the surviving marriage notice and the colonial marriage license exist.

marriages, or 20 of the 31 (64.5 percent) exogamous Huguenot marriages, involved Dutch spouses.[28]

This early exogamy was not bound to wealth and soon transcended being bound to one sex. In New York City males did lead the rush. In only 6 of the 31 (19.4 percent) exogamous Huguenot marriages between 1690 and 1699 did Huguenot women take English or Dutch grooms. However, between 1700 and 1709 women already accounted for half of the exogamous Huguenot marriages (15 of 30). The available records unearth no significant relationship between exogamy and wealth. Whereas rich Huguenots might have been expected to marry outside their Huguenot ranks to increase the family connections so important to business in pre-industrial society, they evinced no greater penchant for exogamy than did other refugees. A few wealthy Huguenots indeed took non-Huguenot brides before 1710. Benjamin D'Harriette married Anna Outmans in 1699, and Stephen DeLancey married Anne Van Cortlandt in 1700. But other wealthy Huguenots—Benjamin Faneuil, Thomas Bayeux, and Gabriel Laboyteaux—took Huguenot spouses. The same pattern emerges among poor and modest New York City Huguenots. Some took non-French spouses early on (Lewis Bougeaud, Michael Bourthier, Peter Cavalier, and Francis Chappelle) while others (Jean Boyer, Jean Hastier, Jean Perlier, and Jacques Vivaux) took Huguenot spouses.

That the early Huguenot turn to exogamy did not stimulate an immediate collapse of cohesion among New York City refugees was due, in good part, to the successful labors of French Church minister Pierre Peiret. Peiret triumphed over the divisions introduced by the Leisler Rebellion, encouraged a remarkable flowering of refugee piety that grew in the wake of the French prison experience of the refugee merchant Elie Neau, and thereby created an unusually strong congregation to stem the tide of secular assimilation and social disintegration.

The political divisions sparked by the Leisler revolt of 1689–90 soon extended to religion. Peiret's arrival in 1687 initially complemented Pierre Daillé's ministry and stimulated construction of the first Huguenot church building in the city in 1688. But cooperation between Peiret and Daillé ceased when Peiret joined with leading New York City merchants and French Church elders to oppose Leisler while Daillé and many New Rochelle Huguenots supported him. In 1692 this disagreement led to the transfer of Huguenot services at Fort George to the new city congregation headed by Peiret. The city's Dutch Reformed minister tried to make the move appear natural by writing that Peiret would now minister to New York City Huguenots while Daillé preached to rural refugees who still lacked ministers, namely the Huguenots at Staten Island and the old Walloons at New Paltz. But the tension introduced by the Leisler revolt soon manifested itself in other church business. Daillé lost his preaching duties at New Paltz under mysterious circumstances to David de Bonrepos in 1693. He also was kept from officiating at the French Church in New York City. Although it is unknown whether perhaps the still embittered Church elders kept Daillé from the Church sanctuary or whether Peiret was responsible for his absence, his name is conspicuously missing from the French Church's baptismal, marriage, and funeral records from 1689 to his departure for Boston in 1696, except for three occasions in May and June of 1693.[29]

Peiret created an unusually strong refugee congregation in New York City despite the bitter legacies left by the revolt. The Huguenots' use of the French Church as a ritual center offers the most obvious evidence of the congregation's health in the 1690s. Pierre Peiret performed 28 marriages there for French couples between 1690 and 1699 and another 12 between 1700 and his death in 1704. Baptisms also increased in the 1690s. They averaged 21 per year between 1690 and 1699 and 23.4 per year between 1700 and 1704. Peiret even recovered some of the Huguenots who took non-Huguenot spouses by baptizing their children in the French Church, these being the children that account for 20 percent of the French Church baptisms in the 1690s and early 1700s.[30]

French Church finances also improved in the 1690s. Aside from an unexplained drop in contributions in 1698, the congregation's receipts rose steadily between 1690 and 1704. It paid its church officers well. It raised Peiret's salary twice in 1694, gave him a gift in 1696, and paid his expenses for a trip to visit his old nemesis, Pierre Daillé, in Boston in 1698. The poor fund received regular contributions from the general membership on the Sabbath and frequently received special contributions from the city's wealthier Huguenots. In 1702 the French Church evidenced its growing strength when its heads of families voted to construct a new and larger building in stone for the expanding congregation. On July 1, 1704, two months before Pierre Peiret's death, New York Governor Lord Cornbury laid the cornerstone for the new building that the French Church occupied for the remainder of the eighteenth century.[31]

Increased baptisms and a new church building were not the only signs of religious renewal within the New York City refugee community in the 1690s. The inner spiritual life of the French Church also deepened and broadened under the leadership of Pierre Peiret and the New York City refugee merchant Elie Neau. For a time Neau influenced refugees on both sides of the Atlantic. Ironically, however, the only activity for which historians have known Neau, his New York City school for African slaves, ended his influence among most New York Huguenots because it resulted in his conformity to the Church of England.

Neau's career demonstrates that Catholic persecution of Huguenots continued unabated in France and extended to those refugees unlucky enough to encounter it again. Neau was born in Saintonge in 1662. He fled to the West Indies with other Protestants in 1679, married a refugee woman named Susanne Paré in Boston in 1686, and settled in New York City in 1690 or 1691. In the course of Neau's business trip to London in 1692, a French privateer captured the ship he was sailing on. The French captain returned Neau to France where French magistrates sentenced him to a life term as one of Louis XIV's unfortunate "galley slaves." When Neau converted a Catholic prisoner to Protestantism, the French authorities transferred him to the infamous prison on the island of If in the Marseilles harbor. From his cell in the basement of the prison, Neau penned numerous letters which he sent to correspondents on the Continent as well as in America, including Pierre Peiret, several New York City merchants, and his wife. Following his release from prison with other Protestants at the end of King William's War in 1698, Neau visited Huguenots with whom he corresponded in Geneva, Holland, and London before returning to New York City in 1699.[32]

Elie Neau's letters from the Marseille prison profoundly affected Pierre Peiret and New York Huguenots and even circulated among English Protestants in the colonies. In 1698, for example, Cotton Mather translated and published an undated letter from Neau to his wife, Susanne Paré, under the title *A Present from a Farr Country*. In it Neau encouraged his wife to be a mother "a second time" so that their children "may be Born again by grace," an injunction that Mather hoped might stir Puritan backsliders as well. He also described the gruesome treatment given to the Marseilles prisoners.[33]

By the mid-1690s Neau's experience and prison letters stimulated a remarkable outburst of religious renewal among Huguenots in New York City. In a 1696 letter Pierre Peiret and the French Church elders wrote Neau that they too suffered in his imprisonment. "How can we be insensible of your affliction, since

3. Elie Neau in the Marseilles Dungeon (anonymous)

you are a member of our body?" Yet Neau's suffering also created spiritual opportunities for them as well as for him. It was an "example of what the grace of God can do," Peiret wrote. "You have been found worthy to suffer for the best cause that ever was; . . . Can the profane pleasures of all the world come up to the joys you are full of?" In the same year an anonymous Huguenot work printed in New York City further developed these themes: *Le Trésor des consolations divines et humaines, ou traité dans le quel le Chrétien peur apprendie à vaincre et à surmonter les afflictions et les misères de cette vie.* It was published in 1696 by William Bradford who, like Boston's Samuel Green in 1690, found the French text difficult to set with English type. The work probably was written or assembled by Pierre Peiret. Certainly the themes paralleled those in the letter to Neau written in the same year by Peiret and his French Church elders. Like Ezéchiel Carré of Boston, Peiret hoped to promote a renewal of piety in the American refugees. But whereas Carré only hinted at how this should be done, *Le Trésor des consolations divines et humaines* offered refugees a detailed guide to the promotion of piety based on Elie Neau's experiences and letters sent from prison. Refugees seeking their own religious rebirth should dwell on suffering, bodily affliction, misery, misfortune, accident, and human tragedy, the centerpieces of Elie Neau's experiences. Affliction turned men and women to prayer. It induced a true love of God. It taught compassion and patience. It diminished love for material things. In short, it affirmed Christian faith even as happiness, contentment, and success destroyed it.[34]

Neau's prison experiences also resulted in two European publications. The first was a brief English tract, *An Account of the Suffering of the French Protestants, Slaves on Board the French King's Galleys* (London, 1699). In it Neau reinforced the popular anti-Catholicism encouraged by William and Mary by describing his capture and the abysmal conditions in Louis XIV's prisons and galleys. Neau also bolstered anti-Catholicism among London's Huguenots by printing the names and home provinces of all French Protestants known to be serving in the galleys as of July 1698 when Neau won his freedom. A more important work appeared in Rotterdam in 1701: *Histoire abbrégée des soufrances du sieur Elie Neau, sur les galères, et dans les cachots de Marseilles.* This was a substantial work of 290 pages prepared by Jean Morin, a Huguenot minister in Holland who may have been related to the New York City merchant Pierre Morin. Morin printed Neau's lengthy introspective prison letters, fifteen original psalms or "cantiques sacrez," and letters Neau received in Marseilles including the 1696 letter from Pierre Peiret and the New York City French Church elders.[35]

Neau's writings and *Le Trésor des consolations divines et humaines* marked a renewal of Huguenot piety in both America and Europe in the 1690s. Paradoxically, European historians have for some time analyzed and appreciated Neau's work while American historians have been unaware of its existence. The distinguished French scholar Emile Léonard describes Neau as "le grand mystique des galères" and writes of him as a major exponent of important mystical and Christocentric themes that developed in the wake of the Huguenot diaspora. Neau's themes charted new territory in French Protestantism. Together with Isaac Lefevre, Jean Mallet, Elie Maurin, and Pierre Serres, Neau emphasized the sufferings of Jesus, private family worship, and the utility of despair. For Léonard "this piety reached its height with Elie Neau." Neau's prison letters adopted the millennialist view of Pierre Jurieu, then exiled in Amsterdam, but also spoke of ecstasy stimulated by personal suffering and agony. Neau described his imprisonment as a gift that brought him religious knowledge for the first time, and he increasingly invoked mystical imagery to describe it. When he likened himself to God's bridegroom— "Endow me with a soul, that I may be thy Spouse, and worthy of that name, and that has its true voice and language"—he promoted themes unprecedented in French Protestantism.[36]

This renewal of Huguenot piety in the 1690s collapsed in the decade after 1700. Elie Neau's failure to expand his publications dimmed his influence on the Continent. The work of other refugee Huguenots—Lefevre, Mallet, Maurin, Serres, as well as Pierre Jurieu—faded in the Netherlands as Jurieu battled the Protestant skeptic Pierre Bayle, and it dissipated in London in the controversy over the so-called French Prophets.[37] In New York, the renewal of refugee piety collapsed following three local calamities: the unexpected death of Pierre Peiret in 1704, the conversion of Elie Neau to Anglicanism several months later, and

the mismanagement of French Church affairs following Peiret's
death. These events also played an important role in the conformity of the important Huguenot congregation at New Rochelle to
the Church of England in 1709. Together, they weakened the
ability of Huguenots to participate in New York society without
also accelerating their disintegration as a cohesive refugee group.

Pierre Peiret's death robbed New York City's French Church of
a remarkable minister and brought on six years of problems for
the congregation. The elders hired Jacques Laborie to replace
Peiret temporarily while they searched for a permanent successor.
The choice proved disastrous, for Laborie was a troublesome
man. He succeeded Daniel Bondet briefly at the Oxford settlement but earlier caused so much trouble in London that the
Threadneedle Street Church warned Boston's Huguenots in 1699
not to hire him as a minister if he tried to gain Pierre Daillé's
position there. Not surprisingly, Laborie and the New York City
elders soon fell to quarreling, and the elders dismissed him in
1706. But rather than hire a replacement with the help of the
Threadneedle Street Church, as Charlestown's Huguenots did in
1700, the elders compounded their problems. They hired David
de Bonrepos to preach, baptize, and perform marriages on a part-
time basis whenever he came to the city and abandoned their
search for a permanent minister.[38] De Bonrepos's part-time ministry produced an alarming decline in lay support for the congregation. This is dramatically evidenced in the temporary decline of
ritual activity in the congregation (see Figure 3 below). Between
1700 and 1704 Peiret baptized an average of 23.4 children in the
French Church each year. But in 1707 de Bonrepos performed
only seven baptisms, and in 1709 he performed only four. Instead
of going to the French Church, Huguenot couples who made up
the congregation took their children elsewhere for baptism. Some
probably went to Trinity Church, the congregation of the Church
of England. But how many did so remains unknown since its early
baptismal records are lost. Others went to the Dutch Reformed
Church in numbers that, again, point up the close bonds that
linked many Dutch and Huguenot residents of the city. Between
1704 and 1710, sixteen couples, all of them Huguenot refugees
who had previously baptized their children in the French Church,
took their infants to the Dutch Church for baptism. Some,

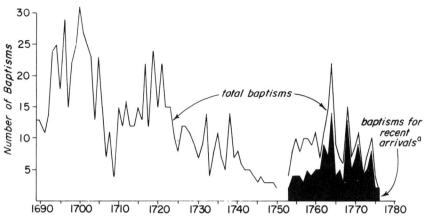

Fig. 3. Baptisms, French Protestant Church, New York City, 1689–1750, 1753–
1776. *Source: Registers of the Births, Marriages, and Deaths of the "Eglise
Françoise à la Nouvelle York," from 1688 to 1804,* ed. Alfred V. Wittmeyer
(Baltimore, Md., 1968).

surprisingly, were prestigious refugees such as Benjamin Faneuil,
Thomas Bayeux, André Stuckey, Jacques le Chevalier, and the
French Church elder Auguste Jay. But others, such as Jean
Lafon, Jean Garreau, Joshua Soulice, Jacob Rezeau, Goudon
Bessonnet, and Pierre Savouret, were poor and modest refugees
whose support for the French Church was equally vital to its
survival.[39]

When the French Church elders finally hired a permanent
minister, Louis Rou, from Amsterdam in 1709, he encouraged
many members of the Huguenot laity to return to the French
Church. Only two of the sixteen couples who baptized children in
the Dutch Church in the previous six years continued doing so
after Rou's arrival. Still, the temporary departure of many
refugees to other congregations may have taught them that those
same congregations could also meet their religious needs. Such a
lesson would be unimportant if the French Church could prevent
further difficulties. But the French Church was not to be so
fortunate.[40]

The disturbing defection of Elie Neau from the French Church
stemmed from his involvement with the Anglican Society for
Promoting Christian Knowledge and his evangelical drive to teach
Christianity to New York's slaves. The S.P.C.K. emphasis on
promoting piety through book publication and societies for

reforming manners apparently impressed Neau, and in August 1700 he became the S.P.C.K.'s lay correspondent in New York. In the next two years Neau also formulated a plan to found a school for slaves in the colony, and in March 1703 the S.P.C.K.'s companion society, the Society for the Propagation of the Gospel in Foreign Parts, authorized payment of £50 per year to Neau to begin teaching New York City slaves. To establish the school formally, however, the S.P.G. demanded that Neau conform to the Church of England and abandon his membership and elder's position in the city's French Church. In October 1704 Neau acknowledged to the S.P.G. "I ought to quit the office of Elder in that church in order to Join myself to the Church of England for the better carrying on of this business." But he hesitated in deference to Peiret's death. When the S.P.G. persisted, Neau resigned to join Trinity Church where he became a vestryman in 1705.[41]

Elie Neau's work with slaves stemmed directly from his personal piety. In an unpublished manuscript he composed about 1718, Neau told the S.P.G. that "the truths and duties that I teach my catechumen" were well summarized in the "cantiques sacrez" he composed in his jail cell in Marseilles. Between 1704 and his death in 1722, Neau regularly taught fifteen to twenty-five "catechumen" each year in his slave school. Neau was not an abolitionist, contrary to the claim of French historian Emile Léonard. In 1706 he successfully petitioned the New York legislature to specify that baptism and Christian conversion did not nullify a slave's status. But in a colony where all Europeans, including Huguenots, were enslaving Africans in astonishing numbers, Neau labored steadily to improve conditions for a people he had not known until his American migration; his experiences as a galley slave and in Marseilles encouraged him to believe he had experienced something of their own captivity and forced labor.[42]

Neau's Anglican conformity, still won him the permanent hatred of many city refugees. Between 1704 and 1722 only a few Huguenots sent their slaves to Neau's school, and they were all supporters of Trinity Church as was Neau. The city's other Huguenots who owned many slaves eschewed the school and its ex-Huguenot master. Neau worsened his position by promoting

Anglicanism with all the vigor of a new convert. When New York Governor Lord Cornbury pressed charges against the Presbyterian minister Francis Makemie in 1707 for preaching in the city without a license, Makemie objected to seating Neau as a juror on the grounds that he "prejudged the cause." According to Makemie, Neau loudly condemned Makemie for preaching in the city and had "justifyed Lord Cornbury's proceedings." It was, said Makemie a sad spectacle "to find one who was so lately dragooned out of France, for his Religion, and delivered out of the Gallies, so soon prove a Persecutor of the same Religion, for preaching a Sermon in this City."[43]

The decade after 1700 also witnessed the conformity of New Rochelle's Huguenot congregation to the Church of England, and the independent New York City and Staten Island congregations might have conformed as well if New York's ecclesiastical situation had been more favorable. In fact, Anglicans could offer New York Huguenots relatively little. Unlike South Carolina, the colony never passed a comprehensive church establishment act. The 1693 New York legislature created only six tax-supported parishes in New York City and the surrounding counties, all of which quickly fell under Anglican control. Thus, New York City Huguenots paid taxes to support Trinity Parish, Staten Island Huguenots supported St. Andrews Parish, and New Rochelle Huguenots supported Westchester Parish.[44]

Anglicans clearly wanted to bring the Huguenot refugees inside the Church of England, however, and soon acted to transcend the limitations of the 1693 Parishes Act. Between 1696 and 1710 the New York Council paid salary supplements to the colony's three Huguenot ministers to curry their favor for the Anglican cause. These included the Anglican-ordained Daniel Bondet at New Rochelle, David de Bonrepos of Staten Island, and Pierre Peiret of New York City, both of whom lacked Anglican ordination. Bondet accepted the supplement for over a decade even though his congregation rejected Anglican conformity until 1709. De Bonrepos accepted only a single payment in 1697. The behavior of Pierre Peiret who accepted the government payments between 1697 and his death in 1704 is more perplexing. As the minister of a successful refugee congregation and author of an important work on piety, Peiret might have been expected to reject these

Anglican overtures. But like his friend Elie Neau, Peiret admired
S.P.G. and S.P.C.K. ecumenical activity, and on the eve of his
death he apparently was involved with Neau and the city's
Anglican and Dutch Reformed ministers in forming an Anglican-
sponsored Society for the Reformation of Manners. This ecumenical instinct and the failure of the Huguenot exile clergy in either
England or America to develop denominational institutions that
could have supported his work probably induced Peiret to accept
the New York government salary supplements even if it did not
move him to Anglican conformity.[45]

New York City and Staten Island Huguenots remained safe
from the Anglican leviathan because they could not be fitted into
the colony's meager parish system and because no powerful
Anglican promoted their cause before London's S.P.G. But the
Anglican politician and manor lord Caleb Heathcote sought the
conformity of New Rochelle's Huguenots for a decade, until they
finally succumbed in 1709. Tellingly, Heathcote's interest in the
Huguenots was personal and political rather than religious. The
New Rochelle refugees simply fitted a plan Heathcote devised to
create a phalanx of Anglican congregations across the counties
north of the city between Connecticut and the Hudson River in
the hope that this would aid his political career. Indeed, it was
Heathcote who lured Daniel Bondet to New Rochelle from
Boston in 1695 on the promise that Bondet would actually earn
his living as the assistant minister at a new parish at nearby Rye.
When this early scheme unraveled, Bondet found himself alone at
New Rochelle with only Huguenot refugees to support him,
refugees who also paid taxes to support the Anglican minister at
Westchester Parish.[46]

Heathcote's first attempt at direct Anglican conformity at New
Rochelle floundered at the death of Pierre Peiret. After the Rye
fiasco with Bondet, Heathcote secured a salary supplement for
Bondet from the New York Council, and then worked to secure
the Anglican conformity of the New Rochelle refugees. Bondet
attached himself to the colony's growing numbers of Anglican
ministers by attending their gatherings and, with Heathcote,
assured the New Rochelle refugees that the S.P.G. would pay his
salary if the congregation would conform to the Church of
England. In the spring of 1704 the congregation agreed to do so.

By midsummer, however, its elders changed their minds under intense pressure from New York City Huguenots worried by Pierre Peiret's death and Elie Neau's departure to Trinity Church. Heathcote wrote the S.P.G. that the New Rochelle elders ultimately rejected Anglican conformity because "the French Congregation at New York were apprehensive that it might be a precedent for them, and for that reason fired the most ignorant of Mr. Bondet's people [against it], and persuaded them to recant from what they had agreed to."[47]

Heathcote continued the pursuit of his New Rochelle quarry with Bondet as his principle aide, whose good will he secured through salary supplements from the New York Council and, occasionally, through the S.P.G. in London. Bondet attended meetings of New York's Anglican clergymen and kept up a close relationship with the Anglican convert Elie Neau. Coupled with the accelerating decline in the New York City French Church after Jacques Laborie's dismissal in 1706, this steady Anglican support for Bondet encouraged him to tell Heathcote in May 1709 that a new attempt at Anglican conformity might now succeed in New Rochelle.[48]

Heathcote orchestrated the Anglican conquest of New Rochelle in masterful fashion. In early June of 1709 Heathcote appeared in New Rochelle flanked by Bondet, the Westchester Parish minister John Bartow, and the Anglican chaplain in Fort George, John Sharpe. Bartow conducted an Anglican Sabbath service, Sharpe preached the sermon (significantly, in English), and Bondet thanked Heathcote profusely for his salary supplements. After receiving instructions from Heathcote, twenty-six heads of families in New Rochelle proclaimed "their resolution of conforming to the rules and discipline of the Church." They petitioned the S.P.G. to permanently guarantee Bondet's salary, and they requested copies of John Durel's *La Liturgie* to use in their church services. Although the twenty-six heads of families represented only half of the family heads who appeared on the New Rochelle census a year later in 1710, they were sufficient for Heathcote and Bondet to proclaim a victory in their quest for the town's allegiance to Anglicanism.[49]

Events in the next year demonstrated how thoroughly New York's Anglican establishment underwrote the conformity of the

New Rochelle Huguenots. Although the lethargy then besetting New York City's French Church mitigated the dangers posed by New Rochelle's Huguenot nonconformists, Caleb Heathcote worked assiduously to preserve his New Rochelle victory. The Fort George chaplain John Sharpe visited with Bondet four times between late October 1709 and early January 1710, when Bondet was inducted as minister of the new congregation in New Rochelle. New York Anglicans also constructed the new stone building in which New Rochelle's conforming Huguenots worshipped. John Sharpe secured a license for the building from Governor Robert Hunter in 1710 and selected a site for it with the help of Bondet and Heathcote. Elie Neau raised the £150 sterling needed to pay for it. Only eight Huguenots contributed to the fund, all of whom were closely linked to Trinity Church in New York City. Neau himself provided the largest single gift of £13 sterling and a "small bell." The remaining contributors represented New York's Anglican leadership and included Governor Hunter, members of the New York Council, the colony's Anglican ministers, vestrymen of New York City's Trinity Church, and British military officers in the colony. Finally, sometime in the fall of 1712, Bondet, Heathcote, Sharpe, and Neau dedicated New Rochelle's new Anglican church building.[50]

In the flush of his New Rochelle victory, Heathcote wrote the S.P.G. that his success could "be a great means to influence the French congregation in New York likewise to conform." Elie Neau went further. He told the S.P.G. that the troubles of the French Church might secure its conformity. It had "been without a minister for three years," and, Neau argued, many of its members "have an affection for the Church of England." Heathcote and Neau proved poor prophets, however. Instead, the conformity of the New Rochelle congregation stimulated the New York City Huguenots to solve their ministerial problems. The French Church finally hired its first permanent minister since 1706 by arranging to bring the thirty-year-old Louis Rou to America with the help of Huguenots in Amsterdam. Rou had married the niece of the New York merchant Gabriel Laboyteaux, and after serving a brief ministerial apprenticeship with the Huguenot refugee congregation in Copenhagen, the Walloon Synod ordained him in August 1709. Rou arrived in New York

City in the spring of 1710 and remained at the French Church until his death in 1750.[51]

The Anglican conformity of the New Rochelle congregation and the hiring of Louis Rou became watersheds in the Huguenot experience in New York. Both events stabilized the religious situation by establishing the forms of the Huguenot congregations that would continue down to the American Revolution. Simultaneously, the different ecclesiastical directions taken by the two congregations point to the strains already produced by assimilation and group disintegration and the principal choices that the refugees faced for the future. They could rebuild traditional Huguenot religious institutions and repair their disintegrating social cohesion, especially in the family, or they could continue their assimilation within the expansive heterogeneous culture of colonial New York in the hope that their distinctive Huguenot religious life might somehow survive as well.

The secular and religious development of eighteenth-century New York should have encouraged the preservation of Huguenot cohesion. Between 1710 and 1760 New York became even more heterogeneous than it was when the Huguenots first arrived in the 1680s. The colony received German-speaking immigrants from the Palatinate, devastated by the last wars of Louis XIV, as well as Scots, Scotch-Irish, other Germans, many English immigrants, and even a few additional Dutch and Jewish settlers. While many of the Palatines moved to Pennsylvania, primarily because of poor planning for a wilderness settlement, other new immigrants clustered together in rural villages and settlements to pursue farming or, like New York City Jews, fitted into the city's merchant and trade economy. All of them fashioned distinctive religious institutions. By 1750 New York contained a New England-dominated Presbytery, several German Reformed congregations, English Presbyterians, Baptists, Quakers, Anglicans, Independents, and an impressive synagogue, the first substantial one built in the mainland colonies. But these new models of ethnic and religious perseverance proved relevant only to later colonists and later Americans, for between 1710 and 1760 New York Huguenots followed the early models of assimilation and internal disintegration they created for themselves as early as the 1690s.[52]

The assimilation of the Huguenots into the New York rural economy after 1710 required little deviation from the patterns laid down in the 1690s. This was true mainly because in these same years the agricultural economy in New York and its northern neighbors grew but did not mature; that is, it expanded on foundations laid down in the late seventeenth century and developed no radically new forms prior to the Revolution. This meant that New Rochelle and Staten Island Huguenots continued the diversified farming practices they first developed in their settlements and kept pace with neighboring farmers without increasing the size of their farms. Staten Island farmers continued to raise livestock including cattle, pigs, and sheep and to harvest small grains. A few New Rochelle Huguenots pursued a living from the sea through fishing and sailmaking, but most farmed. They recorded cattle marks in the town records, argued about fences, and improved their property by clearing, fencing, and sometimes planting apple orchards. Anthony Lispenard's advertisement in the New York *Gazette* in February 1732 typified the description of a relatively large, well-developed New Rochelle farm. Its appeal to a potential buyer rested on its typicality. Lispenard's 200 acres could produce 100 loads of "good English hay." Although it contained twenty acres of woodland, "most of the land is within Fence; there is a good House and Barn, and Orchard of about Five Hundred bearing Apple-trees; there is also an Island near adjacent which contains about Sixty Acres ... [and] a stock of Negroes, Horses, Cattle, Sheep, Hogs, &c., which are also to be sold."[53]

New Rochelle's farmers also continued to own slaves, as Lispenard's advertisement suggests, despite a relative decline in New York's eighteenth-century slave population. The absolute number of slaves in the colony increased, but their proportion in the population remained at about 15 percent through the 1750s, then dropped to 11 percent in 1771. Although a disproportionate number of slaves lived in New York City, farmers held about 80 percent of the colony's slaves throughout the colonial period. Slavery's persistence in New Rochelle suggests that its long-term decline in the colony stemmed from its rejection by new settlers rather than from its abandonment in old communities. The 1710 New Rochelle census finds that slaves then comprised 18.5 percent of the town's population—57 slaves among 251 whites—compared to 18.9 percent in 1698, and that the ratio of slaves to adult whites climbed only slightly from one slave for every 2.3 white adults in 1698 to one slave for every 2.45 white adults in 1710.[54]

The continuing importance of slavery in New Rochelle after 1710, impressionistically suggested in advertisements after 1730, is statistically confirmed in the 1771 census of the so-called "parish" of New Rochelle that included the larger area served by the town's Anglican Church. Where slave-owning declined in the colony as a whole since 1750, it increased in New Rochelle. By 1771 New Rochelle's slaves accounted for fully 21.8 percent of the population—156 slaves amidst 558 whites—and the ratio of slaves to adult whites decreased to one slave for every 1.9 white adults, lower than it had been in either 1698 or 1710. Moreover, Huguenot farmers held proportionately more slaves than did newer English settlers in the parish. Huguenots headed half the parish households in 1771 but owned two-thirds of New Rochelle's slaves. It is scarcely surprising, then, to discover that after the Revolution New Rochelle's Huguenots manumitted slaves very slowly. Like some other slave-owners in New York, if New Rochelle Huguenots freed slaves it was only when they promised not to ask for public assistance after their manumission. Thus the 1790 federal census still found the town to be 16.4 percent black—26 free blacks and 87 slaves among 575 whites—with Huguenots again holding a disproportionate share of the slaves.[55]

It was the urban Huguenots of New York City who offered the most visible evidence of the viciousness that underlay relations between master and slave—evidence that is sometimes more plentiful for that community in New York than it is for South Carolina. Only a single reference to the explosive bitterness generated by slavery has survived for New Rochelle. In 1766 a slave belonging to one of the village's English settlers killed a Huguenot woman, "Miss De Blez . . . by a blow with a small ax on the head," for which he was executed in the town in a public burning. But in New York City, where the precise extent of Huguenot slave-holding is impossible to document after 1703, Huguenots clashed with slaves on numerous occasions and sometimes lost their lives to Africans they angered. Huguenots owned a number of slaves involved in the 1712 New York City revolt—Jean Barberie, John Curé, Pierre Fauconnier, Pierre Morin, and André Stuckey—and two of the eight whites killed in the revolt were Huguenots. The poverty-stricken Auguste Grasset, who came to the city after dismal experiences in London, died when John Curé's slave ran a knife through his neck, and Henry Brasier died when a group of slaves attacked him with a knife.[56]

Huguenots were involved in more subtle ways with the aborted slave rebellion of 1741. Authorities accused slaves owned by eleven Huguenots with direct participation in the reputed plot to destroy the city. James DeLancey's slave Othello and Jean Auboyneau's slave Price were hanged. Slaves owned by a Mrs. Brasier, Peter DeLancey, James Desbrosses, Peter Jay, Charles Le Roux, and John Pintard were sent to the West Indies. A slave owned by the silversmith Simeon Soumain confessed to an involvement in the plot, but his fate is unknown. Auguste Jay's slave Ben became the most fortunate of the accused; he escaped from jail and simply disappeared. Huguenots testified at the trials of the accused slaves and sat on their juries. Finally, prosecutors cited the *History of Popery* by Pierre Jurieu, the Amsterdam refugee and millenarian, to prove that only treacherous Catholics sent to New York from French Canada could have instigated the slave rebellion.[57]

The assimilation of New York City Huguenots in the developing urban economy also continued after 1710 with astonishing thoroughness. This process did not always benefit individual Huguenots or their decendants. One major area of change for the Huguenots as a group was their decline in the city's occupational spectrum. Table 10 reveals how the number of Huguenot freemen involved in the professions and retail and merchant trades dropped significantly after 1710. Whereas about 10 percent of the Huguenots admitted as city freemen before 1710 were professionals, this was true of scarcely 1 percent of the Huguenot freemen admitted between 1731 and 1750. Similarly, the percentage of Huguenot freemen who were retailers dropped by half from 28.3 percent of the Huguenot freemen in the 1690s to 14.3 percent in the 1730s. The reasons for this change are not fully clear but probably centered on one fact. Unlike most refugees of the 1680s, some of the Huguenot professionals and retail merchants of the 1680s and 1690s were older, wealthy men

Table 10. Occupations of applicants for freemanship, New York City, 1694–1740

Occupation	1694–1700	1701–10	1711–20	1721–30	1731–40
Government	1	1	0	0	0
Professions	4	8	0	0	1
Retailers	19	14	6	7	8
Crafts, services	23	9	11	11	12
Industrial trades	13	13	6	16	23
Commerce	6	14	7	4	12
Laborers, agriculture	1	1	0	0	0
Total	67	60	30	38	56

Source: The Burghers of New Amsterdam and the Freemen of New York, 1675–1866, New-York Historical Society Collections, 18 (1885).

who apparently lacked direct family heirs to assume their businesses. The wealth of the merchants Paul Droilhet, Thomas Bayeux, and Gabriel Laboyteaux, who were important in New York City commerce in the 1690s, vanished with little trace after their deaths in the next decade. By contrast, the Jays and DeLanceys continued being important in New York City's merchant economy long after older Huguenot merchant firms had disappeared.[58]

Still, if the occupational distribution of Huguenot freemen changed, it matched change in the city itself. In fact, the occupational distribution of Huguenots granted freemanship in the city between 1741 and 1750 (Table 11) shows astonishing similarities to the occupational distribution of all city freemen. Slighty fewer Huguenot freemen were professionals (2 percent) than was true of English and Dutch freemen (4 percent). But elsewhere Huguenots matched the occupational distribution of the entire city: 31 percent of the Huguenot freemen made their livings in the retail and craft trades compared to 29 percent for the whole city; 29 percent were engaged in the industrial trades compared to 26 percent for all freemen; 22 percent of the Huguenot freemen engaged in maritime commerce compared to 20 percent for all freemen. And when the city began giving freemanship to laborers, Huguenots were admitted in the same ratio as were other laborers. Huguenot laborers comprised 15.7 percent of all Huguenot freemen compared to 19.2 percent of all

Table 11. Occupations of Huguenot and non-Huguenot applicants for freemanship, New York City, 1741–1750 (number
and percent)

Occupation	Huguenots	Non-Huguenots
Government	0 (0.0)	11 (1.6)
Professions	1 (2.0)	26 (3.8)
Retailers	3 (5.8)	20 (2.9)
Crafts, services	13 (25.5)	180 (25.9)
Industrial crafts	15 (29.4)	181 (26.1)
Commerce	11 (21.6)	143 (20.6)
Laborers, agriculture	8 (15.7)	133 (19.2)
Total	51	694

Source: The Burghers of New Amsterdam and the Freemen of New
York 1675–1866, New-York Historical Society, Collections, 18
(1885).

city laborers. Significantly, the most obvious differences, albeit
still minor, bore the legacy of the Huguenots' older occupational
patterns. As late as 1750, slightly more Huguenot freemen in the
city still engaged in the retail trades and crafts than did English
and Dutch freemen while slightly fewer made their livings as
laborers or agricultural workers.

As the ranks of the great Huguenot merchants thinned after
1710, some New York City Huguenots achieved brilliance as
silversmiths between 1710 and 1740. As in Boston and Charlestown, New York's Huguenot silversmiths compared favorably
with refugee silversmiths in England and frequently outshone
other city silversmiths. Bartholomew Le Roux, for example, came
to the city in the 1690s after a brief stint in South Carolina, and
several surviving silver bowls reveal him as a secure if unspectacu-
lar craftsman. His son Charles improved on his father's craft and
won numerous city and provincial government commissions,
among them a graceful silver mace in the shape of an oar made
for the New York Vice Admiralty Court about 1725 and now in
the collections of the Museum of the City of New York. Simeon
Soumain exemplified the best Huguenot silversmith work in the
American colonies, numerous examples of which survive in
American silver collections. The best known is Soumain's marvel-
ously shaped silver sugar dish modeled on a Chinese porcelain

4. Simeon Soumain, Sugar Bowl, c. 1730

bowl. Its design reflects Soumain's familiarity with international artistic fashion, and its craftsmanship and elegant simplicity bespeak an artist of uncommon skill and taste. The American art historian Graham Hood describes Soumain's bowl as the "outstanding example in American silver of a graceful style, at once languid and contained."[59]

As was the case with the Huguenot merchants, the contribution of New York's Huguenot silversmiths remained individual rather than collective. Even in London, the so-called "Huguenot style" of heavy ornamentation favored by the prominent refugee silversmiths Philippe Rollos, Pierre Harache, and Paul de Lamerie never appealed to all Huguenot silversmiths. Not surprisingly then, no significant stylistic differences separate the work of Huguenot from non-Huguenot silversmiths in the colonies. Rather, before 1730 Huguenot silversmiths simply outclassed most of their English or Dutch competitors in New York and elsewhere in America. However, in New York as elsewhere, this gap closed later despite some evidence that Huguenot silversmiths promoted communal cohesion in their shops. Thauvet Besley housed the London Huguenot silversmith Peter Lorin when Lorin visited New York City to sell his wares in the 1730s, and Huguenot silversmiths took Huguenot apprentices more frequently than did other French businessmen in the city. Between 1718 and 1727, four Huguenot silversmiths—Charles Le Roux, Simeon Soumain, Peter Quintard, and John Hastier—took three Huguenots but only one English and one Dutch youth as apprentices. By the 1760s, however, New York City's prominent Huguenot silversmiths had disappeared as thoroughly as had the old Huguenot merchants of the 1690s. Few left their shops in the hands of Huguenot apprentices, and those Huguenot silversmiths who succeeded them failed to dominate the city's silversmith trade as the Le Rouxs and Soumain had once done.[60]

New York City's Huguenot merchants exhibited little ethnic or religious loyalty in their business transactions after 1720. The Jay family maintained trade with their relatives, the Peloquins of Bristol, between 1725 and 1750, and one Jay business letter of 1724 documents a voyage by Peter Jay to La Rochelle in that year, although it is doubtful that the merchants with whom he traded were French Protestants. An account book of Stephen Richard dating from the 1730s reveals no special relationship with Huguenots nor do any of the surviving business papers of the DeLancey family. Similarly, land transaction records of the DeLancey estate on Cortlandt Manor north of New York City between 1761 and 1773 reveal that only one of twenty-five land purchasers there was a Huguenot; the others were English and Dutch farmers. Seemingly, then, like the Faneuils of Boston, New York's Huguenot merchants transcended their Huguenot origins in business after 1720.[61]

Self-conscious attempts by Huguenot merchants and craftsmen to hire Huguenot apprentices also declined after 1710. The trend for Huguenot masters to hire Huguenot apprentices between 1697 and 1707 evaporated after 1715. Between 1718 and 1727 Huguenot masters hired Huguenot apprentices in only three of twenty-two cases. Rather, they hired three Dutch apprentices, and the remaining sixteen came from the city's politically dominant English population. Yet the three Huguenot youths employed by Huguenot masters represented nearly half of all the Huguenot youths whose parents recorded apprenticeship contracts with the city in these years. This suggests both that Huguenot merchants may not have been able to choose Huguenot apprentices frequently even if they wanted them, and that some Huguenot parents still preferred to apprentice their children to Huguenot masters if possible.[62]

The occupational changes occurring among New York City Huguenots affected their relative wealth and, in turn, revealed their further assimilation in the city's evolving economy. The New York City tax records between 1695 and 1735 (see Table 8 above) suggest that the city sustained a remarkably stable distribution of wealth across these important forty years, despite significant population growth and an erratic economy. Gary Nash has found that the top 10 percent of city taxpayers held 45.2 percent of the city's assessed wealth in 1695 and 43.7 percent in 1730 while the poorest 30 percent increased their share from 3.6 percent in 1695 to 6.2 percent in 1730 although, as Nash points out, the figures ignore the expansion of a significant untaxed poor popultion that does not appear on the assessment lists.[63]

The Huguenot shifts within New York City's economic classes reflected the disappearance of old merchant families and a general movement from the professions and merchant trades to smaller retail and craft trades. The percentage of Huguenots in the top 30 percent of city taxpayers remained about the same in 1735 (28.7) as it was in 1695 (22.4 percent) but slipped from the highs recorded between 1709 and 1730 (58.5 percent to 37.8 percent). The most dramatic change occurred in the declining number of poor Huguenot taxpayers. Between 1695 and 1703, 40 percent of all assessed Huguenots ranked in the bottom 30 percent of the city taxpayers. But between 1709 and 1735 only 18 percent to 24 percent of assessed Huguenots found their way into these ranks. These changes account for the rise of Huguenots in the middle 40 percent of city taxpayers. In 1695, 35.8 percent of assessed Huguenots ranked in these middle brackets, but 47.5 percent did so in 1735. In short, the percentage of Huguenots in the top 30 percent of city taxpayers declined through the 1730s from the high reached in 1703 to levels achieved earlier in the mid-1690s. The percentage of assessed refugees who occupied places in the bottom 30 percent of city taxpayers declined dramatically between 1695 and 1735.[64]

These figures reflected the personal fortunes of individuals, some of whom can be traced through the welter of the seventeenth- and eighteenth-century city tax lists, although they are too few to create a statistical index of their performance. Most Huguenots maintained their places in the tax lists between 1695 and 1735 despite the erratic fluctuation of the New York City economy. Only one refugee with an extended appearance on the tax lists matched the economy in its roller coaster ride across the decades. Jean Garreau, probably the grandfather of Anne Faneuil's illegitimate child born in 1726, ranked in the lowest tenth or 1st decile of city taxpayers in 1703, in the top 10 percent or 10th decile in 1709, then in the middle 4th and 5th deciles in 1725 and 1735. Other refugees sometimes improved their position on the lists. Zachary Angevine moved from deciles 2 to 7 between 1695 and 1703; Jean Canon moved from deciles 7 to 10 between 1699 and 1730; the physician Giles Gaudineau moved from deciles 2 to 9 between 1695 and 1703.

Some individuals were remarkably successful. Auguste Grasset, whose dismal London experience led him to migrate to New York in the late 1680s and who was killed in the 1712 slave revolt, moved from deciles 4 to 7 between 1695 and 1709, and the religious author and slave schoolmaster Elie Neau moved from deciles 5 to 9 between 1703 and 1709. Two other Huguenots experienced equally remarkable success. When Henry Jourdain died in 1700 (he ranked in the 4th decile on the 1699 tax list), his widow, Elizabeth, became a tavernkeeper to support herself. In 1703 she had fallen to the lowest decile of city taxpayers. In 1705 she placed a slave in Elie Neau's school. By 1709 she ranked in the top 10 percent of city taxpayers, and she remained in the 6th and 7th deciles through 1735. The silversmith Simeon Soumain discovered that New Yorkers were willing to reward his artistic talent. On the 1695, 1699, and 1703 New York City tax lists Soumain ranked in the 1st or lowest decile. But between 1709 and 1735 he consistently ranked in the 9th or 10th deciles, demonstrating that elite New Yorkers paid well for the silver pieces modern art historians praise so highly.

On the whole, however, the distribution of assessed wealth remained as stationary for most Huguenots as it did for most of the city. Rich refugees remained rich and at the top 10 percent and 20 percent of the city's taxpayers whenever they appeared on the lists—Stephen DeLancey, Auguste Jay, John and Peter Barberie, Elie Boudinot, Gabriel Laboyteaux, Paul and Stephen Richard, François and Jean Vincent, and John Depieu. Middling Huguenots remained in that category and seldom climbed into the ranks of the richest New Yorkers or descended into the bottom ranks. Poor Huguenots, like poor English and Dutch taxpayers, appeared more erratically on the lists. Some moved up, but others moved down and sometimes out, taxed one year, dropped the next, always bobbing in and out of the same low brackets.

Paradoxically, after 1720 Huguenots appeared on the city's poor rolls more often than had been true earlier. The cause obviously was not a dramatic increase in the number of poor Huguenots in the city but rather the decline of the city's French Church. The French Church accounts demonstrate that the congregation supported poor Huguenots regularly through the 1690s, and in 1715 the city's poor wardens supported only one known Huguenot, "Samuel Carlee in the poorhouse." But the continuing decline of the French Church curtailed this aid, especially after 1730. Between 1733 and 1735, for example, the poor wardens regularly supported Elie Chardavoine and his wife, Henry Coelyeux and his wife, a shipwright and former New Rochelle resident named Joshua David, Peter Denis, Peter Lessieur, Anne Magdalen Many, Marguerite Petit, the spinster Elizabeth Targé, and Michel Tennerie. The poor wardens' description of David typified the condition of the Huguenots thrown onto public relief by the decline of the French Church. David needed "a duffles coat and a blanket to keep him from the inclemency of the weather, as he is very old, infirm and past labor."[65]

Huguenot participation in New York politics after 1710 also reflects their continuing assimilation in the colony and was limited only by their concentration in and near New York City. Although New Rochelle added many English and Dutch settlers to its population after 1730, Huguenots still filled most town offices as late as 1770. An important exception was established in the 1730s, however. The town's Huguenots recognized the changing nature of the village and regularly named an English settler as one of New Rochelle's two tax assessors after that date.[66]

Huguenot office-holding at the provincial level reflected the wealth of a few refugees and their continuing concentration in New Rochelle, Staten Island, and New York City. Two wealthy Huguenots dominated refugee membership on the prestigious New York Council between 1700 and the Revolution. The merchant Jean Barberie served on the council from 1705 until his death in 1728; then Stephen DeLancey arranged for the appointment of his son James DeLancey. James DeLancey held this seat from 1729 to 1753; his son James held it from 1755 to 1760; and Oliver DeLancey held it from 1760 until his flight to England as a Loyalist in 1776. Their father and grandfather, Stephen DeLancey, sat in the New York Assembly for over three decades from 1701 to 1737 as the representative of New York City. After 1710, one or two additional Huguenots usually sat in the assembly with DeLancey representing the city, Staten Island, or Westchester County, while descendants of the old Walloons who still comprised most of the New Paltz settlement usually represented Ulster County.[67]

Huguenot participation in New York City government after 1710 accelerated beyond the solid foundation of office-holding created in the 1690s (Table 12). Between 1701 and 1730, New Yorkers elected Huguenots as assistant aldermen fifteen times, as constables thirteen times, and as assessors and tax collectors forty-five times. Between 1731 and 1750, continuing the pattern, city voters elected Huguenots as aldermen nine times, as assistants seven times, as constables twenty-two times, and as tax assessors and collectors forty-seven times.[68]

The assimilation of the city Huguenots appeared also in the deeper sociological parallels among Huguenot, English, and Dutch office-holders. The Huguenots were indistinguishable

Table 12. Municipal offices held by Huguenots, New York City, 1689–1750

Office	1689–1700	1701–10	1711–20	1721–30	1731–40	1741–50
Alderman	0	0	0	0	3	6
Assistant alderman	1	10	2	3	6	1
Assessor, collector	14	15	8	22	24	23
Constable	3	6	3	4	17	5

Source: These figures have been gleaned from the election results in *Minutes of the Common Council of the City of New York, 1675–1776,* ed. Herbert L. Osgood, 8 vols. (New York, 1905).

from English and Dutch city officials or other colonial office-holders. Most Huguenot office-holders came from the upper 30 percent of city taxpayers, and even the poorest of them ranked in the 4th and 5th deciles. Most were merchants or skilled craftsmen, and like other officials they usually served two terms as tax assessors and collectors to maximize efficiency, but tried to limit their terms as constable to one year. One Huguenot, Bartholomew Feurt, served eight terms as an assistant alderman between 1702 and 1710, an uncommon occurrence for any city office-holder and an obvious public recognition of Feurt's political abilities. Finally, Huguenots moved through the New York City public service system like other city residents. Service at the bottom never guaranteed election to top city positions, and most Huguenots who served as assessors, collectors, and constables never held high public office. But nearly all Huguenots who became assistants or aldermen served first in the minor public offices just as their Dutch and English counterparts did.[69]

Little national or religious cohesion can be discerned in Huguenot voting in New York or in their remarkable office-holding record. An exception to this pattern was the disputed 1701 New York City aldermanic election. There, Huguenot voters in the city swung firmly behind an English-dominated anti-Leislerian faction in city politics. Polls from three city wards demonstrate that Dutch voters gave candidates of the so-called Leislerian faction 113 of 138 (82 percent) votes but that English voters gave anti-Leislerian candidates 69 of 77 (89 percent) votes, and Huguenot voters gave them 48 of 53 (91 percent) votes. Beyond this election, however, it is difficult to perceive any special Huguenot influence at work in city politics. Huguenot office-holders in the city came from wards where most Huguenots lived—Dock, South, East, and West—but whether Huguenots voted for them in preference to candidates of other national groups in the city is impossible to tell. Nor is it possible to discern any special Huguenot influence at work in the spectacular political career of Stephen DeLancey and his children—a family that exercised enormous influence in New York's faction-ridden politics from the 1690s to the Revolution. Slurs on the patriotism and loyalty of Benjamin Faneuil by a rival ship captain prompted Faneuil, Stephen DeLancey, and other elders of the French Church as well as Huguenots who had joined the Anglican Trinity Church to denounce the charges in print in 1708. But a blatantly partisan attempt by Governor Robert Hunter to remove Stephen DeLancey from the 1724 Assembly on grounds that DeLancey lacked naturalization apparently elicited no special protest from the New York Huguenots. Nor did the DeLanceys' opponents bring up their Huguenot background against them later; rather, they criticized the DeLanceys' reputed penchant for violence. In 1750 New York Governor George Clinton charged that James DeLancey was using his "two bullies, Peter and Oliver [DeLancey], to frighten those that his artfull Condesention and Dissimulation could not persuade to vote their conscience." But Clinton said nothing about the DeLanceys' Huguenot past.[70]

The post-1710 Huguenot marriage record dramatically sum-marizes Huguenot assimilation in New York and underscores the thorough disintegration of the Huguenots as a cohesive refugee group. Because the records of the French Church at Staten Island have long since disappeared, few New Rochelle marriage records have survived, and its baptismal records exclude spouses' maiden names, it is impossible to obtain a systematic survey of Huguenot intermarriage in either settlement. In New York City, however, although few French Church marriage records exist after 1710, the baptismal records do include spouses names and therefore reveal the marriage pattern of adults presenting children for baptism. Table 13 demonstrates that exogamy gained significant ground in the French Church after 1710. The percentage of

Table 13. Ethnicity of couples presenting children for baptism, French Protestant Church, New York City, 1689–1776

Nationality		1689–	1700–	1710–	1720–	1730–	1740–	1750–	1760–	1770–
Groom	Bride	99	09	11	29	39	49	59	69	76
French	French	61	50	27	8	11	9	20	21	9
French	English	5	5	1	1	4	4	2	3	4
English	French	4	2	1	1	1	3	2	0	1
French	Dutch	2	2	1	4	1	0	2	4	0
Dutch	French	2	0	1	0	1	1	0	1	0
French	Unknown	4	6	22	20	3	0	4	10	1
Unknown	French	0	0	0	0	0	0	1	0	1

Source: Registers of the Births, Marriages, and Deaths, of the "Eglise Françoise à la Nouvelle York," from 1688 to 1804, ed. Alfred V. Wittmeyer (Baltimore, Md., 1968).

exogamous couples participating in baptismal rituals at the French Church ranged from a low of 12.9 percent in the 1710s to a high of 47.1 percent in the 1740s although it declined again in the next several decades.[71]

Records of other city churches and the colonial marriage licenses demonstrate that Huguenot exogamy ran rampant outside the French Church after 1710 (Table 14). Between 1700 and 1709 mixed couples already accounted for 44.8 percent of all recorded marriages involving New York City Huguenots. By 1750, when major gaps in the city marriage records end, Huguenots were marrying each other only as frequently as simple chance allowed. Between 1750 and 1759, 74 of 85 (87.1 percent) Huguenot marriages were exogamous ones, and between 1760 and 1769, the figure was 162 out of 189 (85.7 percent) Huguenot marriages.[72]

New York City Huguenots exhibited only slightly less catholicity in choosing marriage partners after 1710 than earlier. The records of the city's Dutch Reformed Church demonstrate that Huguenot-Dutch marriages certainly continued after 1710. Not unexpectedly, most Huguenots who were married in that Church contracted exogamous marriages to Dutch spouses. But after 1750 Huguenots increasingly chose spouses from the politically dominant English population. Whereas marriages to Dutch spouses accounted for half the exogamous Huguenot marriages

Table 14. Huguenot marriages, New York City, 1750–1784

Nationality					
Groom	Bride	1750–59	1760–69	1770–79	1780–84
French	French	11	27	13	13
French	English	26	55	26	27
English	French	33	68	35	17
French	Dutch	8	16	7	5
Dutch	French	7	21	11	4
French	Unknown	0	1	0	1
Unknown	French	0	1	0	1

Source: New York Marriages Previous to 1784 (Baltimore, Md., 1968), which reprints, with corrections and additions, *Names of Persons for whom Marriage Licenses were issued by the Secretary of the Province of New York, previous to 1784,* [ed. E. B. O'Callaghan] (Albany, 1860). The failure of ministers at New York City's French Church to keep marriage records consistently between about 1715 and 1750 together with the loss of most New York colonial marriage licenses for the same period accounts for the inability to trace marriage patterns among the colony's Huguenots in this period.

recorded between 1690 and 1710 (remembering again that the Anglican records from Trinity Church have been lost), they accounted for only 15 of 74 (20.2 percent) exogamous Huguenot marriages in the 1750s and 37 of 162 (22.8 percent) in the 1760s.

After 1710 gender and wealth had no significant effect on exogamy rates among city Huguenots. Women already accounted for half of the exogamous Huguenot marriages in the first decade of the 1700s, and the records of the Dutch Reformed Church, albeit limited, suggest that their ability and willingness to contract exogamous marriages held firm in the next decades. Between 1720 and 1749 women accounted for 31 of 51 (60.8 percent) of the exogamous Huguenot marriages contracted there. After 1750 women accounted for slightly more than half of the exogamous marriages recorded in the extensive New York colonial marriage licenses—40 of 74 (54.1 percent) in the 1750s and 89 of 162 (54.9 percent) in the 1760s.

It is as difficult in New York as it was in South Carolina to determine how wealth affected exogamy patterns. After 1710 fewer children of New York's wealthiest Huguenot families took Huguenot spouses than did the children of wealthy South

Carolina families, whereas in the 1690s wealthy New York Huguenots still mostly married Huguenots spouses. For example, with one exception, all the DeLancey children who survived to adulthood married children from important English or Dutch families: Stephen DeLancey himself married Anne Van Cortlandt in 1700. His eldest son, James, married Caleb Heathcote's daughter Anne in 1729. His daughter Susannah married Peter Warren. His daughter Anne married John Watts. His son Peter married Elizabeth Colden, daughter of the colony's long-time Lieutenant Governor Cadwallader Colden. The exception, Oliver DeLancey, crossed far greater ethnic and religious boundaries when he married Phila Franks, daughter of the prominent Jewish merchant, Jacob Franks. Phila's mother wept when she learned of her daughter's marriage, which the newlyweds kept secret for six months. But if the DeLanceys too wept (and Oliver DeLancey's secrecy suggests that he worried about their reaction), they were most likely concerned that he married a Jew, not that he had failed to marry a Huguenot. The extent of exogamy among most New York Huguenots including the DeLanceys suggests that marriage to English and Dutch spouses was the norm for Huguenots in the colony long before 1750. This freedom allowed a member of an aristocratic family like the DeLanceys to marry a Jew. But for most New York Huguenots it meant that the family had steadily vanished as a repository of refugee cohesion in the colony.[73]

Finally, the French churches also vanished. The form of their disappearance assumed three now familiar shapes: the failure of dissidents to stand up against Anglican conformity, as at New Rochelle; the failure to preserve any significant French influence in Anglican worship, not even the French language; and the collapse of the independent French congregations in Staten Island and New York City followed by the dispersal of their members to a broad range of denominations.

Lack of early leadership and the dominance of the Anglican faction in town affairs resulted in Anglican success in New Rochelle although only half of the village's Huguenot family heads signed the 1709 petition for Anglican conformity. The travail over Anglican conformity before 1709 and the dispute about it afterwards are difficult to link to personal disputes in the village in the 1690s, the Leisler Rebellion, French regional backgrounds of the town's residents, or even their ages. Some old people supported conformity, for example, and others did not. Whatever its causes—spiritual, intellectual, or economic— dissident strength soon waned because it received no clerical support. Daniel Bondet wholeheartedly supported conformity; David de Bonrepos at Staten Island kept quiet; and Louis Rou, the newly installed minister of the French Church in New York City, only baptized the dissidents' children and seldom preached there. Bondet reported some "troubles and unexpected opposi- tions" in 1711, but in 1714 he applauded the Anglican conformity of several dissidents and a year later claimed only a minority of town residents still opposed conformity.[74]

Opposition to conformity grew after 1718, however, but never became radical or violent as happened in South Carolina. Jean Joseph Brumeau de Moulinars, the assistant minister at New York City's French Church, stimulated the renewal of Huguenot loyalty in New Rochelle. He charged that the Anglican and Catholic churches were "as like one another, as two Sisters can be," and at the same time he cultivated the village's older French-speaking residents who first supported conformity. In 1726 Moulinars moved to New Rochelle after losing a bitter fight with Louis Rou at the French Church in New York City. The New Rochelle nonconformists, now with a permanent minister, constructed a wooden church building for their congregation and somehow wrested control of the old town glebe from the conformist Anglican congregation. Daniel Bondet's successor, Pierre Stoupe, credited Moulinars with about 40 percent of the town's Hu- guenots as supporters in the early 1730s, with most but not all being Huguenots who spoke no English. But the dissident congregation declined after Moulinars' death in 1741. Some members returned to the conformist congregation where their demands for exclusive French language services went unheeded. Other dissidents were forced to accept the ministry of Moulinars' old enemy, Louis Rou, because Rou was the only independent Huguenot minister left in the colony. Rou recorded dwindling numbers of baptisms and marriages in the town until he died in 1750, and when the Anglican congregation regained its glebe in

1765 the dissident congregation disbanded. Some dissidents never accepted Anglican ritual, however, and they joined English and Dutch settlers to organize New Rochelle's first Presbyterian congregation after the Revolution.[75]

French-language worship also slipped away at New Rochelle's conformist Anglican congregation. Of course, conformity brought Anglican ritual to the town at first through the use of John Durel's *La Liturgie.* Daniel Bondet preached in English every third Sunday of the month for nearby English colonists as well as for Huguenots who already used English. As early as 1714, he told the S.P.G. that a successor should be able to preach in both languages because he filled his new church when he preached in English. Pierre Stoupe, who succeeded Bondet in 1724, continued the English services and reported in 1744 that even French-speaking residents, most of whom once supported Moulinars, attended them. When Stoupe died in 1760, the elders obligingly asked the S.P.G. for a French-speaking minister who could "sometimes officiate therein for the Benefit of some of our Ancient People." But their addendum revealed how thoroughly assimilation also marked even this agricultural village: "if this be not practicable we shall be Content to have the Service entirely in the English Tongue, which is by Much the best understood by the greater part of the Congregation." In fact, a French-speaking Anglican minister, Michael Houdin, replaced Stoupe, largely because he already lived in the colony. But by the time of the Revolution, New Rochelle was an English-speaking village with an Anglican congregation whose members happened to carry Huguenot surnames, as also was the case at St. James Santee in South Carolina.[76]

The collapse of Staten Island's French Church again reflected the influence of a Huguenot clergyman partial to the Church of England. Although the French minister, David de Bonrepos, never received Anglican ordination, he supported Anglican work there after 1700. He allowed the Anglican missionary Aeneas MacKenzie to conduct worship in the French Church building in 1709, the year New Rochelle's congregation conformed to the Church of England, and in 1711 he allowed Huguenot children to attend MacKenzie's catechism classes. In the 1720s de Bonrepos, feeling too old for his duties, invited a new Anglican minister, William Harrison, to preach to Staten Island's Huguenots, and in 1733, a year before his death, de Bonrepos wrote the S.P.G. that he had "recommended" his Huguenots "to [Harrison's] Church and Instruction and they have according been most of them his hearers." In fact, as many Staten Island Huguenots already patronized the Anglican St. Andrews Church as their own French Church, and when de Bonrepos died in 1734, the elders simply closed the French Church without making any attempt to replace him. Yet not all of Staten Island's Huguenots became Anglicans. Others found their way into Staten Island's Dutch Reformed Church, usually in the process of being married, and by the 1760s a few had even joined Staten Island's small Moravian Church.[77]

The collapse of New York City's French Church destroyed the colony's last independent Huguenot congregation. It involved three major events—a bitter dispute between the Church elders and Louis Rou, the minister, that began in 1713; a substantial loss of supporters to other congregations; and an unsuccessful decade-long search for a permanent minister that only stimulated additional argument within the congregation. The dispute in New York City's French Church between Louis Rou and the Church elders originated in the scandal of Rou's marriage in 1713 to a fourteen-year-old New Rochelle girl named Renée Marie Gougeon, a year after the death of his first wife and three years after his arrival in the city. The remarriage shocked his congregation. Elie Neau, then observing French Church affairs from a distance, wrote the S.P.G. in London that the remarriage had angered Rou's congregation. "Nobody knows his reasons, for the young Creature has not much." Other New Yorkers found the match equally appalling. Daniel Bondet of New Rochelle refused to marry Rou because the girl was so young, and the Dutch Reformed minister who finally did so pointedly described her in the marriage record as a "young maid."[78] The fertility of Rou's child-bride only added to the embarrassment of his congregation. By 1725 she had presented Rou with seven children, and by 1740 she had given birth to fifteen.

Angered by the marriage, the French Church elders acted against Rou in 1718, when they hired Jean Joseph Brumeau de Moulinars as an assistant minister to carry out many of Rou's duties; their ensuing confrontations energized contests for elders' posts in the congregation. When Rou's supporters failed to win even a single elders' post in 1724, Rou claimed his opponents rigged the election. In response, the elders stopped Rou's salary, denied him use of the church building, and made the assistant minister, Moulinars, the congregation's sole minister.[79]

The dispute quickly became a public spectacle. Opposed by the Church's elders, Rou scoured the city looking for any Huguenots who might support him. One of his petitions suggests that he found them among obscure and poor Huguenots who, as even Rou admitted, had "not thought fit to give open testimony to the truth" during his initial fight with the elders. An even more unusual petition named twenty-five women supporters. Not surprisingly, the name of Rou's wife headed the list. The elders controlled the congregation's most consistent and prestigious supporters including virtually all the Huguenots listed in the top 10 percent of city taxpayers in the 1725 assessment list. Rou, however, used his influence with Governor William Burnet, son of the Anglican bishop Gilbert Burnet, to win a lawsuit he brought against the French Church elders. In response to Rou's suit, Burnet and the New York Council ruled that traditional French Protestant discipline required that ministers be dismissed by colloquies. Since these did not exist in America, they ordered Rou's reinstatement.[80]

The dispute conveyed faint theological overtones. Some participants, especially the assistant minister Moulinars, criticized Rou for harboring Anglican sympathies, a view underscored by Rou's lethargic support for traditional Huguenot worship at New Rochelle and by Governor William Burnet's action on his legal appeal to the New York Council. But persistent embarrassment about Rou's marriage to the Gougeon girl a decade earlier, not theology, fueled the dispute for most Huguenots, and the elders only installed Moulinars because it was the simplest way to replace Rou. Certainly, they never imbibed Moulinars' anti-Anglicanism. Ironically enough, after Rou's forced reinstatement, many of the elders who opposed him—Thomas Bayeux, Stephen DeLancey, Benjamin D'Harriette, Auguste Jay, and Peter Vallete—left the French Church and joined Trinity Church, the Anglican congregation whose principles Rou allegedly favored.[81]

The battle with Rou ushered in two decades of fatal decline in New York City's French Church. In some regards the dispute was incidental to the Church's continuing loss of supporters. After the dispute ended, for example, two elders who had supported Rou joined those who opposed him and joined Trinity Church. The defection of other Huguenots is revealed by the dramatic decline in French Church baptisms after 1730 (Figure 3). Whereas baptisms averaged more than twenty per year between 1690 and 1720 (except from 1704 to 1710), they declined steadily after 1725. By the mid-1730s they were averaging less than ten per year, and by 1745 fewer than five children were being baptized in the congregation each year.[82]

The flight to other congregations demonstrates again that Huguenots exercised broad denominational choices available to them in the city and did not flock to the Anglican Church as historians frequently assume. Huguenots certainly continued to affiliate with the Dutch Reformed Church. Its marriage, baptismal, and burial records demonstrate that Huguenots developed a significant ritual affiliation there after 1710. In earlier years Huguenots who contracted marriages in the Dutch Reformed Church used to return to the French Church to baptize their children. But this seldom happened after 1710. Only two of forty-four such couples returned to the French Church for any ritual activity between 1710 and 1730, and one of them was the French Church minister Louis Rou and his adolescent bride Renée Marie Gougeon. The same records also show that Huguenots still married in the Dutch Reformed Church and had funerals conducted there as well. Between 1726, when the interment records begin, and through the 1790s, the Dutch Reformed ministers buried some sixty persons from at least twenty different Huguenot families, whose affiliation with the Dutch Reformed Church greatly weakened the French Church.[83]

Huguenots affiliated with other congregations in smaller numbers. None seem to have become Quakers and only after 1750 did a few Huguenots associate with the city's Presbyterian Church. Despite the apparent "presbyterian" character of French Protestantism, neither the Huguenot clergy nor the Huguenot laity evidenced significant interest in Presbyterian institutions. No Huguenots appear in the records of New York City's Presbyterian congregation until 1756. Between 1756 and 1769, however, eleven Huguenots solemnized their marriages there, and ten Huguenots, all of them married to English spouses, baptized their children there.[84]

The number and percentage of Huguenots who joined or baptized children at the Anglican Trinity Church before 1740 remains unknown in New York as in Boston. However, early fragmentary records suggest that prestigious members of the community frequently joined the congregation and often held offices there. Some became vestrymen—the physician Giles Gaudineau as early as 1698, the goldsmith Bartholomew Le Roux in 1703, the merchant and slave catechist Elie Neau in 1705, merchants Peter Barbarie, Jr. and Elie Jamain in 1710 and 1711, the silversmith Simeon Soumain in 1712, and the merchant John Auyboyneau in 1718. All of these defections constituted real losses to the French Church. Two had been elders there, four baptized children there, and the rest at least witnessed marriages there.[85]

As in Charlestown, some Huguenots, mostly merchants, maintained dual religious affiliations after 1710, thereby revealing their unease at leaving their native church altogether. John Auyboyneau, Jean Barberie, Elie Boudinot, Stephen DeLancey, Paul Droilhet, Benjamin Faneuil, Abraham Jouneau, and Pierre Morin contributed money to build a steeple for Trinity Church in 1711 at the same time that they still patronized the French Church. A decade later, in 1724, Stephen DeLancey and Elie Grazilier both purchased pews at Trinity Church, even as DeLancey served as an elder and opposed Rou while Grazilier was one of the family heads who backed Rou.[86]

The thorough decline of the French Church seemed to gain a reprieve after 1760. Between 1761 and 1770 baptisms in the French Church suddenly rose from an average of four or five per year in the previous decades to an average of nearly twelve per year in the 1760s (Figure 3). The rise did not stem from reawakened religious loyalties among third or fourth generation Huguenots, however, but from baptisms performed for new immigrants from eastern France and Switzerland. Although their numbers were small in an expanding city society, they offered the French Church a major opportunity to reverse its decline.

Between 1753 and 1760, children born to these new immigrants
accounted for 39.7 percent of all baptisms performed in the
French Church (27 of 68); between 1761 and 1770, the figure was
71 percent (72 of 101 baptisms); and between 1771 and 1776,
when the Church closed, the figure was 81 percent (30 of 37
baptisms). Or, put another way, baptisms of children born to
parents descended from old Huguenot immigrants declined
precipitously in these years from 41 between 1753 and 1760 to 29
between 1761 and 1770 and finally to only 7 between 1771 and
1776.[87]

The new Protestants from eastern France and French-speaking
Switzerland literally resuscitated the ritual life of New York City's
French Church. The elders, however, in their bitterness and
anger against each other, also turned against the immigrants in all
but baptism and soon subtly discouraged even that. Before 1760
several of the new male immigrants married daughters of old
immigrant families, and one of them, Jacques Buvelot, who
arrived in the 1740s and married an English woman, became
treasurer of the French Church in the 1760s. But the post-1760
immigrants encountered a different reception. None found
spouses among children of old Huguenot families, and the settled
colonists seldom witnessed baptisms or marriages for new immigrants. As a result, only two of the eight new immigrant couples
married in the French Church between 1760 and 1776 returned
to the French Church to baptize children. Most important, the old
Huguenots kept the post-1760 immigrants out of church government. Although new immigrants comprised half the number of
persons who signed petitions sent to London, Amsterdam, and
Geneva to support a new minister in 1763, none of them ever
served as an elder or deacon in the French Church between 1760
and 1776.[88]

The disastrous slide of loyalty to the French Church among old
Huguenot families and the cold treatment accorded new immigrants after 1760 doomed the congregation to extinction. Louis
Rou's return to the French Church in 1726 brought a quarter-
century of internal peace to the congregation largely because
Rou's enemies left it. So too did steady numbers of old supporters
whom Rou failed to reclaim or replace. He was a worldly,
sophisticated man far different from his introspective predeces-

sor Pierre Peiret, and in the two decades before his death in 1750 he became better known for wit than for proselytizing. His manuscript sermons reflect a preference for the polite English Enlightenment and for moral principles drawn from classical Roman authors. He sustained friendships with leading New York politicians (and enemies of Stephen DeLancey) including Governors William Burnet, Robert Hunter, and William Cosby, and a now lost parody of imperial politics that circulated in New York City and London in the 1730s illustrated Rou's love of chess and his attraction to Anglo-American political intrigue. It is not surprising, therefore, that another colonial humorist, the secretary of Annapolis's Tuesday Club, the physician Dr. Alexander Hamilton, outlined Rou's character and its consequences for his congregation after a 1744 trip to New York City: "I went this morning to the French Church with Monsr. [Jacques] Bourdillon and heard one Mons. Rue preach. He is reckoned a man of good learning and sense; but being foolishly sarcasticall, he has an unlucky knack att dissobliging the best of his parishioners so that the congregation has now dwindled to nothing."[89]

Louis Rou's death in 1750 brought Jean Carle to New York City from Amsterdam for a decade between 1753 and 1763. Carle served both the French Church in New York City and the Huguenot dissidents in New Rochelle. Despite his labor, both congregations continued to decline, and in 1760 Carle announced his intention to return to Europe. The French Church elders implored him to reconsider, and Carle agreed to do so if they would agree to conform to the Church of England, primarily so they could guarantee his salary. When the elders refused, Carle left.[90]

A thirteen-year search for a successor to Carle produced only embarrassing incidents, arguments among the elders, and finally the closing of the French Church in 1776. In 1764 the elders temporarily hired Jean Pierre Têtard, formerly of Charlestown, but could not agree about offering him their permanent position. In 1765 Amsterdam's Walloon Synod sent the Church a mentally unstable ministerial candidate, Paul Daniel Menauteau, who once had to be locked in his rented rooms to prevent him from preaching. The French ministers at Geneva simultaneously sent a haughty minister named Jacob Daller whom few elders could tolerate. This gave the French Church three ministers, none wanted by a majority of the continually shrinking membership, and further polarized the congregation. Menauteau was returned to Amsterdam, Daller sailed for London, and Têtard retired to a farm near New Rochelle. Amidst much additional argument, the elders tried to hire a German Reformed minister from Pennsylvania only to discover that he did not speak French. Finally they turned to Abraham Keteltas, a Presbyterian of Dutch background who had married the daughter of a former French Church elder. Keteltas agreed to preach to the Huguenots temporarily, but his service ended when he became a member of New York's Provincial Congress in 1776 and left the city when British troops occupied it.[91]

New York City's French Church closed in 1776 with Keteltas's departure. It reopened two decades later in 1796 only to succumb to the new American form of Anglican ecclesiastical order. Although the French Church building survived the Revolutionary War, by the 1790s the congregation had few members and little financial support. Its major potential source of income was a £1000 legacy left by Jacques Desbrosses in 1773 that required conformity to the Church of England. In 1803, the French Church elders, convinced that American independence had wrought major changes in the government of the old Anglican establishment, agreed to accept the denominational authority of the new Protestant Episcopal Church. They thus qualified for Desbrosses's legacy and renamed their congregation the French Church du Saint Esprit. They subsequently used their new Episcopal affiliation to serve New York City's tiny transient French Protestant population and have continued this mission down to the 1980s, a mission whose character and necessity commemorate the assimilation of the original Huguenots of the 1680s into pre-Revolutionary New York society.[92]

Conclusion. Everywhere They Fled, Everywhere They Vanished

The history of both early and modern America is, in part, the background history of its peoples—who they were, how they came, what they wanted. It also is the history of their American experiences—what they did, why they did it, what happened to them in the process. By its very nature, then, the history of America and its peoples is both complex and more than narrowly American. From the colonial period through the modern technological age, it is anchored in rumbling interactions of divergent forces in American society, in the larger texture of Western culture, and, especially after 1850, in an expanding milieu of international economic and political activity.

The disappearance of the Huguenots in America reflects the complexity of interactions among the astonishingly diverse forces that shaped pre-Revolutionary society. It opens important vistas on the evolution of the American colonies, on the broader problems of the massive Huguenot diaspora of the early modern period, and on the conditions under which such refugee groups might survive. From an American perspective, the Huguenot experience illuminates the transformation of small, relatively homogenous agricultural New World enclaves into dramatically different, sophisticated, and heterogeneous societies that would soon break loose from imperial constraints. At the same time, the disappearance of Huguenot identity also illuminates the indelible pathology of seventeenth-century French Protestantism. That pathology had similar effects on Huguenots of the diaspora everywhere and points up the central importance of internal resources among refugee groups in shaping responses to their environments whether in the Old World or in the New.

The Huguenots arrived in America during extraordinarily auspicious times—at the beginning of a period of dramatic growth in Britain's mainland colonies between 1680 and 1760. In these decades, the population expanded nearly ten times from about 250,000 persons to about 2,000,000 persons and became distinctively heterogeneous everywhere outside New England. Small towns became cities in size, urban function, and sophistication. The economy became more complex. It developed tangled regional patterns, yet drew ever closer to Europe. Intellectual life assumed a new breadth and complexity. It fed simultaneously into divergent streams of scientific rationalism, moderate and radical Enlightenment, and evangelical piety. Poverty increased and perhaps even deepened. All the colonies developed powerful, aggressive, politically dominant elites whose support for architecture, painting, the decorative arts, and music transformed the visual and aural culture of pre-Revolutionary America as fully as their political activity transformed the exercise of power and authority in pre-Revolutionary society.[1]

Much in the Huguenot experience in America paralleled the social, economic, and political development of pre-Revolutionary American society. The stereotypical Huguenot merchants who appear so frequently in the histories of American immigration— the Manigaults of South Carolina, the DeLanceys of New York, and the Faneuils of Boston—fitted easily into the ranks of the eighteenth-century colonial aristocracy. Peter Faneuil's enduring gift to Boston, Faneuil Hall, well symbolized their achievement in both politics and business. But even more modest refugees exemplified the extent of the Huguenot economic success in the colonies in the context of a relatively high standard of living for whites throughout pre-Revolutionary America. Huguenot refugees not only persevered, they frequently prospered. Extraordinary numbers of Huguenots established modest farms in New Rochelle and Staten Island, secured substantial places in the evolving urban economies of Boston, New York City, and Charlestown and acquired more than modest lands in South Carolina. Their political success confirmed their material drive. The wealthiest Huguenots capped their careers with seats on the Massachusetts and New York Councils and as Speaker of the South Carolina Assembly. Far more modest Huguenots held committee positions in Boston's eighteenth-century municipal government, sat on the New York City Common Council, served as town officials in New Rochelle and as county officials on Staten Island, and filled seats in the South Carolina Assembly. They provide dramatic evidence of solid Huguenot material success in the British colonies in America.[2]

Huguenots achieved their remarkable material success in America mainly by taking advantage of the attractive economic and political environment created by the general circumstances of the developing colonies and by British colonial governmental policy. Much of their material success can be traced to the timing of their arrival in the 1680s when the mainland colonies were entering a period of swift economic growth. The Huguenots thus became the first major European immigrant group settled in the British colonies to profit from this resurgence and renewal of the economy. Their fate might have been much different had they delayed their arrival until the 1740s, for example. Then they would have experienced significantly more competition from a larger population of well-established colonists and a more stagnant colonial economy, conditions that dramatically affected the emigration and early experiences of German immigrants then arriving in Pennsylvania.[3]

The Huguenots did not enter a particularly homogeneous "colonial America" in the 1680s. Rather, they settled in sharply different provincial societies. Their choice of residence, in turn, determined whether they would enjoy modest or large-scale economic success in America. The Boston case remains undecipherable because we know little about the economic success of refugees there except for the most prominent Huguenots. But the contrasting records of economic success among Huguenots in New York and South Carolina reveal the power of both time and place to shape a people's material destiny in America. New York Huguenots experienced considerable economic success. Between 1695 and 1735 they held their own in the city as the rise of poorer Huguenots into the ranks of middle-class taxpayers compensated for the deaths of important old and wealthy Huguenot merchants who left no heirs to carry on their businesses. Similar middle-class attributes characterized the Huguenot population at New Rochelle and Staten Island. Certainly, some refugees remained or became poor and were forced to take public aid. But in the main it is a record of success.

In South Carolina Huguenots achieved spectacular economic gains, although they differed from New York's Huguenots in no known way. In both colonies, most refugees came from western France, survived dismal experiences in London, often were skilled craftsmen, and were young, usually in their twenties, and unmarried. But the South Carolina Huguenots benefited from government land policies unknown in New York and acquired over 100,000 acres of land from the government alone between 1680 and 1711. As a result, they reaped material rewards that far outstripped the already substantial achievements of the New York Huguenots. They easily surpassed the land acquisition record of New England's seventeenth-century farmers, and they frequently surpassed that of later English settlers in South Carolina itself.

The extent of Huguenot material success suggests as well that the rivulets of early American ethnic prejudice ran swift, not deep. Historians frequently stress the continuity of American ethnic prejudice and find it extensive even in the colonial past. Huguenots certainly experienced bigotry at the hands of English colonists. In the 1680s anxious Boston authorities quickly extracted oaths of allegiance from newly arrived Huguenot refugees, and anti-French sentiment heightened tension between English and Huguenot settlers pursuing rival claims to land in Rhode Island's Narragansett country. In the next decade, South Carolina politicians excluded Huguenots from the colonial assembly and later threatened their legal rights. In 1708 a rival New York ship captain plumbed anti-French sentiment when he questioned Benjamin Faneuil's patriotism, as did Governor Robert Hunter later when Hunter unsuccessfully questioned Stephen DeLancey's naturalization in an attempt to eject him from the New York assembly in 1724.

In fact, this anti-French or even anti-Huguenot prejudice, much of it individual and idiosyncratic, belied a surprising acceptance of Huguenots in the British colonies, especially when viewed from the perspective of government policy. Most British officials ignored the potentially devastating legal problems of Huguenot denization and naturalization and simply treated the refugees as full Crown subjects irrespective of legal technicalities.

Thus New York City and Boston Huguenots won freemanship and political office early, and South Carolina Huguenots easily reentered the colony's assembly after English political infighting abated in 1707. Even the earlier exclusion of Huguenots from the assembly proved relatively short-lived and failed to affect government economic policy toward the refugees; the sale and distribution of land to Huguenots continued uninterrupted during the controversy over assembly membership and laid the foundation for the refugees' subsequent economic success in the colony. Colonial governments likewise encouraged Huguenots to pursue a wide variety of economic activities, whether specialized crafts, the merchant trades, or farming. But because Huguenots so readily replicated the occupations of English colonists—rural refugees farmed in common New World ways and, like English settlers, bought slaves to labor for them while those in the colonial cities pursued the traditional variety of urban occupations—Huguenots largely avoided the debilitating contemporary stereotyping that Jews, Asians, and other immigrants experienced in the next century. It was only historians who later erroneously stereotyped Huguenots as mostly rich merchants and craftsmen.[4]

The treatment of the Huguenots by local and provincial governments in the British colonies was not unique and typified the evolutionary character of American nativism and discrimination. It is true that individuals were not free from prejudice. Benjamin Franklin slurred German immigrants in Pennsylvania in the full confidence that his views were popular. But public response to his attacks also suggests that many English colonists simply did not share his views and that others who did seldom were moved to act on them. Pennsylvania colonists were not always models of Quaker tolerance. Neither were they Know-Nothings, however. Franklin's attempt to promote Charity Schools to anglicize Germans failed not merely because few Germans attended them but also because few Englishmen provided financial support to enable them to continue.[5]

Ethnic tension, indeed, energized disputes between English settlers and Germans, Palatines, Scots, and Swiss immigrants in the colonies. Tension between English settlers and Scots, for example, stood near the center of New Jersey's famous land riots of the 1740s. But ethnic tension in the colonial period was minor compared to the virulent anti-Catholicism that shaped American urban life in the early and mid-nineteenth century, the anti-Semitism of the later nineteenth century, or the vicious anti-Asian racism common to the American West after 1850—to say nothing of the race prejudice sustained and deepened by American slavery. For Africans and Asians, this subsequent American bigotry stimulated efforts to control economic and even religious activity. But for Huguenots, English bigotry rarely resulted in persistent government discrimination.[6]

The mild treatment of Huguenots and other Europeans arriving in colonial America reflected the nature of the immigrants as well as the nature of colonial society—both of them Protestant and white. Indeed, it may be that the increasingly popular English enslavement of Africans, arriving in large numbers in the 1680s, absorbed much colonial anti-foreign prejudice that might otherwise have been directed at the Huguenots. Legislators and merchants were busy spreading slavery across the North American mainland colonies, and the growing slave population required as much policing as the colonial governments could manage. Nor did Huguenots object to slavery. Despite their own experience of religious persecution in France, many of them quickly bought slaves in both New York and South Carolina and reaped significant profits. In fact, their acceptance of slavery became one of the earliest and most tragic signs of their assimilation in colonial American society.

The positive treatment of Huguenots and other European immigrants in the colonies did not flow from a deep reservoir of English goodwill toward others. Rather, it resulted from the inability of English colonists to articulate much of their frequent individual hostility toward strangers and foreigners as social and government policy. One cause for this failure was that the British colonies were early modern societies whose sparse institutional resources made it difficult to pursue the more subtle, complex forms of discrimination that stopped short of slavery and required voluntary cooperation among English settlers. The colonies lacked the panoply of publishing houses, newspapers, missionary societies, religious "reform" groups, and even political parties that underwrote nineteenth-century American nativism, bigotry, and discrimination against Europeans. In addition, the colonies were cultural dependencies themselves. Several historians have noted how the newness of social and political environments in America induced extraordinary anxiety about personal, political, and cultural legitimacy. Colonists were not a sniveling lot; too soon for English taste they would draw their own conclusions about morality, virtue, and political honesty as practiced in the very nation they sought so desperately to emulate. But before 1770 they cast their eyes eastward and across the Atlantic for models in politics, economics, religion, intellectual life, and the fine arts. This cultural insecurity could have been a source of prejudice. The development of slavery, for example, could be interpreted as one of its results, although other interpretations seem more compelling. But in the case of the Huguenots and the other European immigrants to early America, this dependency constrained individual anti-foreign sentiment. Clearly, Huguenots benefited by settling in early and relatively simple New World societies; at least they avoided the aggressive nativism that accompanied America's rise to industrial prowess in the nineteenth century.[7]

If the positive English treatment of the Huguenots and the Huguenots' material success in America failed to encourage Huguenot cohesion, the dynamic relationship that historians have posited between emigration, ethnicity, and religion makes their social and religious disintegration in the colonies even more perplexing. While not all historians treat the relationship between emigration, ethnicity, and religion in identical ways, they certainly treat them as mutually reinforcing. Some have argued that ethnicity energizes religion. Martin Marty calls ethnicity the "skeleton of American religion," and Harry S. Stout argues that ethnicity has been the "vital center" of American religion. Others argue that religion energizes ethnicity. Randall Miller and Tom Marzik call religion the "very bone and sinew of ethnicity" in America. Still others argue that emigration itself stimulates religious commitment. Timothy L. Smith has written that in the nineteenth and twentieth centuries migration "was often a theologizing experience—just as it had been when Abraham left the land of his fathers."[8]

Searching for the causes of the Huguenots' disintegration as a community becomes, in part, a search for general conditions under which immigrant groups preserve social cohesion and religious integrity. Here the first important lesson is that the Huguenot experience constitutes one end of a broad spectrum of immigrant responses to the problem of group preservation and approximates the behavior of other immigrant groups in the American colonies and in nineteenth- and twentieth-century America. This is especially obvious if the analytical focus remains individual rather than institutional. American immigration historians usually establish their argument about the persistence of ethnic cohesion in America first by describing the number of immigrants from, say, Norway who settled in Minnesota, Wisconsin, Illinois, and Iowa in the nineteenth century, then by pointing to the panoply of churches, lodges, newspapers, women's groups, and political organizations that served Norwegian interests. In the case of the New York City Huguenots, an analysis of all the available New York marriage records reveals that the French Church could not prevent refugees from taking non-French spouses despite its preference for endogamy. At least 45 percent of all known Huguenot marriages in the city between 1689 and 1710 were exogamous. Yet the immigration historian examining only the records of the French Church might conclude that the congregation successfully preserved Huguenot cohesion because all but one of the forty-five marriages contracted there in the same years were endogamous.[9]

A look at immigrant populations rather than institutions suggests that ethnic cohesion has not been nearly so ubiquitous in either the colonial or modern periods as historians recently have argued. Immigrant groups have exhibited widely varying rates of attachment to ethnic institutions and flexible attitudes toward exogamy. Despite the existence of a synagogue in New York City since the 1690s and the traditional importance of endogamy among Jews, surprising numbers of the city's small Jewish population married non-Jews in the colonial era, and exogamy in the descendants of Jacob Franks, whose daughter Phila married Oliver DeLancey in 1743, became so frequent that by the end of the eighteenth century none of them remained Jews. Nor were Huguenots the only immigrants for whom migration was not an overwhelming "theologizing experience." Many residents of Germantown in Pennsylvania expressed no special interest in churches after their arrival and remained unmoved by the promotion of religious renewal in the 1740s and 1750s. As a result, scarcely half of the town's adults remained "churched" in any significant sense by the time of the Revolution. Similarly, a recent, massive study of immigrant marriage patterns in modern Wisconsin found surprisingly high exogamy rates in a society saturated with ethnic institutions including churches. By 1910, for example, nearly a third of first-generation Norwegians and nearly half of second-generation Norwegians contracted exogamous marriages. Most important, when the population mixture offered the immigrants real choices between preserving or undermining social cohesion by contracting endogamous or exogamous marriages—that is, when immigrants really were "at risk" to choose one *or* the other—they chose exogamy with a frequency that makes Huguenot intermarriage in colonial Boston, Charlestown, and New York City appear much less extreme.[10]

But perhaps the question of Huguenot cohesion is a moot one. The surprisingly secular character of the Huguenot emigration to America, the dismal refugee experiences in London, and the quick involvement of the immigrants in the colonial economy all might suggest that they never really intended to preserve their social and religious cohesion in the colonies. Or the early social and religious cohesion of the Huguenots in the colonies might be construed as only a temporary response to the language, occupational, and friendship barriers faced by many foreign immigrants. When these barriers fell, so to did the cohesion they supported.

Yet it cannot be said that the Huguenots lacked a long-term interest in preserving their social and religious cohesion. The motives for Huguenot migration to America were as complex as those of the seventeenth-century English Puritans or twentieth-century Asians, Cubans, and Haitians. Huguenots came to America for material gain; they also came to pursue spiritual ends; further, they wished the company of their fellow refugees. They clustered together in rural New England, New York, and South Carolina as well as in urban Boston, New York City and Charlestown. They supported refugee congregations, hired ministers they liked, fired ministers they disliked, and sometimes pursued religious renewal through the vigorous promotion of a new, unique, refugee piety. When ministers and some refugees in rural South Carolina and New York approved conformity to the Church of England, others resisted, sometimes violently, suggesting that many Huguenots were willing to preserve traditional French Protestant worship if only their ministers would lead them.[11]

The question of the disappearance of Huguenots in America should perhaps look for an answer beyond the New World, to the Huguenot diaspora in early modern Europe and to the Huguenot experience in seventeenth-century France. Certainly none of the obvious features of their experience in the American colonies offer a satisfactory explanation for their social and religious disintegration. The Huguenots' rapid assimilation into stunningly different economic and political systems in Boston, South Carolina, and New York should have strengthened rather than diminished their chances for survival. As Jews did later, successful Huguenots could have promoted group cohesion at the same time as they also partcipated fully in the larger societies in which they lived. Greater discrimination might have fostered group cohesion, but as with African slaves who suffered from prejudice in its most severe form, discrimination might also have reshaped the very culture and religion Huguenots were seeking to preserve. On the other hand, positive treatment by British colonial governments did not in itself stimulate Huguenot social and religious disintegration. Huguenots could and did promote social and religious cohesion within the context of a pluralistic social model that the British accepted, at least implicitly, throughout eighteenth-century America. In any case, those Huguenots who left their traditional church and family structure exercised individual judgment in these matters, however eagerly English and Dutch colonists lured them away.

The spectacular material success of the wealthiest Huguenot refugees, such as the Faneuils, DeLanceys, and Manigaults, also did not guarantee Huguenot disintegration. Wealthy Huguenots frequently maintained dual religious affiliations that provided the French churches of Boston, New York City, and Charlestown with substantial financial resources, and perhaps some social prestige. Furthermore, even in the deferential political milieu of early American society, it is not at all clear that these wealthy refugees set patterns that other refugees followed. In Boston, many modest refugees preceeded the Faneuils in their departure from the French Church, and none of the evidence from New York and Charlestown suggests that the behavior of wealthy Huguenots affected the religious or marriage patterns of other Huguenots.

However, the loss of extensive support from immigrant refugees of modest means proved devastating to Huguenot religious and social cohesion. Huguenots could survive the departure of the wealthiest refugees, especially when they qualified their exodus from the French churches with financial aid. But neither the churches nor the Huguenot family could survive the alienation of middle-class and lower-class Huguenots, and this alienation, best measured in exogamous marriages, happened in all the places where non-Huguenot spouses were easily available to them.

The failure of Huguenot clerical leadership exacerbated the disastrous loss of lay loyalty to family and church among the Huguenot refugees. No refugee minister took up Pierre Peiret's quest for religious renewal among the American refugees after Peiret's death in 1704, and Elie Neau's conformity to the Church of England in the same year ended his influence among the Huguenot laity. The refugee ministers never established regional or intercolonial denominational institutions, though some of them developed personal relationships. For example, in the late 1690s, Pierre Peiret and Pierre Daillé ended the hostility developed a decade earlier during the Leisler Rebellion, and Daillé apparently raised one of Peiret's children after the father's death. But these personal relationships remained just that. They never produced signifcant, supportive intercongregational ties.

Relations with European exile congregations remained equally idiosyncratic. The three urban Huguenot congregations in Boston, New York City, and Charlestown used London's Threadneedle Street Church to hire ministers before 1750, and New York City's French Church received additional help for the same need from the French Protestant ministers in Geneva and Amsterdam in 1710 and in the 1760s. These congregations could have developed mature links to the exile Huguenots in Europe. For example, they could have followed the model of transatlantic denominational relations developed by New York's Dutch Reformed congregations; the latter accepted the authority of the Dutch Reformed Synod in Amsterdam in return for the Synod's supplying ministers and assistance with discipline and organizational problems. The relationship was far from perfect, and it became especially difficult after 1740. But for a century it established an institutional framework for settling numerous vexing difficulties in New York's far away Dutch congregations. The refugee Huguenot congregations developed no formal, sustained relationships with their exile counterparts in Europe. They wrote to them for ministers and then stopped their correspondence until a new crisis, usually over hiring a minister, stimulated another equally narrow exchange of letters.[12]

In the end, the Huguenot migration to America could be viewed as too small to sustain group cohesion, particularly in the face of institutional lethargy and rapid lay alienation from the church and family. Certainly the Huguenot emigration to America was small; no more than 2,000 persons arrived by 1700, making it far smaller than historians have previously realized. Such a tiny refugee population might have offered little room for dispute, decay, and failure. Few enough refugees existed to sustain Huguenot cohesion, fewer still were present to take up the slack when some refugees turned their loyalties elsewhere. The paucity of Huguenots in the colonies provided no cushion for failure, and too few resources remained to renew efforts to salvage refugee cohesion as Huguenot loyalties decayed.

Yet it is this simple and attractive explanation for the Huguenots' disappearance in America that also returns us to the larger problem of the Huguenot diaspora in early modern Europe, and to the importance of internal resources that migrating groups require if they hope to preserve themselves in new environments. Huguenots disappeared everywhere they fled, not merely in America. Great Britain received at least 20,000 refugees between 1680 and 1700, perhaps more, and most of them settled in London. Yet by 1730 many of the London Huguenot congregations had closed, and the number of Huguenots patronizing the remaining congregations was falling rather than rising. By the time rioting broke out among the Spitalfields weavers in 1769, nearly as little that was distinctively French survived in London as survived in the far away American settlements of St. James Santee

Parish in South Carolina or New Rochelle in New York. Huguenots persisted longer in Germany where some 30,000 refugees arrived between 1680 and 1700. The community sustained endogamous marriages and independent churches through the 1750s, but its cohesion decayed rapidly thereafter until, by 1800, most Huguenots practiced exogamy and ignored the few remaining French Protestant congregations. About 50,000 Huguenots fled to the Netherlands. Their disintegration is less well documented but, apparently, followed the now familiar pattern. Wealthy refugees moved into the ranks of the Dutch aristocracy, educated Huguenots assumed significant places in government, trade, and in the country's intellectual life, and Huguenots of all kinds left their refugee congregations to move into Dutch or Walloon ones or to drift into erratic relationships with churches as happened in Germany and the American colonies as well.[13]

The disappearance of the Huguenots in Europe was particularly remarkable because the Huguenot diaspora on the Continent was massive, not small. It was the most explosive forced migration to occur in Western society between the Renaissance of the fifteenth century and the rise of industrialism in the nineteenth century. It involved the escape from France of no less than 160,000 Protestants, and it occurred when a traditional agrarian, small craft economy dominated France and Europe and long before new industrial labor systems, technologies, and political bureaucracies underwrote the massive migrations of the nineteenth century. Yet everywhere Huguenots settled they disappeared. By 1750 Huguenots no longer existed as a significant religious, national, or ethnic minority in most of their places of exile; by 1800 they had disappeared in all of them. Clearly, then, the disappearance of the Huguenots in America was not an isolated or unique New World event. Rather, it was linked firmly to broader processes of decay in French Protestantism evident throughout the early modern West.

To some small extent, the failure of Huguenots to sustain their religious and social cohesion in Europe and America stemmed from problems associated with the deepening national provincialism of seventeenth-century European Protestanism. In the sixteenth century, especially between 1520 and 1560, Catholic persecution helped turn local and provincial quests for religious reform into an international Protestant movement. Exiles in Geneva, Strasbourg, Amsterdam, and London strengthened their faith, deepened their theology, and improved techniques of proselytization through an interchange of ideas made possible by exile itself. The exiles followed international religious developments closely when they returned home. English Dissenters informed contemporaries about France's Protestant religious model by publishing important Huguenot documents in English, such as the 1623 Charenton Synod proceedings, the 1642 digest of French Protestant polity, and, in 1692, the complete synod proceedings of France's sixteenth- and seventeenth-century Huguenots in the two-volume *Synodicon in Gallia Reformata*. But this interest became more superficial after 1660 as persecuted Protestants in both England and France turned inward. England's Presbyterians, Independents, Baptists, and Quakers scarcely cooperated among themselves in resisting Restoration persecution and sustained notably less interest in Continental Protestant affairs than they had before 1650. France's beleaguered Protestants retreated into provincial synods following the demise of their national synod in 1659 and pursued few international contacts beyond their long-standing connections to Geneva.

The results proved disastrous. By the 1680s Huguenots in England and America had no significant relationship with Britain's Dissenters, including English and Scottish Presbyterians. At the same time, the Dissenters not only offered Huguenots little material aid but provided a poor model for them to emulate, since all groups but the Quakers suffered serious institutional erosion and membership losses after 1660. In this context, Anglican worry about the potential Huguenot-Dissenter alliance proved unfounded. The Church of England faced no significant competition in wooing exile Huguenot clergymen. In exchange for steady financial support, the Huguenot ministers agreed to recognize the ecclesiastical authority of the Archbishop of Canterbury; as a result, no Huguenot denomination-in-exile ever appeared in England.

The Huguenot inability to preserve social and religious cohesion in Europe as well as in the American colonies reflected the nature of French Protantism in the seventeenth century.

France's Protestants were poorly prepared to exercise the instruments of church government in exile. The abandonment of national synods after 1659 meant that internal problems, difficulties in church-state relations, and common theological and ecclesiastical difficulties received no sustained national attention in the quarter-century before the Revocation. As a result, too many exile Huguenots were unfamiliar with the simple mechanics of national church government. They possessed no experience in making decisions beyond the local and provincial level, and they possessed even less experience in correcting erroneous decisions.

The clerical dominance of ministers in seventeenth-century French Protestantism further limited leadership in the exile Huguenot congregations. Despite their adherence to the abstract principle of the "priesthood of all believers," the Huguenot laity in both the sixteenth and seventeenth centuries allowed and encouraged the same coterie of clerics to manage religious reform in France as managed religious reform in Germany, Holland, and England. Bourgeois and aristocratic laymen gave the reformers financial support, managed business affairs for congregations, and played important roles in the Huguenots' regional colloquies. But clergymen had consistently dominated theological and ecclesiastical affairs in the movement and left the Huguenot laity poorly prepared to assume religious leadership in the movement in exile.

Both Huguenot ministers and laymen of the diaspora also proved uncritically submissive to government authority, even when their acquiescence quashed important instruments of Huguenot cohesion. This concern for the wishes of the state developed in seventeenth-century France. The French monarchy had given them the Edict of Nantes in 1598 and could revoke it if the Huguenots proved disobedient. Therefore Huguenots submitted to the restrictions placed on them by Louis XIV after 1660. Huguenots similarly obeyed the governments of the countries to which they fled in the 1680s. Sometimes this proved advantageous. If they remained more united in Prussia than elsewhere, it was because Frederick I legally guaranteed their minority status, offered them direct government aid in business and housing, allowed special courts for them, and established a Huguenot ecclesiastical organization through the Potsdam Decree. But not even Prussian efficiency could guarantee Huguenot cohesion, which finally decayed there as elsewhere.

In England, however, Anglican authorities opposed a separate Huguenot religious establishment, and the exiled Huguenot clergymen never organized one. Virtually all the French clergymen in the nation accepted Anglican reordination. The Huguenot ministerial association in London, the only one in the country, consisted of Anglican-ordained clergymen who gathered for fraternal and advisory purposes. They eschewed church government functions and did not ordain new ministers. London's Huguenot laity resisted the loss of traditional French Protestant worship in the 1690s just as they did later in America. They accepted the Anglican-ordained ministers but insisted on retaining their traditional liturgy. Anglican authorities acceded to this compromise, in part because it was dangerous to oppose it and, in part, because their control of the Huguenot clergy forestalled formation of a Huguenot denomination-in-exile. The Huguenot laity never pressed for such a denomination. As in rural South Carolina and New Rochelle, they thought only of salvaging traditional worship. In accordance with Anglican wishes and following its traditional role, the Huguenot laity also failed to stimulate the formation of a denomination-in-exile that could have strengthened refugee congregations and promoted secular cohesion.

Paradoxically, while French Protestantism failed in exile, it survived at home, though it did not survive intact. French Protestantism never claimed more than 1 percent of France's population after 1700, although before 1660 it claimed between 5 percent and 10 percent of the French population. The political influence of the movement shrank dramatically, and it experienced profound internal changes. After 1700 the movement became thoroughly bourgeois and lost its earlier important support from working-class Frenchmen, peasants, and farmers everywhere except in Languedoc. Still, despite a drastic reduction in numbers and a shifting membership composition, the religious, political, and intellectual forces of French society that brought Protestantism into being in the sixteenth century and that shaped it in the seventeenth century carried a miniature version of it into the eighteenth century and, ultimately, into modern times.

But the diaspora that brought Huguenots across France's borders to new societies and to the New World also removed them from the old and the familiar. Nor did they begin their task with the fresh enthusiasm of new groups like Count Zinzendorf's Moravians or Anne Lee's Shakers, groups whose very lack of history served as a springboard for an innocent and vital idealism. The two centuries of historical experience that did accompany them into exile also lacked the stolid but secure institutional foundations on which groups like New York's Dutch Reformed colonists or Pennsylvania's German Lutheran and Reformed immigrants based their continuing cohesion in the New World. Rather, the dispiriting evolution of seventeenth-century French Protestantism offered Huguenot refugees few resources with which to salvage their religious practice and preserve their social cohesion. They attempted to do both in America as well as in Europe. But on both continents Huguenots found themselves entrapped in broad, deep processes of social and religious change. Everywhere Huguenots were lured away from their traditions. Everywhere they found themselves unable to secure their religious and social cohesion. And everywhere, in the Old World as well as in the New, they became and chose to become new men and new women as individuals. Their historical experience in seventeenth-century France dictated the necessity of the choice; the nature of the new societies they entered determined its substance.

Appendix. "Huguenot" Settlements in Eighteenth-Century American Colonies

Between 1700 and 1766 French-speaking European Protestants settled four additional communities in the British colonies of North America: Manakin in Virginia (1700), Purrysburg in South Carolina (1732), New Bordeaux in South Carolina (1765), and Campbell Town in British West Florida (1776). None of these settlements grew out of the original Huguenot emigration of the 1680s and none developed significant ties with the older Huguenot communities. All four remained independent of each other. Indeed, Purrysburg never was a Huguenot settlement, that is, a settlement of Protestants from France, although historians often describe it as such. Instead, its settlers were Swiss Protestants, only some of whom emigrated from the French-speaking portions of western Switzerland. Still, in their histories these settlements paralleled those of America's seventeenth-century Huguenot communities in remarkable ways, particularly in their agricultural economies and slave-holding, their religious instability, and, ultimately, their disintegration and disappearance.[1]

The initial strengths and weaknesses of three of the eighteenth-century settlements resulted from their origin in colonization schemes designed to procure profit or political advancement for their promoters. Manakin's founders, an Englishman named Dr. Daniel Coxe and two Huguenots, the Marquis de la Muce and Charles de Sailly, as well as Purrysburg's organizer, the Neuchâtel entrepreneur Jean Pierre Purry, intended to sell land to their immigrants, while the governor of British West Florida hoped simply to people his new colony. They successfully lured settlers to America with extravagant promises of New World riches. But they failed to make their own fortunes through these schemes. The Virginia Council refused to allow the Manakin group to settle on Coxe's lands near the North Carolina border and forced them onto colony lands near the James River falls; Jean Pierre Purry sold no significant part of his personal lands at Purrysburg and was dead by 1736 in any case; Campbell Town collapsed from poor leadership and miserable physical conditions in 1768, only two years after its settlement, and British West Florida officials never reestablished the community. Only the 1765 New Bordeaux settlement met its organizers' expectations. Led by Jean Louis Gibert, a provincial Huguenot leader, its settlers came to America in good part to advance the evangelical Protestanism then emerging among Enlightenment-era French Protestants. Gibert received no commercial privileges or special land grants for bringing his settlers to South Carolina, and he was the only eighteenth-century settlement leader to retain his immigrants' respect after their American settlement.

The eighteenth-century immigrants differed in important ways from the Huguenots of the 1680s. The Purrysburg, New Bordeaux, and Campbell Town settlers did not leave Europe until a half-century or more after the Revocation. Even Manakin's settlers endured European exile for as long as two decades before sailing for Virginia. Many were, in fact, "second generation" refugees, young children or infants when their parents removed them from France or children born in the European exile centers; few had lived in France for more than a few years and some never lived there at all.

The Manakin, Purrysburg, and New Bordeaux settlers also brought children to their colonies, thereby behaving quite differently from the refugees of the 1680s who seldom brought children to America. As early as July 1700 children under sixteen years accounted for between 38 and 44 of Manakin's 205 settlers (18.5 percent and 21.5 percent), for at least 16 of Purrysburg's 47 French-speaking Swiss (34.0 percent) in 1732, and for 43 of the 173 emigrants (24.9 percent) who sailed with Jean Louis Gibert for New Bordeaux from Bristol, England, in November 1763.

On the other hand, the eighteenth-century emigrants possessed occupational skills that strongly resembled those of their predecessors of the 1680s. The urban background of many Manakin settlers meant that they probably brought craft and trade skills but little direct agricultural experience to Virginia, although little evidence about their European occupations survives. Yet they too were young, adaptable, and able to do the work that was needed. New Bordeaux's settlers and perhaps even those at Purrysburg and Campbell Town represented a broader occupational spectrum. About half of New Bordeaux's males had earlier pursued nonagricultural occupations in Europe as mariners and in the cloth trades and teaching. Occupations of most other New Bordeaux settlers intertwined easily with the dominant agrarian economy of both Europe and America—wine growers, barrel-makers, carpenters, and general laborers who likely had worked in the fields at planting and harvest times.

Manakin's, Purrysburg's, and New Bordeaux's economic development also followed patterns established by the first Huguenots in America. These ranged from experimentation with viticulture and silk production to the development of a familiar economy based on slavery. Silk production at Purrysburg and New Bordeaux outlasted Manakin's viticulture, and even in the 1750s Purrysburg's farmers still produced some 500 pounds of silk each year. But immigrants in each settlement quickly diversified their agriculture to grow food and make some small profit with grains and beans, native fruits and vegetables, and fatted cattle. They also began pursuing the larger local economic patterns that turned out tobacco, wheat, and cattle at Manakin and rice, grains, and cattle at Purrysburg. This led them to slave-holding. Manakin's slave population expanded from two or three slaves among some seventy-five French adult males in 1709 to more than seventy slaves among some eighty adults in 1735. At Purrysburg, indentured European laborers common through the 1740s similarly gave way by the 1750s to large numbers of slaves. There, as elsewhere, owning slaves was not without its dangers. Charles Purry, son of the promoter Jean Pierre Purry, acquired more and more slaves as his merchant business at Beaufort prospered in the 1740s, and was murdered by them in 1754.

Only New Bordeaux preserved or extended even a minimal measure of religious independence for any significant period after its formation. Manakin's Huguenots found themselves subtly linked to the Church of England even at their departure from Europe, with ministers who had already undergone Anglican ordination or reordination. The Virginia burgesses tightened those bonds at their arrival by creating King William Parish to serve Manakin's church needs. But religious life at Manakin still proved unstable. Manakin's ministers fought with each other and with the laity.[2] Worse, the parish funds were inadequate to support a minister, largely because the parish was only a fifth the size of most Virginia parishes, and after 1715 the King William vestrymen could secure only part-time preaching from neighboring ministers. As a result, neither Anglicanism nor any independent Huguenot church life prospered, and some parish residents drifted into Virginia's growing ranks of Dissenters, especially after 1750. Likewise, two French ministers who served briefly at Purrysburg in the 1730s had received Anglican reordination before leaving London for America, and in 1746 the South Carolina legislature turned the church building they used into a place of worship for the new St. Peter's Parish. Even New Bordeaux's Huguenots found it difficult to maintain their ecclesiastical independence. By 1771, six years after their settlement, some of them petitioned the S.P.G. for an Anglican-ordained minister who was supported by the Society, while after the Revolution others helped establish a Presbyterian congregation, a denominational connection that was rarely pursued by the first Huguenot refugees, with the exception of Boston's André le Mercier.

Under these circumstances, it is scarcely surprising that the eighteenth-century settlements soon lost their cohesiveness. Campbell Town literally vanished within two years of its formation. New Bordeaux and Purrysburg, laid out in isolated portions of South Carolina, nonetheless soon found English settlers living amongst them, while some of their own immigrants were moving into other South Carolina counties, alone or with only a few additional immigrants. Even Manakin, settled in 1700 on the Virginia frontier, lost its narrow Huguenot identity and many residents. By 1735 about a quarter of Manakin's whites bore English surnames as many children of original settlers moved into nearby and sometimes far distant Virginia counties. By the time of the American Revolution, the eighteenth-century French settlements had also experienced the disintegration of internal cohesion and assimilation into colonial society well known to the original Huguenot refugees of the 1680s.

Notes

Abbreviations

Annales, ESC	*Annales: Economies, Sociétés, Civilisations*
BosRCR	*Reports of the Record Commissioners of the City of Boston*
BSHPF	*Bulletin de la société de l'histoire du protestantisme français*
HSLProc	Huguenot Society of London, *Proceedings*
HSLPubl	Huguenot Society of London, *Publications*
HSSCT	Huguenot Society of South Carolina, *Transactions*
MHSColl	Massachusetts Historical Society, *Collections*
MHSProc	Massachusetts Historical Society, *Proceedings*
MinCCNY	*Minutes of the Common Council of the City of New York, 1675–1776*
NYColDocs	*Documents Relative to the Colonial History of the State of New York*
NYGBR	*New York Genealogical and Biographical Record*
NYHSColl	New-York Historical Society, *Collections*
PROSC	*Records of the British Public Record Office Relating to South Carolina*
SCHGM	*South Carolina Historical and Genealogical Magazine*
SPG mss	Society for the Propagation of the Gospel in Foreign Parts, London, manuscripts

Introduction

1. Cotton Mather, *A Sermon wherein is Showed that the Church of God is sometimes a Subject of Persecution* (Boston, 1682), 18.

2. Robert Mandrou et al., *Histoire des protestants en France* (Toulouse, 1977), 463.

3. Nancy L. Roelker, *The French Huguenots: An Embattled Minority* (St. Louis, 1977), 9.

4. James G. Leyburn, *The Scotch-Irish: A Social History* (Chapel Hill, N.C., 1962); R. J. Dickson, *Ulster Emigration to Colonial America, 1718–1775* (London, 1966); Duane Meyer, *The Highland Scots of North Carolina, 1732–1776* (Chapel Hill, N.C., 1961); Jacob R. Marcus, *Early American Jewry* (Philadelphia, 1951–1953); Edwin Wolf II and Maxwell Whiteman, *The History of the Jews of Philadelphia from Colonial Times to the Age of Jackson* (Philadelphia, 1957); David de Sola Pool, *Portraits Etched in Stone: Early Jewish Settlers, 1682–1831* (New York, 1952); W. A. Knittle, *The Early Eighteenth Century Palatine Emigration* (Philadelphia, 1936); Albert B. Faust, "Swiss Emigration to the American Colonies in the Eighteenth Century," *American Historical Review*, 22 (1916): 21–44; Mildred Campbell, "English Emigration on the Eve of the American Revolution," *American Historical Review*, 41 (1955): 1–20; David Galenson, *White Servitude in Colonial America: An Economic Analysis* (New York, 1981).

1. French Protestantism and the Revocation of 1685

1. David Parker, "The Huguenots in Seventeenth-century France," in *Minorities in History*, ed. A. C. Hepburn (New York, 1979), 11–30, provides a superb short introduction to its subject, and Samuel Mours, *Essai sommaire de géographie du protestantisme réformé français au xviie siècle* (Paris, 1966), provides the best guide to the distribution of France's Protestants before 1685.

2. The best short description of these developments is Robert Mandrou, "Pourquoi se réformer?" in Mandrou et al., *Histoire des protestants en France* (Toulouse, 1977), 7–44. For greater detail regarding the reformation in sixteenth-century France see, among others, Robert Kingdon, *Geneva and the Coming of the Wars of Religion in France (1555–1563)* (Geneva, 1956); Kingdon, *Geneva and the Consolidation of the French Protestant Movement (1564–1572): A Contribution to the History of Congregationalism, Presbyterianism and Calvinist Resistance Theory* (Geneva, 1967); Nancy L. Roelker, *Queen of Navarre: Jeanne d'Albret, 1528–1572* (Cambridge, Mass., 1968); and Janine Garrison-Estebe, *Protestants du midi, 1559–1598* (Toulouse, 1981).

3. Daniel Ligou, "La peau de chagrin (1598–1685)," in Mandrou et al., *Histoire des protestants en France*, 118–122; Emile-G. Léonard, "Le protestantisme français au xviie siècle," *Review historique*, no. 200 (1948): 153–179; Léonard, *A History of Protestantism* (London, 1967), II, 162–171; Roland Mousnier, *Les institutions de la France sous la monarchie absolue, 1589–1789* (Paris, 1974), I, 300–301; P. Beuzart, "L'edit de Nantes, creation ou aboutissement," *BSHPF*, 91 (1942): 16–24; George A. Rothrock, "Some Aspects of Early Bourbon Policy toward the Huguenots," *Church History*, 29 (1960): 17–24.

4. Jean Orcibal, *Louis XIV et les protestants* (Paris, 1951); A. Th. Van Deursen, *Professions et métiers interdits: un aspect de l'histoire de la révocation de l'edit de Nantes* (Groningen, 1960); Léonard, "Le protestantisme français au xviie siècle," *Revue historique*, (1948), 164–179; Léonard, *History of Protestantism*, II, 409–414.

5. Mours, *Essai sommaire de géographie du protestantisme*, 40–41; Leónard, *History of Protestantism*, II, 414–431; Georges Frêche, "Contre-Reforme et dragonnades 1610–1789: pour une orientation statistique de l'histoire du protestantisme," *BSHPF*, 119 (1973): 362–383.

6. Mathieu Lelièvre, *De la révocation à la révolution: étude sur l'histoire morale et religieuse du protestantisme français pendant un siècle: premiere periode (1685–1715)* (Paris, 1911), especially pp. 1–22, 37, 116; Léonard, *History of Protestantism*, II, 365–371, 413, and Léonard, "Le protestantisme français au xviie siècle," *Revue historique* (1948): 164–179; Ligou, "La peau de chagrin," in Mandrou et al., *Histoire des protestants*, 117–122; Brian G. Armstrong, *Calvinism and the Amyraut Heresy: Protestant Scholasticism and Humanism in Seventeenth-Century France* (Madison, Wisc., 1969), 88–119.

7. Darrett B. Rutman, *American Puritanism: Faith and Practice* (Philadelphia, 1970), 10–28; David D. Hall, *The Faithful Shepherd: A History of the New England Ministry in the Seventeenth Century* (Chapel Hill, N.C., 1972), 3–20, 270–278; J. William T. Youngs, *God's Messengers: Religious Leadership in Colonial New England, 1700–1750* (Baltimore, Md., 1976), 1–39, 64–91; Jon Butler, *Power, Authority, and the Origins of American Denominational Order: The English Churches in the Delaware Valley, 1680–1730* (Philadelphia, 1978), 5–27.

8. Emmanuel Le Roy Ladurie, *The Peasants of Languedoc*, tr. John Day (Urbana, Ill., 1974), 149–171, 203–210; A. N. Galpern, *The Religions of the People*

in Sixteenth-Century Champagne (Cambridge, Mass., 1976), 16–68; E. William Monter, *Witchcraft in France and Switzerland: The Borderlands during the Reformation* (Ithaca, N.Y., 1976), 167–190. Descriptions of parallel situations in Germany and England are found in Gerald Strauss, *Luther's House of Learning: Indoctrination of the Young in the German Reformation* (Baltimore, Md., 1978), and Keith Thomas, *Religion and the Decline of Magic* (New York, 1971).

9. Mours, *Essai sommaire de géographie du protestantisme;* Ligou, "La peau de chagrin," in Mandrou et al., *Histoire des protestants,* 122–125.

10. Le Roy Ladurie, *The Peasants of Languedoc,* 158–171; Pierre Channu, "Une histoire religieuse sérielle à propos du diocése de La Rochelle (1648–1724) et sur quelques examples normands," *Revue d'histoire moderne et contemporaine,* 12 (1965): 5–36; Ligou, "La peau de chagrin," in Mandrou, et al., *Histoire des protestants,* 125–127; Louis Perouas, *Le diocèse de La Rochelle de 1648 à 1724* (Paris, 1964), 130–144, 294–307, 309–352; Perouas, "Sur la demographie rochelaise," *Annales, ESC,* 16 (1961): 1131–1140.

11. William Minet, "The Church at Calais and its Poor Fund," *HSLProc,* 6 (1898–1901): 138–171; Janine Estebe, "Vers une autre religion," in Mandrou, et al., *Histoire des protestants,* 105–107.

12. Pierre Bolle, "Structure sociale d'une paroisse réformée en Dauphiné au xviiᵉ siècle: Mens-en-Trièves," *LXXXVᵉ congrès national des sociétés savantes, 1960, section d'histoire moderne et contemporaine* (Paris, 1960), 419–432; Mousnier, *Les institutions de la France sous la monarchie absolue,* I, 310.

13. Jonathan H. Webster, "The Merchants of Bordeaux in Trade to the French West Indies, 1664–1717" (Ph.D. diss., University of Minnesota, 1972), 192–203; Mousnier, *Les institutions de la France sous la monarchie absolue,* I, 309–314. Léonard argues for a "laicisation of French Protestantism" in the *History of Protestantism,* II, 172–178, but his evidence is weak. Certainly the reform failed to erase class distinctions important in French Protestantism since the sixteenth century. For a glimpse at that period see the article by Henry Heller, 'Famine, Revolt and Heresy at Meaux: 1521–1525," *Archiv für Reformationsgeschichte,* 68 (1972): 133–156, and Garrison-Estebe, *Protestants du midi.*

14. Bolle, "Structure sociale d'une paroisse réformée," *LXXXVᵉ congrès national des sociétés savantes,* 426; Samuel Mours, "La vie synodale en Vivarais au xviiᵉ siècle," *BSHPF,* 92 (1946): 55–103; Solange Bertheau, "Le consistoire dans les églises réformées du Moyen-Poitou au xviiᵉ siecle," *BSHPF,* 116 (1970): 332–359, 513–549; Michelle Ludemann-Magdelaine, "La discipline de l'église réformée française de Sainte-Marie-aux-Mines (1660)," *BSHPF,* 124 (1978), 133–141. Ligou stresses the suppleness of Huguenot institutions in "La peau de chagrin," in Mandrou et al., *Histoire des protestants,* 127–129.

15. Arnold Lloyd, *Quaker Social History, 1669–1738* (London, 1950), 157–165; Butler, *Power, Authority, and the Origins of American Denominational Order,* 17–21; Léonard, *History of Protestantism,* II, 108–109, 133–142, 365–366, 394–396.

16. Léonard, *History of Protestantism,* II, 405–409, 416–420.

17. Daniel Ligou and Philippe Joutard, "Les deserts (1685–1800)," in Mandrou et al., *Histoire des protestants,* 189–199; Lelièvre, *De la révocation à la révolution,* 33–36, 37–42, 135–140; Léonard, *History of Protestantism,* II, 420–436; Pierre Gaxotte, *The Age of Louis XIV,* tr. Michael Shaw (New York, 1970), 189–217.

18. Quoted in Charles W. Baird, *History of the Huguenot Emigration to America* (New York, 1885), II, 116–117.

19. An English translation is printed in Orest Ranum and Patricia Ranum, eds., *The Century of Louis XIV* (New York, 1972), 358–363.

20. Le Roy Ladurie, *Peasants of Languedoc*, 265–286; Lelièvre, *De la révocation à la révolution*, 512–540.

21. Leonard, *Histoire générale du protestantisme*, III, 59–70; Lelièvre, *De la révocation à la révolution*, 280–370.

22. "Sur la demographie rochelaise," *Annales, ESC* (1961); Frêche, "Contre-Reforme et dragonnades," *BSHPF* (1973): 362–383.

23. Frêche, "Contre-Reforme et dragonnades," *BSHPF* (1973); Daniel Ligou, "L'Eglise réformée du desert, fait éconmique et social," *Revue d'histoire economique et sociale*, 32 (1954), 146–167; Ligou and Janine Garrison-Estebe, "La bourgeoisie réformée montalbanaise à la fin de l'ancien régime," *Revue d'histoire econmique et sociale*, 33 (1955): 377–404; Channu, "Une histoire religieuse sérielle à propos du diocèse de la Rochelle," *Revue d'histoire moderne et contemporaine* (1965); Emile-G. Léonard, *Problémes et experiences du protestantisme français: l'urbanisation, l'embourgeoisement, les deviations ecclésiastiques, l'attrait Catholique* (Paris, 1940).

24. Sylvie Cadier-Sabatier, *Les Protestants de Pont-de Veyle et lieux circonvoisins au xviie siècle* (Trevoux, France, 1975); André Corviser, "Les Religionaires employés dans les manufactures de la generalité de Rouen de 1700," *BSHPF*, 120 (1974): 282–296; Daniel Ligou, "La structure sociale du protestantisme montalbanais à la fin du xviiie siècle," *BSHPF*, 100 (1954): 93–106; Roger Mazauric, "Etude sur les consequences de la révocation de l'Edit de Nantes au pays messin: Un siècle de resonnance dans le village de Courcilles-Chaussy," *BSHPF*, 120 (1974): 257–281; Robert Pic, "Les protestants d'Aubais de la révocation a la révolution," *BSHPF*, 126 (1980): 53–108; Alice Wemyss, *Les protestants du Mas-D'Azil: histoire d'une resistance, 1680–1830* (Toulouse, 1961); Alfred Levoux, *Les religionnaires de Bordeaux de 1685 à 1802* (Bordeaux, 1920).

25. Samuel Mours, "Les pasteurs à la révocation de l'édit de Nantes," *BSHPF*, 114 (1968): 67–105, 292–316, 521–524.

26. Samuel Mours, "Essai d'evaluation de la population protestante réformée aux xviie et xviie siècles," *BSHPF*, 104 (1958): 1–24; Orcibal, *Louis XIV et les protestants;* Léonard, "Le protestantisme français au xviie siècle."

27. Helmut Erbe, *Die Hugenotten in Deutschland* (Essen, 1937); Wilhelm Beuleke, *Die Hugenotten in Niedersachen* (Hildesheim, 1960); Lothar Zogner, *Hugenottendorfer in Nordhessen* (Marburg, 1966).

28. Marie-Claude Buxtorf-Laplanche, "La communauté huguenote de Kasel de 1685 à la fin du xviiie siècle," *Ecole de Chartes, positions de theses* (Paris, 1971), 37–42.

29. See especially Stefi Jersch-Wenzel, *Juden und "Franzosen" in der Wirtschaft des Raumes Berlin/Brandenburg zur Zeit des Merkantilismus* (Berlin, 1978), and Scoville, *Huguenots and French Economic Development*, 348–357.

30. *Register of the Walloon Church of Cazand in Holland, 1685–1724, HSLPubl*, 39 (1934): 64–66; H. H. Bolhius, "La Hollande et les deux refuges," *BSHPF*, 115 (1969): 407–428; André Paul, "Les refugiés huguenots et wallons dans le xvie siècle à la révolution," *Revue historique*, no. 157 (1928): 264–276; Alice C. Carter, "Some Huguenots in Professional and Administrative Functions in the Netherlands in the Eighteenth Century," *HSLProc*, 21 (1965–1970), 550–568.

31. Gerald Cerny, "The Crisis in Late Seventeenth-Century French Protestant Thought: Jacques Basnage and the Moderate Huguenot Refugees in

Holland" (Ph.D. diss., University of California, Berkeley, 1974), 78–89; D. F. Poujol, *Histoire et influences des églises wallonnes dans les Pays-Bays* (Paris, 1902).

32. Cerny, "The Crisis in Late Seventeenth-Century French Protestant Thought," 89–93; Elisabeth Labrousse, *Pierre Bayle* (The Hauge, 1963–1964); Walter Rex, *Essays on Pierre Bayle and Religious Controversy* (The Hague, 1965); Lelièvre, *De la révocation à la révolution*, 492–495, 533–534; Guy H. Dodge, *The Political Theory of the Huguenots of the Dispersion, with Special Reference to the Thought and Influence of Pierre Jurieu* (New York, 1947); F. R. J. Knetsch, "Pierre Jurieu, Theoloog en pulitiken der Refuge," English synopsis in *Acta Historiae Neerlandica* (Leiden, 1971), 213–242; C. R. Gibbs, "Some Intellectual and Political Influences of the Huguenot Emigres in the United Provinces, c. 1680–1730," *Bijragenen en Mededlingen betreffende de Gischiedenis der Nederlanden*, 90 (1975), 255–287.

33. *His Majesty having been pleased, . . . to Renew His Brief to the Distressed French Protestants, . . .* [London, 1688], copy at the Newberry Library, Chicago; [Charles Mossom], *An Account of the Disposal of the Money Collected upon the Late Brief for the French Protestants* [London, 1688]; Thomas Firmin, et al., *The Case of the Poor French Refugees* [London, 1689?]; Roy A. Sundstrom, "Aid and Assimilation: A Study of the Economic Support Given French Protestants in England, 1680–1727" (Ph.D. diss. Kent State University, 1972), 18–22, 42.

34. "A List of the French Chapels in the Diocese of London and Their Respective Ministers" [c. 1700], Lambeth Palace mss.; Robin D. Gwynn, "The Distribution of Huguenot Refugees in England," *HSLProc*, 21 (1965–1970): 404–436, and 22 (1971–1975): 509–567; Gwynn, "The Arrival of Huguenot refugees in England," *HSLProc*, 23 (1976–1980): 366–373; Irene Scouloudi, "Alien Emigration into and Alien Communities in London, 1558–1660," *HSLProc*, 16 (1935–1940): 27–49; E. R. Briggs, "Reflexions upon the First Century of the Huguenot Churches in England," *HSLProc*, 23 (1976–1980): 100–119.

35. *French Protestant Refugees Relieved through the Threadneedle Street Church, London, 1681–1687*, ed. A. P. Hands and Irene Scouloudi, *HSLPubl*, 49 (1971); *Registers of the French Church of La Patente, Spitalfields, London, HSLPubl*, 11 (1898), xiv; *Registers of the French Churches of the Tabernacle, Glasshouse Street, and Leicester Fields, London, HSLPubl*, 29 (1926), xxvi.

36. Royal Bounty ms. 7, Nov. 20, 1689, mss. coll., Huguenot Society of London. This is one of many surviving account books for Royal Bounty funds, but is unusually complete, legible, and exhaustive. See *The Records in the Huguenot Library: The Royal Bounty and Connected Funds, The Burn Donation, The Savoy Church*, ed. by Raymond Smith, *HSLPubl*, 51 (1974), and A. H. Thomas "The Documents Relating to the Relief of French Protestant Refugees, 1693 to 1718, Preserved in the Records Office of the Guildhall, London," *HSLProc*, 12 (1922): 263–287. The most extensive analysis of aid given to the refugees is Sundstrom, "Aid and Assimilation," but his account should be supplemented by Irene Scouloudi's important article, "L'aide apportée aux refugiés protestants français par l'église de Threadneedle Street, l'église de Londres, 1681–1687," *BSHPF*, 115 (1969): 429–444, and by Raymond Smith's brief critique of Sundstrom's dissertation in "Financial Aid to French Protestant Refugees 1681–1727: Brief and the Royal Bounty," *HSLProc*, 22 (1971–1975): 248–256.

37. Because women and the elderly were precisely the persons most likely to receive charitable assistance it is possible that the 1687 aid account exaggerates

their numbers among the Huguenot refugees in England. However, the relief committee always claimed that virtually all refugees were in need of aid and that it tried to aid all of them. Most important, the account is the only major source yet discovered that systematically gives exact ages of large numbers of refugees.

38. *Calendar of State Papers, Domestic, 1686–1687,* 130, 296; Sundstrom, "Aid and Assimilation," 38–41; Malcolm R. Thorp, "The Anti-Huguenot Undercurrent in Late-Seventeenth-Century England," *HSLProc,* 22 (1971– 1975): 569–580; D. C. Agnew, *Protestant Exiles from France . . . in the Reign of Louis XIV,* 2nd ed. (London, 1871), I, 30.

39. Malcolm R. Thorp, "The English Government and the Huguenot Settlement, 1680–1702" (Ph.D. diss., University of Wisconsin, 1972), 59–111; Sundstrom, "Aid and Assimilation," 44–91.

40. The most succinct recent discussion of this problem is found in James H. Kettner, *The Development of American Citizenship, 1607–1879* (Chapel Hill, N.C., 1978), chap. 1.

41. "Collections for Poor Protestants of France," 88–89, box 17b, mss. coll., Corporation of London Record Office (Guildhall); Sundstrom, "Aid and Assimilation," 40–65; Thorp, "English Government and the Huguenot Settlement," 131–132.

42. John Latimer, *Annals of Bristol in the Eighteenth Century* (Bristol, 1893), 411; Thorp, "English Government and the Huguenot Settlement," 209–210; Thorp, "The Anti-Huguenot Undercurrent in Late-Seventeenth-Century England."

43. *Calendar of State Papers, Domestic, May 1684–February 1685,* 310–311, 330, 363; Max Beloff, *Public Order and Popular Disturbances 1660–1714* (London, 1938), 61, 63, 82; Edward Carpenter, *The Protestant Bishop, Being the Life of Henry Compton, 1632–1713, Bishop of London* (London, 1956), 333–334.

44. Thorp, "English Government and the Huguenot Settlement," 70–80, 86–94, 105–107; Sundstrom, "Aid and Assimilation," 207–229. The role of the Huguenot refugees in the development of the English economy has never been adequately studied. The concept of the market economy is described in C. B. MacPherson, *The Political Theory of Possessive Individualism, Hobbes to Locke* (Oxford, 1962) and criticized in Alan Macfarlane, *The Origins of English Individualism: The Family, Property, and Social Transition* (New York, 1978). Thomas Firmin, one of the actors in MacPherson's description of the drive for achievement of England's market economy, was active in the Huguenot relief committees.

45. Carpenter, *The Protestant Bishop,* 333–334; *Plymouth Church Records, 1620–1859,* Colonial Society of Massachusetts, *Publications,* 22 (1920): xxi, 36; *Articles Agreed on in the Nationall Synode of the Reformed Churches of France Held at Charenton neere Paris in the Moneth of September, 1623* (Oxford, 1623); *The Ecclesiasticall Discipline of the Reformed Churches of France or, The Order whereby They Are Governed* (London, 1642); *A Warning Peece for London* (London, 1642); *Synodicon in Gallia Reformata; or the Acts . . . and Canons of . . . National Councils of the Reformed Churches in France,* tr. and ed. John Quick (London, 1692).

46. Beloff, *Public Order and Popular Disturbances,* 11–31; *Calendar of State Papers, Domestic, 1660–1661,* 529; ibid., *1685,* 287; ibid., *1686–1687,* 147, 287; William Minet, "The Fourth Foreign Church at Dover, 1685–1731," *HSLProc,* 4 (1891–1893): 99; James Fontaine, *Memoirs of a Huguenot Family* (New York, 1872), 142–143; Carpenter, *The Protestant Bishop,* 325. A charter issued to ten

Huguenot ministers to organize several nonconformist congregations signaled no change in government and Anglican opposition to a French Protestant denomination-in-exile, as Thorp explains in "The English Government and the Huguenot Settlement," 148–150. The ministers all had been reordained by Anglican authorities and accepted the ecclesiastical authority of the Archbishop of Canterbury.

47. Quoted in Sundstrom, "Aid and Assimilation," 178; Ronald Mayo, "The Bristol Huguenots, 1681–1791," *HSLProc*, 21 (1965–1970): 445–446. The close watch kept on Huguenot ministers is revealed in the fine gradations by which they were categorized in the Huguenot relief accounts. See Royal Bounty ms. 7; "A List for the Distribution of Her Majesty's Bounty" [c. 1700], Lambeth Palace mss.; "The Number of Ancient French Ministers without Employ with Their Wives and Children," British Library, loan 29/48.

48. "A List of the French Chapels in the Diocese of London and of Their Respective Ministers" [c 1700], Lambeth Palace mss.; Gwynn, "Distribution of Huguenot Refugees in England," 561–562.

49. John Durel, *The Liturgy of the Church of England Asserted in a Sermon* (London, 1662); Durel, *A View of the Government and Publick Worship of God in the Reformed Churches beyond the Seas . . .* (London, 1662).

50. *The Exeter Assembly: The Minutes of the Assemblies of the United Brethren of Devon and Cornwall, 1691–1717, . . .* ed. Allan Brockett, *Publications*, Devon and Cornwall Record Society, n.s., 6 (1963): 5, 15, 16, *passim; The Note Book of the Rev. Thomas Jolly*, ed. Henry Fishwick, *Remains Literary and Historical*, Chetham Society, n.s., 33 (1894); Joseph Hunter, *The Rise of the Old Dissent Exemplified in the Life of Oliver Heywood . . . 1630–1702* (London, 1842); William C. Braithwaite, *The Second Period of Quakerism*, 2nd ed. (Cambridge, 1961), 594.

51. The London association never has received systematic study. That its activity pales by comparison with traditional French synods and colloquies or even by comparison with the colloquy of French exile churches in England that met from the 1580s through 1660 can be seen in the comments by Robin D. Gwynn in *A Calendar of the Letter Books of the French Church of London from the Civil War to the Restoration, 1643–1659*, ed. Gwynn, *HSLPubl*, 54 (1979): 2–26, and in the surviving records of the earlier colloquies, *Les Actes des colloques des églises françaises et des synodes des églises étrangères refugiées en Angleterre 1581–1654*, ed. Adrian C. Chamier, *HSLPubl*, 2 (1890). See "Records of the French Assemblies, 1720–1800," mss. coll., Huguenot Society of London. A bitter comment on its alleged influence can be found in *Michel Malard: His Address and Representation of Grievances* (London, 1720), 113–116.

52. *Le livre des conversions et des reconnoissances faites a l'église françoise de la Savoye, 1684–1702, HSLPubl*, 22 (1914); *French Protestants Relieved through the Threadneedle Street Church*, ed. Hands and Scouloudi, 190–192, 228–230; Carpenter, *The Protestant Bishop*, 339; Ronald Mayo, "The Bristol Huguenots, 1681–1781," *HSLProc*, 21 (1965–1970): 438–439. Figures for the distribution of aid per refugee are taken from Royal Bounty ms. 7, mss. coll., Huguenot Society of London, and from figures cited by Sundstrom, "Aid and Assimilation," 56–91. Sundstrom argued that the relief committee distributed its funds equitably because aid given to each social class was very nearly equal between 1698 and 1708 and because aid given poor refugees increased in these years. However, the number of poor refugees always was greater than the number of middle class and upper class refugees, meaning that the per capita aid always was

significantly less for poor refugees than for others. See also *Register of the Church of St. Martin Orgars with Its History and that of Swallow Street*, HSLPubl, 37 (1935): xi–xxvii; William Minet, "History of the Leicester Fields Church 1687–1786 from the Actes du Consistoire," *HSLProc*, 4 (1898): 596–612; William C. Waller, "The French Church of Thorpe-le-Soken," ibid., 265–297, but especially pp. 292–297, which describe implicit links between social class and charity in the congregation.

53. Hillel Schwartz, *The French Prophets: The History of a Millenarian Group in Eighteenth-Century England* (Berkeley, Calif., 1980). See also Ronald Knox, *Enthusiasm: A Chapter in the History of Religion with Special Reference to the XVII and XVIII Centuries* (Oxford, 1950), 356–371; Daniel Ligou and Philippe Joutard, "Les Deserts (1685–1800)," in Mandrou, et al., *Histoire des protestants en France*, 189–215, and Joutard, *Les Camisards* (Paris, 1976).

54. Some figures for baptisms by decade are included in Robin D. Gwynn, "The Distribution of Huguenot Refugees in England," *HSLProc*, 21 (1965–1970), 404–436. See also *Register of the French Church of La Patente, Spitalfields, London*, HSLPubl, 11 (1898): xxv; *Registers of the French Churches of the Savoy, Spring Gardens, and Les Grecs, London*, HSLPubl, 26 (1919): iv–v; *Registers of the French Churches of the Tabernacle, Glasshouse Street, and Leicester Fields, London*, HSLPubl, 29 (1926): xxvii; *Registers of the French Church of Rider Court, London*, HSLPubl, 30 (1927): xiv–xv; *Register of the French Church of Hungerford Market, later Castle Street, London*, HSLPubl 31 (1928): xliii.

55. A few articles and essays describe the refugees in England after 1700. Among them are C. F. A. Marmoy, "The Huguenots and Their Descendants in East London," *East London Papers*, 13 (1970–1971): 72–99; Marmoy, "L'entraide des refugiés français en Angleterre," *BSHPF*, 115 (1969): 591–604; Roy A. Sundstrom, "French Huguenots and the Civil List, 1696–1727: A Study of Alien Assimilation in England," *Albion*, 8 (1976): 219–235; Alice C. Carter, "The Huguenot Contribution to the Early Years of the Funded Debt, 1694–1714," in Carter, ed., *Getting, Spending, and Investing in Early Modern Times* (Aasen 1975), 76–122; Francis H. W. Sheppard, "The Huguenots in Spitalfields and Soho," *HSLProc*, 21 (1965–1970): 355–365; William C. Waller, "Early Huguenot Friendly Societies," *HSLProc*, 6 (1899–1901): 201–233; Marmoy, "La soupe: La maison de charité de Spitalfields," *HSLProc*, 23 (1979), 134–147; Norma Perry, "John Vansommer of Spitalfields: Huguenot, Silk-designer, and Correspondent of Voltaire," *Studies on Voltaire and the Eighteenth Century*, 40 (1968): 289–310; Perry, "Voltaire's London Agents for the *Henriade:* Simond and Benezet, Huguenot merchants," *Studies on Voltaire*, 102 (1973): 265–299.

2. The Huguenot Emigration to America, 1680–1695

1. Arthur H. Hirsch, *The Huguenots of Colonial South Carolina* (Durham, N.C., 1928), 3–8; Charles W. Baird, *History of the Huguenot Emigration to America*, 2 vols. (New York, 1885), I, 28–78.

2. Dale Miquelon, *Dugard of Rouen and Montreal French Trade to Canada and the West Indies, 1729–1770* (Montreal, 1978), 72, 163; John F. Bosher, "French Protestant Families in Canadian Trade, 1740–1760" *Histoire Sociale/Social History*, 7 (1974): 179–201; Baird, *Huguenot Emigration to America*, I, 79–147.

3. Ibid.; Gabriel Debien, *Le peuplement des Antilles françaises au xvii siècle: Les engagés partis de la Rochelle (1683–1715)* (Cairo, 1942), 53–58; Petitjean-Roget,

"Les protestants à la Martinique sous l'Ancien Régime," *Revue française d'histoire d'outre-mer*, 42 (1955): 220–265; M. Delafosse, "La Rochelle et les isles," *Revue française d'histoire d'outre-mer*, 36 (1949): 238–281, "Deportation en Amérique," Papiers Rey-Lescure, Library of the Société de l'histoire du protestantisme Français, Paris; M. Besson, "Les Huguenots à Saint-Christophe et à la Tortue," *BSHPF*, 75 (1926): 324–326; M. Bernard, "Journal de voyage aux Indies de Thomas-Simon Berard, 1712," *BSHPF*, 90 (1941): 239–262.

4. Petitjean-Roget, "Les protestants à la Martinique sous l'Ancien Régime," 235–240, 251–265.

5. David T. Konig, "A New Look at the Essex 'French': Ethnic Frictions and Community Tensions in Seventeenth-Century Essex County, Massachusetts," *Essex Institute Historical Collections*, 110 (1974): 167–180; Baird, *Huguenot Emigration to America*, II, 190–192, 200–201; "First Church Records, Salem, Massachusetts, 1629–1660," Aug. 11, 1678, f. 32, mss. coll., Essex Institute, Salem. Mary Maples Dunn kindly furnished the reference from the Salem Church records.

6. Baird, *Huguenot Emigration to America*, I, 148–200; Ralph LeFevre, "The Huguenots: The First Settlers in the Province of New York," *New York State Historical Association Journal*, 2 (1912): 177–185; H. de Peyster, "A l'occasion d'un centenaire: Les origines françaises et flamandes de New York," *BSHPF*, 73 (1924): 89–110; John A. Maynard, *The Huguenot Church of New York: A History of the French Church of Saint Esprit* (New York, 1938).

7. Konig, "A New Look at the Essex 'French'"; Marion Starkey, *The Devil in Massachusetts: A Modern Enquiry into the Salem Witch Trials* (Garden City, N.Y., 1969), 146, 178–179, 255–256, 267–268; Paul Boyer and Stephen Nissenbaum, *Salem Possessed: The Social Origins of Witchcraft* (Cambridge, Mass., 1974), 131–132, 181–182, 210.

8. *Journal of Jaspers Danckaerts, 1679–1680*, ed. Bartlett B. James and J. Franklin Jameson (New York, 1913), 374; Chinard, *Les refugiés Huguenots en Amérique*, 37–57.

9. J. J. Clute, *Annals of Staten Island, from Its Discovery to the Present Time* (New York, 1877), 39; Charles W. Leng and William T. Davis, *Staten Island and Its People: A History, 1609–1929* (New York, 1930) I, 432–435; William T. Davis et al., *The Church of St. Andrew, Richmond, Staten Island, Its History, Vital Records, and Gravestone Inscriptions* (Staten Island, N.Y., 1925), 15–21.

10. LeFevre, "The Huguenots: The First Settlers in the Province of New York"; G. D. B. Hasbrouck, "The Huguenot Settlement in Ulster County," *New York State Historical Association Proceedings*, 11 (1921): 88–103.

11. St. Julien R. Childs, "The Petit-Guerard Colony," *SCHGM*, 43 (1942): 1–17; R. A. Brock, *Documents Chiefly Unpublished Relating to the Huguenot Emigration to Virginia*, *Coll.*, Virginia Historical Society, 5 (1886).

12. Stephan Thernstrom, ed., *Harvard Encyclopedia of American Ethnic Groups* (Cambridge, Mass., 1980), 381; Max Savelle and Darold D. Wax, *A History of Colonial America*, 3rd ed. (Hinsdale, Ill., 1973), 552; Darrett B. Rutman, *The Morning of America, 1603–1789* (Boston, 1971), 86, estimates 9,000 refugees in 1700.

13. "New Rochelle Census, 1698," N.Y. Colonial mss., v. 42, p. 60, New York State Library, Albany. It is printed accurately in *The New York Genealogical and Biographical Record*, 59 (1928): 105–107. The 1698 New Paltz census is reprinted in E. B. O'Callaghan, ed., *Documentary History of the State of New York*

(Albany, N.Y., 1850–1855), III, 96. The only copy of the 1703 New York City census is in ibid., I, 611–624. The manuscript was destroyed during a fire at the New York State Library in 1911. The Staten Island census probably dates from about 1706 and is reprinted in John E. Stillwell, *Historical and Genealogical Miscellany*, 4 vols. (New York, 1906–1932), I, 149–156.

14. The 1699 estimate of Huguenots in South Carolina in 1699 is reprinted in *PROSC*, IV, 75. The lists of Huguenots applying for benefits under South Carolina's 1697 naturalization act have been printed many times. I have used the edition in "Liste de françois et suisses," *HSSCT*, 24 (1926): 27–46. The original manuscript apparently has been lost. The names of French-surnamed persons receiving land grants have been extracted from *Warrants for Lands in South Carolina, 1672–1711* (Columbia, S.C., 1973).

15. The best guides to Boston's Huguenot population are Baird, *Huguenot Emigration to America*, II, 188–254, and Percival Merritt, "The French Church in Boston," *Proceedings of the Colonial Society of Massachusetts*, 26 (1926): 323–348. For information on the Oxford settlement see Baird, *Huguenot Emigration to America*, II, 255–290, and George F. Daniels, *The Huguenots in the Nipmuck Country* (Boston, 1880). The best secondary account of the Narragansett settlement still is Baird, *Huguenot Emigration to America*, II, 291–310, although it was written without knowledge of the settlement's church records. See "Records of the French Church at Narragansett, 1686–1691", ed. and tr. L. Effingham de Forest, *NYGBR*, 70 (1939): 236–241, 359–365; 71 (1940): 51–61.

16. Edith W. Birch, "The Huguenot Settlers of Pennsylvania," *Berks County Historical Review*, 6 (1941): 78–82; Charles I. Landis, "Madame Mary Feree and the Huguenots of Lancaster County," *[Lancaster County] Historical Papers and Addresses*, 21 (1917): 101–124; Adrian C. Leiby, *The Huguenot Settlement of Schraalenberg: The History of Bergenfield, New Jersey* (Bergenfield, N.J., 1964).

17. Thernstrom, ed., *Harvard Encyclopedia of American Ethnic Groups*, 379–388.

18. Judith Giton Manigault's narrative is cited in Baird, *Huguenot Emigration to America*, II, 112–114, 182, 183, 296–297, but I have used the more recent translation in Slann L. G. Simmons, ed. and tr., "Early Manigault Records," *HSSCT*, 59 (1954): 25–27.

19. These examples are drawn from an exhaustive survey of birth, baptismal, and marriage records of London's French congregations in the *Publications* of the Huguenot Society of London. A complete list of the volumes is printed at the conclusion of each volume.

20. The lack of government policy regarding foreign immigration to America is best indicated by the confusion surrounding naturalization. This is superbly described by James H. Kettner, *The Development of American Citizenship, 1608–1870* (Chapel Hill, N.C., 1978), 106–114. See also Maldwyn A. Jones, *American Immigration* (Chicago, 1960), 39–44.

21. "First Brief of James II, accounts for grants," ms. 2.1; March 5, 1687–April 11, 1687; ms. 2.2, May 4, 1687; ms. 2.3, May 5–July 20, 1687; ms. 2.4, Aug. 8, 1687; ms. 2.5, Aug. 3,–Nov. 12, 1687; ms. 2.6, Nov. 12 1687–Feb. 29, 1688; ms. 2.7, Feb. 29–June 16, 1688; Library, Huguenot Society of London. See also *French Protestant Refugees Relieved through the Threadneedle Street Church, London, 1681–1687*, ed. A. P. Hands and Irene Scouloudi, *HSLPubl*, 49 (1971): 17–18, 223, 227, and Edward Carpenter, *The Protestant Bishop, Being the Life of Henry Compton, 1632–1713, Bishop of London* (London, 1956), 342.

22. Class bias did not always affect aid given to the refugees, however. Between April 11–May 30, 1687, the relief committee recorded gifts to Peter Giraud, "ploughman," for £20 to take himself, his wife, and his niece to America, and gave the blacksmith Lewis Guyon £19 to take himself, his wife, and two children to America. See Royal Bounty ms. 2.2.

23. *The Papers of William Penn*, ed. Richard Dunn and Mary Maples Dunn (Philadelphia, 1981), I, 32; William Penn to James Harrison, 25/6 mo./[1681], in ibid., II, 107–109; Moses Charras to Penn, August 25, 1682, in ibid., II, 284–287; Chinard, *Les réfugiés huguenots en Amérique*, 63–64; William Richardson et al., to George Fox, 16/2 mo./1685, Port.16.29, ms. coll., Friends House, London.

24. Melvin B. Endy, Jr., *William Penn and Early Quakerism* (Princeton, N.J., 1973), 98–100; *Narratives of Early Pennsylvania, West New Jersey, and Delaware, 1630–1707*, ed. Albert C. Myers (New York, 1912), 227–228, 287. See also Joseph E. Illick, *William Penn the Politician: His Relations with the English Government* (Ithaca, N.Y., 1965) and Edith Philips, *The Good Quaker in French Legend* (Philadelphia, 1932).

25. Chinard, *Les réfugiés Huguenots en Amérique*, 62–63; Hope Francis Kane, "Colonial Promotion and Promotion Literature of Carolina, 1660–1700" (Ph.D. diss., Brown University, 1930), 73–77, 107–119; *PROSC*, I: 62–63, 73–74, 96; II: 81, 96, 120, 165, 209; III: 131, 133, 150; Salley, *Warrants for Land in South Carolina*, 26, 31, 39, 138; II, 203, 206, 209; St. Julien R. Childs, "The Petit-Guerard Colony," *SCHGM*, 43 (1942): 88–97, 117; Converse D. Clouse, *Economic Beginnings in Colonial South Carolina, 1670–1730* (Columbia, S.C., 1971), 73–74.

26. "Remarks on the New Account of Carolina by a French Gentleman— 1686," *The Magnolia*, n.s., 1 (1842): 226–230. This English translation has survived while no copy of the original French edition is known to exist. See also Chinard, *Les réfugiés Huguenots en Amérique*, 63.

27. The data are drawn from surveys of the "Liste de françois et suisses," and "Records of the French Church at Narragansett," as well as Childs, "The Petit-Guerard Colony." Baird's *Huguenot Emigration to America*, chaps. 5–8, still contains the best description of the origins of the refugees despite the additional materials on the life of the refugees in America uncovered since he wrote a century ago.

28. "Records of the French Church at Narragansett, 1686–1691," *NYGBR*, 70 (1939): 238–239; 71 (1940): 55; Salley and Oldsberg, eds., *Warrants for Land in South Carolina*, II, 31, 107, 138.

29. Joyce D. Goodfriend, "'Too Great a Mixture of Nations': The Development of New York City Society in the Seventeenth Century" (Ph.D. diss., University of California at Los Angeles, 1975), 158–165; cf. Thomas J. Archdeacon, *New York City, 1664–1710, Conquest and Change* (Ithaca, N.Y., 1976), 49–57.

30. These individuals can be located in *French Protestant Refugees Relieved through the Threadneedle Street Church*, whose editors provide an alphabetical listing of all refugees who received aid.

31. Ibid.

32. "Décès de refugiés français à Genève de 1681 à 1710," *BSHPF*, 58 (1909): 50–65; Alfred Perrenoud, *La population de Genève aux xvi–xix siècles: étude démographique*, in *Mémoirs et documents, société d'histoire et d'archeologie de Genève*, 47 (Geneva, 1979): 291–324.

33. L. Effingham de Forest, ed. and tr., "Records of the French Church at Narragansett," *NYGBR*, 71 (1940): 61.

34. "New Rochelle census, 1698," N.Y. Colonial mss., vol, 42, p. 60, New York State Library, Albany. This description of New Rochelle's population differs considerably from that of Robert Wells, *Population of the British Colonies in America before 1776* (Princeton, N.J., 1976), 115–119. Wells combined the 1698 censuses of New Rochelle and Bedford to obtain his population profile despite the fact that the structure of the population of each town differs greatly.

35. "Liste de françois et suisses." For comparison see also Amy Ellen Friedlander, "Carolina Huguenots: A Study in Cultural Pluralism in the Low Country, 1679–1768" (Ph.D. diss., Emory University, 1979), 88–96.

36. Baptismal records for the following persons can be found in *Registers of the French Church of Threadneedle Street, London,* in *HSLPubl,* 13 (1899): Antoine Boureau and Jeanne Beraut, 275; Isaac Baton and Marie de Lorme, 202, 207, 214, 221, 229; Louis Pasquereau and Madeline Chardon, 278; Isaac Porcher, 262, 278; Louis Thibou, 226, 231; Jacques Varein and Suzanne Horry, 215, 220, 228; and Pierre Videau, 280.

37. *Recueil de diverses pièces, concernant la Pensilvanie* (The Hague, 1684); "Collection of Various Pieces concerning Pennsylvania," tr. Samuel W. Pennypacker, *Pennsylvania Magazine of History and Biography,* 6 (1882): 311–328; *Nouvelle relation de la Caroline, par un gentil-homme françois arrivé depuis mois, de ce nouveau pais* (The Hague, 1686).

38. See *French Protestant Refugees Relieved through the Threadneedle Street Church* for alphabetical lists of refugees receiving aid.

39. For Augustus Grasset's 1695 tax assessment see *Tax Lists of the City of New York, [1695, 1699, 1791],* in *NYHSColl,* 43 (1910): 19, and for his murder see Kenneth Scott, "The Slave Insurrection in New York in 1712," *New-York Historical Society Quarterly,* 45 (1961): 48.

40. "Records of the French Church at Narragansett, 1686–1691," *NYGBR,* 70 (1939): 237; Baird, *Huguenot Emigration to America,* II, 291–302; Francis Jennings, *The Invasion of America: Indians, Colonialism, and the Cant of Conquest* (Chapel Hill, N.C., 1975), 278–280, 306–307; Robert C. Black, III, *The Younger John Winthrop* (New York, 1966), 195–198.

41. Baird, *Huguenot Emigration to America,* II, 301–302, 306–308.

42. "Records of the French Church at Narragansett, 1686–1691," *NYGBR,* 70 (1939): 240, 360, 361; 71 (1940): 53.

43. *NYGBR,* 70 (1939): 238–239, 241, 362, 363; 71 (1940): 54–60.

44. Ibid., 57, 59–61; Baird, *Huguenot Emigration to America,* II, 291–310.

45. "Delineation of the Town of Oxford," Bernon Papers; affidavit of Banja[min] Faneuil, et al., Sept. 4, 1696, ibid.; Baird, *Huguenot Emigration to America,* II, 255–290; "Mr. Daniel Bondet's Representation referring to N. Oxford, July 6th, 1691," in Abiel Holmes, "Memoir of the French Protestants who settled at Oxford, Massachusetts, A.D. 1686," *MHSColls.,* 3d ser., 2 (1830): 61; Jennings, *The Invasion of America,* 40, 149, 298–312.

46. Baird, *Huguenot Emigration to America,* II, 281–285, 288–290, 316–327.

47. *Livre synodal contenant les articles résolus dans les églises wallonnes des Pays-Bays, 1686–1688* (The Hague, 1904), 789, 811; Van den Bosch to Bishop Henry Compton, July 4, 1685, in Worthington C. Ford, "Ezéchiel Carré and the French Protestant Church in Boston," *MHSProcs.,* 52 (1919): 122–123; Merritt, "French Protestant Church in Boston," 324; *Abstract and Index of the Records of the Inferior*

Court of Pleas (Suffolk County Court) Held at Boston, 1680–1698 (Boston, 1940), 127; Pierre Daillé to Increase Mather, May 2, 1686, in Baird, *Huguenot Emigration to America,* II, 398–399; Samuel Sewall, "Diary, 1674–1729," *MHSColls.,* 5th ser., 5 (1878–1882): 98.

48. The charges against Van den Bosch and Van den Bosch's defense are found in the De Peyster mss., New-York Historical Society. See also Merritt, "French Protestant Church in Boston," 323–329, and Nelson W. Rightmyer, *Maryland's Established Church* (Baltimore, Md., 1956), 216.

49. Baird, *Huguenot Emigration to America,* II, 225–226.

50. Minutes, French Protestant Church of New Rochelle, Dec. 18, 1691, June 16, July 10, Aug. 7, Aug. 14, Aug. 17, 1692, Sept. 26, Oct. 16, Oct. 29, 1693, mss. coll., New-York Historical Society; Consistory of the Church of New York to the Consistory of the Church of New Rochelle (July 1692), and David de Bonrepos et al., to the Consistory of the Church of New York, July 3, 1692, in ibid.

51. Hirsch, *Huguenots of Colonial South Carolina,* 50–52, 60–62; Merritt, "French Protestant Church in Boston," 323–340; Maynard *Huguenot Church of New York,* 67.

3. If All the World Were Boston

1. For descriptions of late seventeenth and early eighteenth-century Boston see G. B. Warden, *Boston, 1689–1776* (Boston, 1970); Gary B. Nash, *Urban Crucible: Social Change, Political Consciousness, and the Origins of the American Revolution* (Cambridge, Mass., 1979), 3–4 *passim;* Perry Miller, *The New England Mind: From Colony to Province* (Cambridge, Mass., 1953); and Bernard Bailyn, *The New England Merchants in the Seventeenth Century* (Cambridge, Mass., 1955), 143–198.

2. Thomas Cobbett to Increase Mather, March 18, 1682, *MHSColls.,* 4th ser., 8: 293–296. For descriptions, often quite different, of the failure of the Puritan dream in America see Miller, *The New England Mind;* Darrett B. Rutman, *Winthrop's Boston: Portrait of a Puritan Town* (Chapel Hill, N.C., 1963); and Paul R. Lucas, *Valley of Discord: Church and Society along the Connecticut River, 1636–1725* (Hanover, N.H., 1976).

3. Ichabod Chauncy to Increase Mather, Feb. 17, 1681, *MHSColls.,* 10th ser. 8: 617–619; Thomas Cobbett to Increase Mather, March 18, 1682, ibid., 4th ser., 8: 293–296; Samuel Baker to Increase Mather, Jan. 30, 1682[/3], ibid., 509–512; Nathaniel Mather to Increase Mather, Feb. 10, 1683, ibid., 41–44; Joshua Moody to Increase Mather, March 20, 1683, ibid., 363; Samuel Cradock to Increase Mather, March 21, 1688, ibid., 643–644; *Diary of Cotton Mather,* ed. by Worthington C. Ford (New York, 1957), I, 134, 263, 321; Cotton Mather, *A Sermon wherein is showed that the Church of God is sometimes a Subject of Persecution* (Boston, 1682); Cotton Mather, *A Present from a Farr Country* (Boston, 1698); Giorgio Spini, "Remarques sur la reforme française dans l'historiographie puritainne de la Nouvelle Angleterre," in Philipe Joutard, ed., *Historiographie de la Réforme* (Paris, 1977), 99–107.

4. Charles W. Baird, *History of the Huguenot Emigration to America* (New York, 1885), I, 195–201.

5. James H. Kettner, *The Development of American Citizenship, 1608–1870* (Chapel Hill, N.C., 1978), 69. 86–88; *BosRCR,* 10: 60, 61, 62, 76, 80.

6. "Records of the French Church at Narragansett, 1686–1691," *NYGBR*, 71 (1940): 52. For descriptions of colloquies and synods in France see Estebe, "Vers une autre religion et une autre église (1536–1598)?", in Robert Mandrou et al., *Histoire des protestants en France* (Toulouse, 1977), 82–85; and Mours, "La vie synodale en Vivarais au xviie siècle," *BSHPF*, 92, (1946): 55–103.

7. Worthington C. Ford, "Ezechiel Carré and the French Church in Boston," *MHSProcs.* 52 (1919): 121–132.

8. Ezéchiel Carré, *The Charitable Samaritan*, tr. Nehemiah Walter (Boston, 1689), 17, 21; on post-Revocation religious literature see Emile-G. Léonard, "La piété de 'l'église des gallères' sous Louis XIV" *Mélanges offerts à M. Paul-E. Martin, mémoirs et documents*, Société d'histoire et d'archéologie de Genève, 40 (Geneva, 1971): 97–111.

9. Percival Merritt, "The French Protestant Church in Boston," *Publications*, Colonial Society of Massachusetts, 26 (1926): 323–337; "Records of the French Church at Narragansett," *NYGBR*, 71 (1940): 54; *Registers of the Churches of La Patente de Soho, PublHSL*, 45 (1956): 4; *Registre de l'Eglise Wallonne de Southampton, HSLPubl*, 4 (1890): 67. This is the first appearance of Bondet in the Minutes, French Protestant Church of New Rochelle, July 15, 1696.

10. Robert M. Kingdon, "Pourquoi les réfugies huguenots aux colonies américaines sont-ils devenus épiscopaliens?" *BSHPF*, 115 (1969): 487–509, and a slightly revised English version, "Why did the Huguenot Refugees in the American Colonies Become Episcopalian?" *Historical Magazine of the Protestant Episcopal Church*, 49 (1980): 317–335; Patrice Higonnet, "French," in *Harvard Encyclopedia of American Ethnic Groups*, ed. Stephan Thernstrom (Cambridge, Mass., 1980), 385.

11. Timothy L. Smith, "Religious Denominations as Ethnic Communities: A Regional Case Study," *Church History*, 35 (1966): 207–226; Randall Miller and Tom Marzik, eds., *Immigrants and Religion in Urban America* (Philadelphia, 1977); Ned Landsman, "Scottish Communities in the Old and New Worlds" (Ph.D. diss., University of Pennsylvania, 1979); Stephanie G. Wolf, *Urban Village: Population, Community, and Family Structure in Germantown, Pennsylvania, 1683–1800* (Princeton, N.J., 1976), 229–242.

12. Henry W. Foote, *Annals of King's Chapel* (Boston, 1882–1886), I, 98; Chandler A. Robbins, *A History of the Second Church, or Old North, in Boston* (Boston, 1852), 232, 261.

13. Population estimates are drawn from surveys of the tax lists in *BosRCR*, 1: 158–170, and from "A List of Inhabitants in Boston, 1695," *Publications*, Bostonian Society, 10 (1913): 81–94; see also Merritt, "French Protestant Church in Boston," 337–343, which digests all the available information on Daillé's background.

14. Samuel Sewall, *Diary, 1674–1729, MHSColls.* 5th ser., 5: 491; 6: 153, 407; *Diary of Cotton Mather,* 2: 94, 256.

15. Daillé to S.P.G., in Baird, *Huguenot Emigration to America*, 2: 401; *Historical Collections Relating to the American Colonial Church*, ed. William S. Perry (Hartford, Conn., 1870–1873), 3: 80–81; *Calendar of State Papers, Colonial Series, America and West Indies* (London, 1856–1955), 13: 353–354, 387–388; 15: 99–100; *BosRCR*, 11: 43.

16. James Savage, *A Genealogical Dictionary of the First Settlers of New England* (Boston, 1860), I, 221; Abram E. Brown, *Faneuil Hall and Faneuil Hall Market* (Boston, 1901), 1–10; Baird, *Huguenot Emigration to America*, II, 219, 248–250.

17. *BosRCR*, 8: 29, 38, 41, 45, 60, 75.

18. *The Manifesto Church: Records of the Church in Brattle Square, Boston, 1699–1872* (Boston, 1902), 100, 148; Foote, *Annals of King's Chapel,* I, 186, 260.

19. David M. Heer, "Intermarriage," *Harvard Encyclopedia of American Ethnic Groups,* 513–521; Milton Gordon, *Assimilation in American Life: The Role of Race, Religion, and National Origins (New York, 1964)* 121–124; Richard M. Bernard, *The Melting Pot and the Altar: Marital Assimilation in Early Twentieth-Century Wisconsin* (Minneapolis, Minn., 1980), xii–xxviii; Wolf, *Urban Village,* 132, 296–300.

20. J. Hector St. John de Crèvecoeur, *Letters from an American Farmer* (New York, 1957), 39. For impressionistic comments on intermarriage among European immigrants in the colonies see Walter A. Knittle, *Early Eighteenth-Century Palatine Emigration: A British Government Redemptioner Project to Manufacture Naval Stores* (Philadelphia, 1937), 91–98; James G. Leyburn, *The Scotch-Irish: A Social History* (Chapel Hill, N.C., 1962), 133–139, 143, 153, 331. Wolf, *Urban Village,* 132, measures intermarriage among Germantown's eighteenth-century residents with a single statistic that reveals neither changes in rates across time nor differences in rates among men and women. For a discussion of the "at risk" concept in historical analysis see Daniel Scott Smith, "A Perspective on Demographic Methods and Effects in Social History," *William and Mary Quarterly,* 3d ser., 39 (1982): 442–468.

21. Based on a compilation of marriages involving Huguenot spouses drawn from the Boston marriage records of 1700–1751 printed in *BosRCR,* 21.

22. Merritt, "French Protestant Church in Boston," 343–344; "Brief Memoir of Andrew Le Mercier," 315, 319; Samuel Sewall account book, June 19, 1716, p. 59, ms. coll. Massachusetts Historical Society, Boston.

23. Based on a survey of Huguenot marriages drawn from the Boston marriage records of 1700–1751 printed in *BosRCR,* 21.

24. Based on a survey of Huguenot office-holding drawn from the Boston town records printed in *BosRCR,* 8, 12, 14.

25. Foote, *Annals of King's Chapel,* I, 260, 421; II, 43, 98, 118–122, 153–154, 585–587, 605–610.

26. *The Records of the First Church in Boston, 1630–1868, Publications,* Colonial Society of Massachusetts, 39 (1961): 109, 343–343; Robbins, *History of the Second Church,* 226–291, contains names of persons baptized and admitted to the congregation.

27. On the problem of lagging church membership in eighteenth-century New England see Edward M. Cook, Jr., *The Fathers of the Towns: Leadership and Community Structure in Eighteenth-Century New England* (Baltimore, Md., 1976), 127–129, and for a recent discussion of the general problem that overestimates popular commitment to organized religion see Patricia U. Bonomi and Peter R. Eisenstadt, "Church Adherence in the Eighteenth-Century British American Colonies," *William and Mary Quarterly,* 3d ser., 39 (1982): 245–286.

28. Lawrence Towner, ed., "The Indentures of Boston's Poor Apprentices: 1734–1805," *Publications,* Colonial Society of Massachusetts, 43 (1956–63): 417–468. The four were Mary Anne LePierre (1740), Elisabeth Barjere (1742), Alexander LeBlond (1743), and Mary Devereux (1758). On the role of Huguenot silversmiths in Boston see Esther Forbes, *Paul Revere and the World He Lived In* (Boston, 1942), 3–11; John M. Phillips, "The Huguenot Heritage in American Silver at Yale University," *Legion of Honor Magazine,* 11 (1940): 67–74; and Kathryn Buhler, *Colonial Silversmiths, Masters and Apprentices* (Boston, 1956).

29. Abram E. Brown, *Faneuil Hall and Faneuil Hall Market or Peter Faneuil*

and His Gift (Boston, 1900), 14, 15, 37–48; Allan Forbes and Paul F. Cadman, *Boston and Some Noted Emigrés* (Boston, 1938), 9–16; John Lovell, *A Funeral Oration [for] . . . Peter Faneuil* (Boston, 1743).

30. Bernard Bailyn and Lotte Bailyn, *Massachusetts Shipping 1697–1714* (Cambridge, Mass., 1959), 36, 72–73, 128–131; Peter Faneuil mss., 1716–1739, Baker Library, Harvard University; Andrew Faneuil et al., to [Boston Selectmen], July 17, 1735, ms. coll., Massachusetts Historical Society, Boston; Stephen Boutineau to Sir William Pepperell, March 25, 1746, ms. coll., Massachusetts Historical Society, Boston.

31. "Data Relative to the Faneuil Family," *NYGBR*, 47 (1916): 123–124; *Registers of the Births, Marriages, and Deaths of the "Eglise Françoise à la Nouvelle York,"* 188.

32. "Data Relative to the Faneuil Family," 124.

33. "Brief Memoir of Andrew Le Mercier," 316–318; Merritt, "French Protestant Church in Boston," 344; Alexander Blaikie, *A History of Presbyterianism in New England* (Boston, 1881), 36–37, 56–73, 82–94, 106–108; Charles A. Briggs, *American Presbyterianism* (New York, 1885), 228; Richard Webster, *A History of the Presbyterian Church in America* (Philadelphia, 1857), 119.

34. The documents in the 1748 French Church disputes are printed in "Brief Memoir of Andrew Le Mercier," 319–321.

35. Ibid.

36. Ibid.; Merritt, "French Protestant Church in Boston," 348.

4. South Carolina; Refugees in Slavery's Elysium

1. "John Martin Boltzius' Trip to Charleston, October 1742," ed. and tr. George F. Jones, *SCHGM*, 82 (1981): 101.

2. On the origins and development of early South Carolina, see M. Eugene Sirmans, *Colonial South Carolina: A Political History, 1663–1763* (Chapel Hill, N.C., 1966), 3–100; Peter H. Wood, *Black Majority: Negroes in Colonial South Carolina from 1670 through the Stono Rebellion* (New York, 1974), 3–34; Converse D. Clowse, *Economic Beginnings in Colonial South Carolina, 1670–1730* (Columbia, S.C., 1971), 69–138.

3. Arthur H. Hirsch, *The Huguenots of Colonial South Carolina* (Durham, N.C., 1928), 14–24; Henry A. M. Smith, "French James Town," *SCHGM*, 9 (1908): 220–227.

4. St. Julien R. Childs, "The Petit-Guerard Colony," *SCHGM*, 43 (1942): 1–17, 88–97. For Antoine Poitevin's influence at Orange Quarter see Francis Le Jau to S.P.G., April 22, 1708, in *The Carolina Chronicle of Dr. Francis Le Jau, 1706–1717*, ed. Frank J. Klingberg (Berkeley, 1956), 39, and S.P.G. to Le Jau, July 25, 1709, in S.P.G. papers at Lambeth Palace, London, v. 16, 246–249; Samuel Mours, "Les pasteurs à la Révocation de l'Édit de Nantes," *BSHPF*, 114 (1968); Lawrence Van den Bosch to Henry Compton, Bishop of London, July 4, 1685, in Ford, "Ezechiel Carré and the French Protestant Church in Boston," 122–123.

5. Alexander Crottet, *Histoire des églises réformées de Pons, Gemozac, et Mortagne, en Saintonge* (Bordeaux, 1848), 130–140; Royal Bounty mss. 2.2, no. 9, April 11, 1687–May 30, 1687, ms. coll., Huguenot Society of London.

6. Prioleau ms., South Caroliniana Library, University of South Carolina, Columbia.

7. Hirsch, *Huguenots of Colonial South Carolina*, 61; *Transcript of the Registers of the Protestant Church at Guines from 1668 to 1685, HSLPubl*, 3 (1891): vi; Sidney C. Bolton, "The Anglican Church of Colonial South Carolina, 1704–1754; A Study in Americanization" (Ph.D. diss., University of Wisconsin, 1973), 30; Thomas Smith to Robert Stevens, Jan. 16, 1708, S.P.G. papers at Lambeth Palace, London, v. 16, 193–194; George Howe, *History of the Presbyterian Church in South Carolina* (Columbia, S.C., 1870), I, 100–116. The information on Pierre Robert was kindly furnished by Thomas O. Lawton, Jr., of Allendale, S.C.

8. Louis Thibou to [Gabriel Bontefoy], Sept. 20, 1683, mss. coll., South Caroliniana Library, University of South Carolina, Columbia. The identification of Thibou's correspondent is based on Thibou's statement that he was writing to the godfather of his son Gabriel. Gabriel Thibou was baptized Jan. 13, 1678, in London's Threadneedle Street Church with Gabriel Bontefoy as his godfather.

9. *The Laws of the Province of South Carolina*, comp. Nicholas Trott (Charleston, 1736), 62.

10. B. H. Slicher Van Bath, *The Agrarian History of Western Europe, 500–1850*, tr. Olive Ordish (London, 1963), 206–220; Jerome Blum, *The End of the Old Order in Rural Europe* (Princeton, N.J., 1978), chaps. 6–9.

11. Based on a survey of the records in A. S. Salley, Jr., and R. Nicholas Olsberg, eds., *Warrants for Land in South Carolina, 1672–1711* (Columbia, S.C., 1973).

12. For land distribution patterns elsewhere in the colonies see Kenneth A. Lockridge, *A New England Town: The First Hundred Years* (New York, 1970), 71; Philip J. Greven, *Four Generations: Population, Land, and Family in Colonial Andover, Massachusetts* (Ithaca, N.Y., 1970), 58–60; Charles S. Grant, *Democracy in the Connecticut Frontier Town of Kent* (New York, 1971), 13–16, 18–20, 56–62.

13. Lewis C. Gray, *History of Agriculture in the Southern United States to 1860* (Washington, D.C., 1933), I, 184–190; Arthur H. Hirsch, "French Influence on American Agriculture in the Colonial Period with Special Reference to Southern Provinces," *Agricultural History*, 4 (1930): 1–9.

14. Hirsch, "French Influence on American Agriculture"; Hirsch, *Huguenots of Colonial South Carolina*, 196–205.

15. Thomas Ashe, *Carolina, or a Description of the Present State of that Country*, in Salley, ed., *Narratives of Early Carolina*, 143.

16. Hirsch, *Huguenots of Colonial South Carolina*, 196–205.

17. Thibou to Bontefoy, Sept. 20, 1683.

18. A. S. Salley, ed., "Stock Marks Recorded in South Carolina, 1695–1721," *SCHGM*, 13 (1912): 227; Clarence L. Ver Steeg, *Origins of a Southern Mosaic* (Athens, Ga., 1975), 114–116.

19. Samuel G. Stoney, "Nicholas de Longemare, Huguenot Goldsmith and Silk Dealer in Colonial South Carolina," *HSSCT*, 55 (1950): 38–69.

20. H. A. Wyndam, *Problems of Imperial Trusteeship: The Atlantic and Slavery* (London, 1935), 234; David Brion Davis, *The Problem of Slavery in Western Culture* (Ithaca, N.Y., 1966), 109–110, 201.

21. Wood, *Black Majority*, Thibou to Bontefoy, Sept. 20, 1683. The inventories of the estates of Peter Perdriau and Arnaud Bruneau (1695) are in the Records of the Secretary of State, misc. records, main ser., 1671–1973, v. 17–18, South Carolina Archives. See also Salley and Olsberg, *Warrants for Land in South Carolina*, 245, 320, 336, 337.

22. Wood, *Black Majority*, 97, 149; James Gignilliat to S.P.G., May 28, 1710, SPG mss, Letters, ser. A, v. 5, no. 119.

23. Sirmans, *Colonial South Carolina*, 40–54; Ver Steeg, *Origins of a Southern Mosaic*, 30–39.

24. Craven et al., to Laurent Trouillart et al., April 12, 1693, *PROSC*, III, 103–104; Sirmans, *Colonial South Carolina*, 42; Hirsch, *Huguenots of Colonial South Carolina*, 106–108.

25. *PROSC*, III: 166–167, 177, 196; IV: 43, 76–77; *Commissions and Instructions from the Lords Proprietors of Carolina to Public Officials of South Carolina, 1685–1715*, ed. A. S. Salley (Columbia, S.C., 1916), 63–64, 80–81, 84–85.

26. Deposition of Isaac Cailleboeuf, May 25, 1696, in *HSSCT*, (1897): 20–21; *Laws of the Province of South Carolina*, 60–62. Huguenot membership in the early Assembly is most conveniently traced through the *Biographical Directory of the South Carolina House of Representatives*, ed. Walter B. Edgar (Columbia, S.C., 1974).

27. Huguenots endenized in London are listed in *Letters of Denization and Acts of Naturalization for Aliens in England and Ireland, 1603–1700, HSLPubl*, 18 (1911).

28. *PROSC*, IV: 43, 76–77; *Commissions and Instructions from the Lords Proprietors*, ed. Salley, 87–88, 93–94, 96–100; *Journals of the Commons House of Assembly of South Carolina for 1702*, ed. A. S. Salley (Columbia, S.C., 1932), 52–57.

29. *Journal of the Commons House of Assembly [for 1707]*, ed. A. S. Salley (Columbia, S.C., 1940), 23–24.

30. Ibid., 25, 56–57.

31. Johnston quoted in Hirsch, *Huguenots of Colonial South Carolina*, 303; see also pp. 139–146; Sirmans, *Colonial South Carolina*, 148–154.

32. Jack P. Greene, *The Quest for Power: The Lower Houses of Assembly in the Southern Royal Colonies, 1689–1775* (Chapel Hill, N.C., 1963), 20, 475–488; Katheryn B. Mazyck, "Notes on the Mazyck Family," *HSSCT*, 37 (1932): 56.

33. Margaret S. Middleton, *Henrietta Johnston of Charlestown, South Carolina: America's First Pastellist* (Columbia, S.C., 1966), 49–74.

34. Drawn from a survey of the following sources: *The Annals and Parish Register of St. Thomas and St. Denis Parish, in South Carolina, from 1680 to 1884*, ed. Robert F. Clute (Charleston, 1884); *Register of St. Philip's Parish, 1720–1758*, ed. A. S. Salley, (Columbia, S.C., 1971); *Register of St. Philip's Parish, 1754–1810*, ed. A. S. Salley and D. E. Huger Smith (Columbia S.C., 1971); *The Register Book for the Parish Prince Frederick Winyaw* (Baltimore, Md., 1916); "The Register of Christ Church," ed. Mabel L. Webber, *SCHGM*, 18 (1917): 50–53, *passim;* "Parish Register of St. James Santee, 1758–1788," ed. Mabel L. Webber, *SCHGM*, 15 (1914), 133–43, *passim;* "Register of St. Andrew's Parish, Berkeley County, South Carolina, 1719–1774," ed. Mabel L. Webber, *SCHGM*, 12 (1911), 172–182, *passim.*

35. Hirsch, *Huguenots of Colonial South Carolina*, 79–80; Salley and Olsberg, *Warrants for Land in South Carolina;* Mazyck, "Notes on the Mazyck Family," 55–58.

36. Actes, ms. coll., Threadneedle Street Church, London, May 19, 1700; Aug. 21, 1700; Nov. 23, 1701; Hirsch, *Huguenots of Colonial South Carolina*, 51–54.

37. *Lettres inedites addressées de 1686 à J. A. Turrettini, theologien genevois*, ed. Eugene G. T. De Bude (Paris and Geneva, 1887), II, 201–231; Turrettini mss. (ms. fr. 488), Bibliothéque publique et universitaire, Geneva.

38. Gideon Johnston to S.P.G., July 5, 1710, in *Carolina Chronicle: The Papers*

of Commissary Gideon Johnston, 1706–1716, ed. Frank J. Klingberg (Berkeley, Calif., 1946), 42–43; Eamon Duffy, "'Correspondence Fraternelle': the SPCK, the SPG, and the Churches of Switzerland in the War of the Spanish Succession," in *Reform and Reformation: England and the Continent c1500–c1750,* ed. Derek Baker (Oxford, 1979), 251–280; William Minet "The Fourth Foreign Church at Dover, 1685–1731," *HSLProc,* 4 (1891–1893): 135–136. L'Escot did not return to Charlestown's French Church between 1731 and 1734 as reported in Hirsch, *Huguenots of Colonial South Carolina,* 54, but died in Dover in 1724. On L'Escot see also Johnston, "The Present State of the Clergy in South Carolina," in ibid., 297–309.

39. Paul L'Escot to J. A. Turrettini, May 25, 1719, Turrettini mss.; Gideon Johnston to S.P.G., July 5, 1710; Gideon Johnston, "The Present State of the Clergy in South Carolina," [1713], in Hirsch, *Huguenots of Colonial South Carolina,* 297–309.

40. Sidney C. Bolton, "South Carolina and the Reverend Doctor Francis Le Jau: Southern Society and the Conscience of an Anglican Missionary," *Historical Magazine of the Protestant Episcopal Church,* 40 (1971): 63–79; Arthur H. Hirsch, "Reverend Francis Le Jau, First Rector of St. James Church, Goose Creek S.C.," *HSSCT,* 34 (1929): 25–47; most of Le Jau's letters have been collected and edited in *The Carolina Chronicle of Dr. Francis Le Jau,* ed. Frank J. Klingberg (Berkeley, Calif., 1956). A request for an Anglican-ordained minister at St. James Santee in a letter from Paul L'Escot to a Mr. Bonet, March 24, 1708, S.P.G. papers at Lambeth Palace, London, v. 16, 244, does not mention Pierre Robert; nor does James Gignilliat's first report to the S.P.G., May 28, 1710, SPG mss, Letters, ser. A, v. 5, no. 119. Pierre Trouillart of Canterbury is frequently described as Laurent Trouillart's father. But the 1692 marriage record for a Marie Trouillart and Philippe Margot at Canterbury provides a description of her parents that matches the description Laurent Trouillart gave for his parents on the 1697 South Carolina naturalization lists. Both name their parents as Pierre and Marie Trouillart, and both describe them as deceased. However, the Pierre Trouillart who was at Canterbury was married to Susanne Regnier Janssen and also baptized children there in 1687, 1689, 1691, 1693, 1695, and 1696. Most likely this Pierre Trouillart, the Marie Trouillart married in 1692, and the Laurent Trouillart who emigrated to South Carolina, were all children of the Pierre Trouillart who taught at the Protestant academy at Sedan and who, apparently, was dead by the early 1690s. See *Registers of the Wallon or Strangers Church at Canterbury, HSLPubl.,* 5 (1891): 316, 317, 324, 325, 334, 347, 352, 540, 610, and Hirsch, *Huguenots of Colonial South Carolina,* 80.

41. For a general history of the Huguenot congregations see Hirsch, *Huguenots of Colonial South Carolina,* 47–89.

42. Analysis of the South Carolina establishment dispute is hampered by the fact that most of the literary evidence comes from the so-called Dissenter party. The best discussions of the general problem are found in Ver Steeg, *Origins of a Southern Mosaic,* 30–53; Sirmans, *Colonial South Carolina,* 86–90; Friedlander, "Carolina Huguenots," 147–155; Hirsch, *Huguenots of Colonial South Carolina,* 103–130; Bolton, "Anglican Church of Colonial South Carolina," 35–52.

43. *Journal of the Commons House of Assembly [for 1706],* ed. A. S. Salley (Columbia, S.C., 1937), 41.

44. The 1706 Church Act is printed in *Laws of the Province of South Carolina,*

129–144; Ver Steeg, *Origins of a Southern Mosaic*, 47–48; Sirmans, *Colonial South Carolina*, 89.

45. James Gignilliat to S.P.G., May 28, 1710, SPG mss, Letters ser. A, v. 5, no. 119, and July 15, 1711, ibid., v. 6, no. 105; Albert Pouderous to S.P.G., Jan. 20, 1723, ibid., ser. B, v. 4, no. 135; "The Present State of St. James Santee Carolina served by Albert Pouderis French Minister [1723]," ibid., ser. A, v. 17, pp. 72–73.

46. Gideon Johnston, "The Present State of the Clergy of South Carolina" (the year of 1713), in Hirsch, *Huguenots of Colonial South Carolina*, 297–309; John La Pierre to S.P.G., June 24, 1710, SPG mss, Letters, ser. A, v. 5, no. 132; Elizabeth A. Poyas, *Our Forefathers* (Charleston, 1860), 111–112.

47. Hillel Schwartz, *The French Prophets: The History of a Millenarian Group in Eighteenth-Century England* (Berkeley, Calif., 1980), 54–62, 72–79, 113–153.

48. John La Pierre to Rev. C. G. de la Mothe, Aug. 18, 1714, in *The Aufrere Papers*, ed. Winifred Turner, *HSLPubl*, 40 (1940): 211–212. The London tracts on the French Prophets are in the library of the Huguenot Society of South Carolina, Charleston.

49. John La Pierre to S.P.G., Feb. 15, 1716, SPG mss., Letters, ser. A, v. 11, pp. 142–144; La Pierre to S.P.G. May 15, 1716, ibid., pp. 155–157 and ser. B, v. 4, no. 69 (two versions of this letter exist); Thomas Hassell to S.P.G., Dec. 27, 1716, ibid., ser. A, v. 12, pp. 155–159.

50. John La Pierre to S.P.G. April 5, 1719, SPG mss., Letters, ser. A, v. 13, pp. 208–210; Thomas Hassell to S.P.G., Oct. 20, 1722, ibid., v. 16, pp. 80–82; Francis Varnod to S.P.G., ibid., ser. B, v. 4, no. 132; Hassell to S.P.G. April 15, 1724, ibid., no. 174.

51. Alexander Garden, *Take Heed How Ye Hear* (Charlestown, 1741), 29–38. Garden used the episode to attack the religious enthusiasm of George Whitefield. Elizabeth A. Poyas, *The Olden Time of Carolina* (Charleston, 1855), 192, reports that John Dutartre built a chapel of ease in St. James Goose Creek Parish in 1721. English readers learned of the Dutartre affair in Zachary Grey, *A Serious Address to Lay-Methodists, to Beware of the False Pretences of their Teachers* (London, 1745), 22–29, who quoted from Garden's 1741 sermon. South Carolina's Anglican ministers briefly described the Dutartre affair in a letter they sent to the bishop of London, Oct. 1, 1724, in Fulham Papers, Lambeth Palace, v. 9, f. 154–155.

52. Garden, *Take Heed How Ye Hear*, 29–38; Poyas, *Olden Times of Carolina*, 192; *PROSC*, II, 237, 240; Schwartz, *The French Prophets*, 113–122.

53. Francis Varnod to S.P.G., Jan. 15, 1723, SPG mss, Letters, ser. B, v. 4, no. 132; Memorial of the Rev. Mr. Bull, Aug. 16, 1723, ibid., ser A, v. 17, pp. 36–41; William Bull to S.P.G., Aug. 16, 1723, ibid., ser. C, v. 7; Thomas Hassell to S.P.G., Jan 5, 1724/5, ibid., ser. A, v. 19, p. 54; Albert Pouderous to S.P.G., April 16, 1723, ibid., ser.B, v. 4, no. 145; Peter Robert, et al., to S.P.G., April 2, 1723, ibid., no. 143; Pouderous to S.P.G., Jan. 20, 1723, ibid., no. 135; Francis Ladron et al., to S.P.G., May 13, 1723, ibid., ser. B, v. 4, no. 147; Rene Ravenel et al., to S.P.G., Feb. 6, 1721, ibid., no. 100; "A List of Children Baptized by Mr. Maury at Goose Creek So. Carolina" [1722], ibid., ser. A, v. 16, pp. 131–133; Poyas, *Olden Times of Carolina*, 187, 190.

54. Analysis of Huguenot estates is based on a survey of Huguenot inventories in Estate inventories, 1736–1770, South Carolina Archives, Columbia, S.C. For the Huger estate see William B. Lees, "The Historical Development

of Limerick Plantation, a Tidewater Rice Plantation in Berkeley County, South Carolina, 1683–1945," *SCHGM*, 82 (1981): 48–50.

55. Wood, *Black Majority*, 131–166; Estate inventories, 1736–1770, South Carolina Archives.

56. W. Robert Higgins, "Charles Town Merchants and Factors Dealing in the External Negro Trade, 1735–1775," *SCHGM*, 65 (1964): 205–217.

57. South Carolina *Gazette* Dec. 9, 1732, Oct. 28, 1732, Oct. 7, 1732, Wood, *Black Majority*, 333–339; Daniel C. Littlefield, *Rice and Slaves: Ethnicity and the Slave Trade in Colonial South Carolina* (Baton Rouge, La., 1981), 124, 126.

58. Richard Waterhouse, "South Carolina's Colonial Elite" (Ph.D. diss., The Johns Hopkins University, 1973), 179–183, 189–92; Estate inventories, 1736–1770, South Carolina Archives. On the South Carolina economy see Sirmans, *Colonial South Carolina*, 146–155, 225–229, 265–270, and Clowse, *Economic Beginnings in Colonial South Carolina*, 184–250.

59. Philip D. Morgan, ed., "A Profile of a Mid-Eighteenth Century South Carolina Parish: The Tax Return of Saint James', Goose Creek," *SCHGM*, 81 (1980): 51–65. This return, which consists of two of the three original pages, is found in the SPG mss, Letters, ser. C, v. 7, p. 149, where, for unknown reasons, it was sent in 1745 or 1746.

60. *Warrants for Land in South Carolina*, ed. Salley and Oldsberg, 506–507; Slann L. C. Simmons, "Early Manigault Records," *HSSCT*, 59 (1954): 24–42; Maurice A. Crouse, "Gabriel Manigault: Charleston Merchant," *SCHGM*, 68 (1967), 220–231.

61. Crouse, "Gabriel Manigault"; Sirmans, *Colonial South Carolina*, 169, 228–229, 248, 252–253, 314; Greene, *Quest for Power*, 38, 206, *passim;* Alice H. Jones, *Wealth of a Nation to Be: The American Colonies on the Eve of the Revolution* (New York, 1980), 148, 170–180. Peter Manigault's estate inventory is printed in Alice H. Jones, *American Colonial Wealth: Documents and Methods*, 2d ed. (New York, 1977), 1543–1557.

62. Estate inventories, 1736–1770, South Carolina Archives; Parish of St. Philip's, Charlestown, Vestry book, 1732–1755, WPA transcript, South Caroliniana Library, 164, 172. Stephen E. Wiberley, Jr., "Four Cities: Public Poor Relief in Urban America, 1700–1775" (Ph.D. diss., Yale University, 1975), 78–85, 132–139.

63. Sirmans, *Colonial South Carolina*, 38, 142–143.

64. Based on a survey of the assembly election results found in Edgar, ed., *Biographical Directory of the South Carolina House of Representatives*.

65. Estate inventories, 1736–1766, State Archives; Greene, *Quest for Power*, 475–488.

66. For the role of ethnicity in Pennsylvania politics see Dietmar Rothermund, "The German Problem of Colonial Pennsylvania," *Pennsylvania Magazine of History and Biography*, 84 (1960): 3–21; Alan Tully, "Englishmen and Germans: National-Group Contact in Colonial Pennsylvania, 1700–1755," *Pennsylvania History*, 45 (1978): 237–256; Wayne L. Bockelman and Owen S. Ireland, "The Internal Revolution in Pennsylvania: an Ethnic-Religious Interpretation," ibid., 41 (1974): 125–159; Stephanie G. Wolf, *Urban Village: Population, Community, and Family Structure in Germantown, Pennsylvania, 1683–1800* (Princeton, N.J., 1976), 127–303.

67. South Carolina *Gazette*, March 25, 1732; Oct. 28, 1732; Nov. 18, 1732; Feb. 16, 1734; June 1, 1734; Nov. 20, 1734; Hirsch, *Huguenots of Colonial South*

Carolina, 153–164; Frederick P. Bowes, *The Culture of Early Charleston* (Chapel Hill, N.C., 1942), 131–136.

68. E. Milby Burton, *South Carolina Silversmiths, 1690–1860* (Rutland, Vt., 1968); Kathryn Buhler, *Colonial Silversmiths, Masters and Apprentices* (Boston, 1956); David R. McFadden, "Alexander Petrie and David Willaume, Jr.: Recent Acquisitions in Silver," *Bulletin*, Minneapolis Institute of Arts, 61 (1974): 35–19.

69. Based on a survey of records in *Register of St. Philip's Parish, 1720–1758*, ed. Salley, and *Register of St. Philip's Parish, 1754–1810*, ed. Salley and Huger Smith.

70. See *Annals and Parish Register of St. Thomas and St. Denis Parish*, comp. Clute.

71. Mazyck, "Notes on the Mazyck Family"; Myrta J. Hutson, "Early Generations of the Motte Family of South Carolina," *HSSCT*, 56 (1951), 57–63.

72. Friedlander, "Carolina Huguenots," 198. On the duties of vestrymen see the 1706 Church Act in *Laws of the Province of South Carolina*, 129–144; William A. Bultman stresses the benevolence of S.P.G. aid for Huguenots in "The S.P.G. and the French Huguenots in Colonial America," *Historical Magazine of the Protestant Episcopal Church*, 20 (1951): 156–172.

73. SPG mss, Journals, v. 1, Aug. 18, 1704; Phyllis Bultman and William A. Bultman, "Claude Grosteste de la Mothe and the Church of England, 1685 to 1713," *HSLProc*, 20 (1958–1964): 89–101; *A Chapter in English Church History: Being the Minutes of the Society for Promoting Christian Knowledge . . . 1698–1704*, ed. Edmund McClure, (London, 1888), 94, 218, 219, 249, 267–268.

74. John La Pierre to S.P.G., Jan. 20, 1722, SPG mss, Letters, ser. B. v. 4, no. 136; Thomas Hassell to S.P.G., April 15, 1724, ibid. no. 174; Hirsch, *Huguenots of Colonial South Carolina*, 55–59; *Annals and Parish Register of St. Thomas and St. Denis Parish*, comp. Clute, 12–15.

75. John La Pierre to S.P.G., April 5, 1719, SPG mss, Letters, ser. A, v. 13, pp. 208–210; Albert Pouderous to S.P.G. n.d., [1720], ibid., ser. A, v. 14, pp. 41–42; Pouderous to S.P.G. Jan. 20, 1723; ibid., ser. B, v. 4, no. 135; Peter Robert et al., to S.P.G., April 2, 1723, ibid., no. 143; S.P.G. to Pouderous, Oct. 2, 1725, ibid., ser. A, v. 19, p. 115. P. Morritt to S.P.G., May 3, 1741, ibid., ser. B, v. 4, no. 244; Hirsch, *Huguenots of Colonial South Carolina*, 60–66.

76. Hirsch, *Huguenots of Colonial South Carolina*, 52–59; Daniel Ravenel, "Historical Sketch of the Huguenot Congregations of South Carolina," *HSSCT*, 7 (1900): 49–62.

77. Hirsch, *Huguenots of Colonial South Carolina*, 59–60; Ravenel, "Historical Sketch," 59–60; South Carolina *Gazette*, Jan. 24, 1736; Howe, *History of the Presbyterian Church in South Carolina*, 218, 272; *Records of the Court of Chancery of South Carolina, 1671–1779*, ed. Anne K. Gregorie (Columbia, S.C., 1950), 430, 461.

78. "The Records of the Quakers in Charlestown," *SCHGM*, 28 (1927): 192; Leah Townsend, *South Carolina Baptists* (Florence, S.C., 1935), 39, 55, 56, 113; Elizabeth A. Poyas, *A Peep into the Past* (Charleston, 1853), 195–196; "Register of the Independent or Congregational (Circular) Church, 1732–1738," ed. Mabel L. Webber, *SCHGM*, 12 (1911): 27–37, 53–59, 135–140.

79. Ravenel, "Historical Sketch," 55–56; Parish of St. Philip's Charlestown, Vestry book, 1732–1755, WPA transcript, p. 1; Church commissioners book, 1717–1742, Oct. 1, 1717, South Carolina Archives, Columbia. The persons signing the 1731 request for a minister are listed in John S. Burn, *The History of*

the French, Walloon, Dutch and other Protestant Refugees Settled in England (London, 1846), 19.

80. Based on a survey of the St. Philip's records described in note 68.

81. For comments on erratic but not necessarily irreligious behavior in South Carolina see "John Tobler's Description of South Carolina," *SCHGM*, 71 (1970): 152; William Dunn to S.P.G., Nov. 17, 1707, S.P.G. papers at Lambeth Palace, v. 16, pp. 182–185; Gideon Johnston to [bishop of London?], Sept. 20, 1708, ibid., pp. 228–331; Levi Durand to S.P.G., [Nov. 1746], SPG mss, Letters, ser. B, v. 16, pp. 171–172. The number of baptisms performed by Charles Woodmason and Woodmason's occasional worry about the way parents used and abused the rite are revealed in his remarkable journal. See *The Carolina Backcountry on the Eve of the Revolution,* ed. Richard J. Hooker (Chapel Hill, N.C., 1953), 4–64. James A. Henretta, *The Evolution of American Society, 1700–1815: An Interdisciplinary Analysis* (Lexington, Mass., 1973), 26–33, conveniently digests colonial American demographic patterns, although much of the work is on the New England colonies.

82. Based on a survey of Huguenot wills printed occasionally in *HSSCT*, vols. 10–54. The Mazyck will is printed in ibid., 14 (1907): 26. Woodmason's comment is in *The Carolina Backcountry on the Eve of the Revolution,* 74.

83. James le Chantre inventory, Aug. 25, 1732, Charleston County inventories, 1732–1736, pp. 82–88, South Carolina Archives, Columbia; Philip Combe inventory, Aug. 14, 1737, ibid., H–1736–1739, pp. 78–80; Isaac Porcher inventory, March 7, 1743, ibid., KK–1737–1739; Noah Serre inventory, April 4, 1746, ibid., LL–1744–1746, pp. 223–229; Peter Porcher inventory, [1754], ibid., 1753–1756, v. 2, pp. 101–107; *A Catalog of Books belonging to the Charles-Town Library Society in Charles-Town, South-Carolina* (London, 1750); *A Catalog of Books belonging to the Charlestown Library Society* (Charleston, 1770).

84. Peter Porcher inventory, [1754], Charleston County Inventories, 1753–1756, v. 2, pp. 101–107; *George Whitefield's Journals* (London, 1960), 384–385, 442; South Carolina *Gazette*, June 21, 1742; Bowes, *Culture of Early Charleston*, 27; [Charles Chancy], *The Wonderful Narrative, Or, A Faithful Account of the French Prophets, Their Agitations, Extasies, and Inspirations* (Boston, 1742); Garden, *Take Heed How Ye Hear;* for Jonathan Edwards's awareness of the alleged link between revivalists and the French Prophets see C. C. Goen, ed., *The Works of Jonathan Edwards* (New Haven, Conn., 1972), iv, 313, 330, 341.

85. South Carolina *Gazette*, Oct. 3, 1774; Ravenel, "Historical Sketch," 56–57; Hirsch, *Huguenots of Colonial South Carolina*, 54, 85. J. Barton Starr, "Campbell Town: French Huguenots in British West Florida," *Florida Historical Quarterly*, 54 (1975–1976): 532–547.

86. Ravenel, "Historical Sketch," 61–62.

87. Ibid., 62–74; Marguerite Couturier Steedman, *The Huguenot Church of Charleston, South Carolina* (Charleston, 1970), 4–10.

5. New York: Refugees in an Ethnic Caldron

1. "Gov. Dongan's Report to the Committee of Trade on the Province of New-York, dated 22d February, 1687," *Documentary History of the State of New York,* ed. Edmund B. O'Callaghan (Albany, 1849), I, 186; Michael Kammen, *Colonial New York, A History* (New York, 1975), 44–47, 58–62, 75, 91; Oliver A. Rink, "The People of New Netherland: Notes on Non-English Immigration to

New York in the Seventeenth Century," *New York History*, 62 (1981): 5–42; David S. Cohen, "How Dutch were the Dutch of New Netherland?", ibid., 44–60.

2. Gary B. Nash, *Urban Crucible: Social Change, Political Consciousness, and the Origins of the American Revolution* (Cambridge, Mass., 1979), 106–109, *passim;* Ira Berlin, "Time, Space, and the Evolution of Afro-American Society of British Mainland North America," *American Historical Review*, 85 (1980): 44–78; Edgar J. McManus, *A History of Slavery in New York* (Syracuse, N.Y., 1966), 23–41; Thomas J. Archdeacon, *New York City, 1664–1710: Conquest and Change* (Ithaca, N.Y., 1976), 46–47, 52–54, 93–94; Kammen, *Colonial New York*, 58–59, 181–182.

3. "Records of the First Presbyterian Church of the City of New York," *NYGBR*, 8 (1877): 347; *The Burghers of New Amsterdam and the Freemen of New York, 1675–1866*, *NYHSColl*, 18 (1885): 218. John Laboyteaux's grandfather, Gabriel Laboyteaux, married Marquise Fleuriau in New York City's French Church in April 1689, but the marriage of his parents is not recorded, nor is the baptism of any Laboyteaux child between 1699 and 1763. John Laboyteaux's wife, Hannah Smith, had no known Huguenot ancestors. The use of George Washington as a given name is discussed is Peter Karsten, *Patriot-Heroes in England and America: Political Symbolism and Changing Values over Three Centuries* (Madison, Wis., 1978), 84–91.

4. John Miller, *New York Considered and Improved, 1695*, ed. Victor H. Paltsits (New York, 1903), 54.

5. Based on an analysis of the 1695 and 1699 tax lists printed in "Tax Lists of the City of New York, December, 1695–July 15th, 1699," *NYHSColl*, 43 (1910): 1–35; 44 (1911): 279–315.

6. Miller, *New York Considered*, 54; John A. Maynard, *The Huguenot Church of New York: A History of the French Church of Saint Esprit* (New York, 1938), 59–69, 73–77.

7. New York City freemanship figures are drawn from *Burghers of New Amsterdam*. See also Kammen, *Colonial New York*, 105, 119; James H. Kettner, *The Development of American Citizenship, 1608–1870* (Chapel Hill, N.C., 1978), 86.

8. Kenneth Scott and Kenn Stryker-Rodda, *Denizations, Naturalizations, and Oaths of Allegiance in Colonial New York* (Baltimore, Md., 1975); "The Oath of Abjuration, 1715–1716," *New-York Historical Society Quarterly*, 3 (1919): 35–40; *The Colonial Laws of New York from the Year 1664 to the Revolution* (Albany, N.Y., 1894–1896), I, 858–865.

9. *Records of the Town of New Rochelle, 1699–1828*, ed. Jeanne A. Forbes (New Rochelle, N.Y., 1916), 451–499; J. J. Clute, *Annals of Staten Island, from its Discovery to the Present Time* (New York, 1877), 68; *The Earliest Volume of Staten Island Records, 1673–1813* (New York, 1942); Morgan H. Seacord, *Biographical Sketches of the Huguenot Settlers of New Rochelle 1687–1776* (New Rochelle, N.Y., 1941), 53–54.

10. *MinCCNY*, I, 424; Bruce M. Wilkenfeld, "The New York City Common Council, 1689–1800," *New York History*, 54 (1966): 249–273; Archdeacon, *New York City, 1664–1710*, 78–96. Election results for New York City are scattered through *MinCCNY*.

11. See chap. 2, note 13. Robert Bolton, *The History of the Several Towns, Manors, and Patents of the County of Westchester* (New York, 1881), I, 686–687; Kammen, *Colonial New York*, 161–171.

12. *Records of the Town of New Rochelle*, ed. Forbes, 3–6; John Bodin

inventory, Feb. 11, 1695, Jacques Pouillion inventory, Feb. 11, 1695, John Le Conte inventory, April 6, 1698, ms. estate inventories, Klapper Library, Queens College, New York City.

13. See the inventories above as well as that of Nicholas Crosheron, Dec. 14, 1696, in ms. estate inventories, Klapper Library. Kammen, *Colonial New York*, 58–59; Joyce D. Goodfriend, "Burghers and Blacks: The Evolution of a Slave Society at New Amsterdam," *New York History*, 59 (1978): 125–144.

14. New Rochelle ms. census, 1698. Although the census taker grouped slaves in "family" units, internal inconsistencies make it impossible to link slaves and owners.

15. Joyce D. Goodfriend, "Too Great a Mixture of Nations: The Development of New York City Society in the Seventeenth Century" (Ph.D. diss. University of California, Los Angeles, 1975), 165–168; cf. Archdeacon, *New York City, 1664–1710*, 89–90.

16. Nash, *Urban Crucible*, 4–19, *passim;* Goodfriend, "Too Great a Mixture of Nations," 142–150; Archdeacon, *New York City, 1664–1710*, 52–54.

17. Goodfriend, "Too Great a Mixture of Nations," 146–148.

18. Based on a survey of freemanship applications in *Burghers of New Amsterdam.*

19. Archdeacon, *New York City, 1664–1710*, 42–43, 73; David Peloquin to Peter Jay, Sept. 19, 1724, March 25, 1725; François Mouchard to Peter Jay, March 31, 1724, July 7, 1724, May 6, 1725; John Jay mss., Columbia University, New York City. Listings of Huguenot ship captains and merchants can be found in *An Account of Her Majesty's Revenue in the Province of New York, 1700–1709: The Customs Records of Early Colonial New York*, ed. Julius M. Bloch et al. (Ridgewood, N.J., 1966).

20. "New York City Apprentices, 1697–1707," *NYHSColl*, 13 (1898): 47–69.

21. Jerome R. Reich, *Leisler's Rebellion: A Study of Democracy in New York, 1664–1720* (Chicago, 1953); Archdeacon, *New York City, 1664–1710;* David Lovejoy, *The Glorious Revolution in America* (New York, 1972), 251–257, 294–303.

22. Rev. Godfridus Dellius to Amsterdam Classis, Oct. 21, 1700, in *Ecclesiastical Records of the State of New York*, ed. Edward T. Corwin (Albany, N.Y., 1901–1916), 1397–1398; Reich, *Leisler's Rebellion*, 98, 112, 139; Archdeacon, *New York City, 1664–1710*, 47–48.

23. Affidavit of Catherine DuBois, June 9, 1690, *NYColDocs*, III, 743; Stephen Van Cortlandt to Sir Edmund Andros, May 19, 1690, ibid., 716; Petition of Stephen DeLancey et al., to William and Mary, May 19, 1690, ibid., 748–749.

24. Johannes Van Giesen et al., to Amsterdam Classis, Oct. 16, 1698, *Ecclesiastical Records of the State of New York*, 1246–1261; *Journal of the Votes and Proceedings of the General Assembly of the Colony of New York, 1691–1765* (New York, 1764–1766), 9–10; Bolton, *History of the Several Towns of Westchester*, I, 582–587.

25. Clute, *Annals of Staten Island*, 66–67; Reich, *Leisler's Rebellion*, 77, 120–121.

26. Based on an analysis of the New York City ms. tax lists, 1694–1735, Klapper Library; cf. Nash, *Urban Crucible*, 395.

27. Maynard, *Huguenot Church of New York*, 77–81; French Church of New

York City, ms. accounts, 1698–1710, 1692/3–1699, New-York Historical Society.

28. Archdeacon, *New York City, 1664–1710*, 48. The marriage figures here are based on a survey of the following materials: *Registers of the Births, Marriages, and Deaths, of the "Eglise Françoise à la Nouvelle York"; New York Marriages Previous to 1784* (Baltimore, Md., 1968); *Marriages from 1639 to 1801 in the Reformed Dutch Church*, in *Collections*, New York Genealogical and Biographical Society, 9 (1940); and "Earliest Trinity Church Marriages," *NYGBR*, vols. 69–72.

29. Maynard, *Huguenot Church of New York*, 71–74; Hasbrouck, "The Huguenot Settlement in Ulster County," 97.

30. See note 28 above.

31. French Church of New York City, ms. accounts, 1687–1700, July 4, Oct. 3, 1698; Maynard, *Huguenot Church in New York*, 81–89, 94–95.

32. Sheldon Cohen, "Elias Neau, Instructor to New York Slaves," *New-York Historical Society Quarterly*, 55 (1971): 7–27.

33. Cotton Mather, *A Present from a Farr Country* (Boston, 1698), 1–21; Giorgio Spini, "Remarques sur la réforme française dans l'historiographie puritaine de la Nouvelle Angleterre," Philipe Joutard, ed., *Historiographie de la Réforme* (Paris, 1977), 99–107.

34. *Le Trésor des consolations divines et humaines, ou traité dans le quel le Chrétien peur apprendre à vaincre et à surmonter les afflictions et les misères de cette vie* ... (New York, 1696); *Histoire abbrégée des soufrances du sieur Elie Neau, sur les galères, et dans les cachots de Marseille* (Rotterdam, 1701), 212–219. The English translation is taken from "A Short Account of the Life and Sufferings of Elias Neau," tr. John Christian Jacobi, in Thomas Mason, *The Book of Martyrs, or the History of the Church* (London, 1747), II, separately paginated, p. 14. A separate edition of this translation was published in London in 1749.

35. *Histoire abrégée des soufrances du sieur Elie Neau*, 27.

36. Ibid.; Emile Léonard, "La piété de l'église des galères' sous Louis XIV," *Mélanges offerts à M. Paul-E. Martin*, in *Mémoirs et documents*, Société d'histoire et d'archéologie de Genève, 40 (Geneva, 1961): 97–111; Matthieu Lelievre, *De la révocation a la révolution; étude sur l'histoire morale et religieuse du protestantisme français pendant un siècle; première periode (1685–1715)* (Paris, 1911), 306–317; Samuel Mours, "Note sur les galériens protestants," *BSHPF*, 116 (1970): 184–185; Emile G. Léonard, *Histoire générale du protestantisme* (Paris, 1955–1964), III, 61–64.

37. Hillel Schwartz, *The French Prophets: The History of a Millenarian Group in Eighteenth-Century England* (Berkeley, Calif., 1968), 54–71; see also Elisabeth Labrousse, *Pierre Bayle* (The Hague, 1963–1964) and F. R. J. Knetsch, "Pierre Jurieu, Theoloog en politiken der Refuge," English synopsis in *Acta Historiae Neerlandica*, V (Leiden, 1971), 213–242.

38. Notice of the death of Pierre Peiret, mss. 40.190.173, Museum of the City of New York; *Registers of the "Eglise Françoise à la Nouvelle York,"* 101–102; Maynard, *Huguenot Church of New York*, 114–119.

39. Based on comparisons of baptismal records in *Registers of the "Eglise Françoise à la Nouvelle York"* with *Baptisms from 1639 to 1730 in the Dutch Reformed Church, New York*, in New York Genealogical and Biographical Society, *Collections*, 2 (1901).

40. Maynard, *Huguenot Church of New York*, 120–122.

41. Cohen, "Elias Neau"; Elie Neau to S.P.G., Oct. 13, 1704, SPG mss,

Letters, ser., A, v. 2, no. 20; *A Chapter in English Church History*, ed. McClure, 78, 82–84, 143; S.P.G. ms. journal, March 19, 1703, vol. 1, p. 103, in SPG mss.

42. "Les 'hymnes ou cantiques sacrez' d'Elie Neau; un nouveau manuscrit du 'grand mystique des galères,'" ed. Jon Butler, *BSHPF* 124 (1978): 416–423; Frank J. Klingberg, *Anglican Humanitarianism in Colonial New York* (Philadelphia, 1940), 124–139; Cohen, "Elias Neau"; Winthrop Jordan, *White Over Black: American Attitudes Towards the Negro, 1550–1812* (Chapel Hill, N.C., 1968), 259.

43. Francis Makemie, *A Narrative of a New and Unusual American Punishment* (New York, 1707), 19. For lists of Neau's students see, among others, Neau to S.P.G., Oct. 3, 1705, SPG mss, Letters, ser. A, v. 2, no. 124; "A List of the Slaves Taught by Mr. Neau since the year 1704," ibid., v. 10, pp. 220–223; "A List of the Negroes Taught by Mr. Neau, December the 23d 1719," ibid., v. 14. pp. 141–143.

44. John W. Pratt, *Religion, Politics, and Diversity: The Church-State Theme in New York History* (Ithaca, N.Y., 1967), 26–48.

45. Payments to the Huguenot ministers by the New York government can be traced through the *Calendar of [New York] Council Minutes, 1668–1783, Bulletin,* New York State Library, 58 (1902): 131, *passim,* and *An Account of Her Majesty's Revenue in the Province of New York,* ed. Bloch et al., 80, *passim.* Neau wrote the S.P.C.K. in 1701 that Peiret's interest in a Society for the Reformation of Manners stemmed from his disgust with his French Church members who were "incorrigible men" who "laugh at Excommunicators and Excommunications." Whether Neau's comments were accurate and whether this made the city's Huguenots significantly different from other New Yorkers is impossible to determine. Neau to S.P.C.K., June 13, 1701, in *A Chapter in English Church History,* ed. McClure, 348.

46. See Fox, *Caleb Heathcote, Gentleman Colonist,* chap. 8, for a superb description of Heathcote's attitude toward religion, the Church of England, and politics.

47. Caleb Heathcote to S.P.G., April 10, 1704, SPG mss, Letters, ser. A, v. 1, no. 182; Evan Evans et al., to S.P.G., Oct. 17, 1704, ibid., v. 2, no. 22; Heathcote to S.P.G., [1705], ibid., no. 117; John Bartow to S.P.G., May 25, 1703, ibid., v. 1, no. 105; Heathcote to S.P.G., Nov. 9, 1705, in *Documentary History of the State of New York,* ed. O'Callaghan, III, 117–128.

48. Heathcote to S.P.G., April 16, 1706, SPG mss, Letters, ser. A, v. 2, no. 164; Heathcote to S.P.G., Dec. 18, 1707, ibid., v. 3, no. 161; Daniel Bondet to S.P.G., Jan. 28, 1708, ibid., pp. 478–479; Evan Evans et al., to S.P.G., [1708], ibid., v. 4, no. 128; Bondet to S.P.G., Feb. 17, 1709, ibid., no. 99; "Journal of Rev. John Sharp." *Pennsylvania Magazine of History and Biography,* 49 (1916): 268, 276.

49. Elias Badeau et al., to S.P.G. [June 1709] in Caleb Heathcote to S.P.G., June 10, 1709, SPG mss, Letters, ser. A. v. 5, no. 5; Daniel Bondet to S.P.G., June 13, 1709, ibid., no. 2; Heathcote to S.P.G., June 13, 1709, ibid., no. 5; Elie Neau to S.P.G., June 6, 1709, ibid., no. 6; Neau to S.P.G., July 5, 1709, ibid., v. 4, no. 151; Neau to S.P.G., June 21, 1709, ibid., no. 155; John Bartow to S.P.G., June 10–14, 1709, ibid., v. 5, no. 9.

50. "Journal of Rev. John Sharpe," 276, 280, 283, 286, 293; "An Account of the Money Collected by the Reverend Mr. John Sharp and Mr. Elias Neau ... 1711–1712," in SPG mss, Letters, ser. B, v. 8, pp. 260–262. An incomplete version of Neau's account is in Bolton, *History of the Several Towns of Westchester,* II, 620–621.

51. Elie Neau to S.P.G., June 21, 1709, SPG mss, Letters, ser. A, v. 4, no. 155; Caleb Heathcote to S.P.G., June 10, 1709, ibid., v. 5, no. 5. Neau also believed the New Rochelle episode might induce New York City's Dutch Reformed residents to conform to the Church of England. His unrealistic assessment apparently was produced by his extraordinary concern for Christian unity. See also Neau to S.P.G., July 5, 1710, ibid., v. 5, no. 139; Maynard, *Huguenot Church of New York*, 120–123; Fox, *Caleb Heathcote, Gentleman Colonist*, 217–225.

52. Kammen, *Colonial New York*, 177–180, 216–241.

53. New York *Gazette*, Feb. 6, 1732; April 29, 1736; *Records of the Town of New Rochelle*, ed. Forbes, 56, 59, 85, 130.

54. Berlin, "Space, Time, and the Evolution of Afro-American Society in British Mainland North America," 44–54; Kammen, *Colonial New York*, 181–182; New Rochelle ms. census, 1710.

55. "The Number of Inhabitants in the Parish of New Rochelle, Anno 1771," in James Pitcher ms. farm book, New-York Historical Society; *Heads of Families at the First Census of the United States Taken in 1790: New York* (Washington, D.C., 1908), 201. Field Horne of Sleepy Hollow Restorations, Tarrytown, N.Y., kindly provided the copy of the census from the Pitcher farm book.

56. Scott, "Slave Insurrection in New York in 1712," 48, 56–57, 62–67; Bolton, *History of the Several Towns of Westchester*, II, 671.

57. Daniel Horsmanden, *The New-York Conspiracy*, ed. Thomas J. Davis (New York, 1971; orig. publ. New York, 1744), 37, 41, 48, 51, 421–431, 467–473.

58. I have categorized occupations of Huguenot freemen according to the superb scheme developed in Jacob M. Price, "Economic Function and the Growth of American Port Towns in the Eighteenth Century," *Perspectives in American History*, 8 (1974): 177–183. The freemanship applications are in *The Burghers of New Amsterdam*.

59. Graham Hood, *American Silver: A History of Style 1650–1900* (New York, 1971), 101–103. For city council commissions to Charles Le Roux see *MinCCNY*, III, 239, 323, 439, 460. For names of other Huguenot silversmiths in the city see Rita S. Gottesman, comp., *The Arts and Crafts in New York, 1726–1776*, NYHSColl, 69 (1963).

60. Hayward, *Huguenot Silver in England*, 7; Gottesman, comp., *Arts and Crafts in New York*, 137; "Indentures of Apprentices, 1718–1727," *NYHSColl*, 42 (1909), 111–199.

61. François Mouchard to Peter Jay, March 31, 1724, Jay mss., Columbia University; see also the DeLancey mss. and Stephen Richard ms. account book, New-York Historical Society; Sung Bok Kim, *Landlord and Tenant in Colonial New York: Manorial Society, 1664–1775* (Chapel Hill, N.C., 1978), 423–424.

62. "Indentures of Apprentices, 1718–1727," 111–199.

63. Nash, *Urban Crucible*, 117–118, 395.

64. Based on an analysis of the 1709, 1725, 1730, and 1735 tax lists in the New York City ms. tax lists, 1694–1735, Klapper Library, Queens College.

65. Kenneth Scott, ed., "The Church Wardens and the Poor in New York City, 1693–1747," *NYGBR*, 101 (1970): 164–173. The minutes of the French Church in the city record a payment to "Madame Chardavoine" on Oct. 13, 1728, and an accounting of the congregation's poor fund by Antoine Pintard on June 4, 1729, but no additional dealings with the poor through 1754.

66. *Records of the Town of New Rochelle,* ed. Forbes, 451–499, esp. 462–464.

67. Patricia U. Bonomi, *A Factious People: Politics and Society in Colonial New York* (New York, 1971), 93–97, 111–117, 140–149, *passim;* Archdeacon, *New York City, 1664–1710,* 64–65, 88, 157.

68. Based on a survey of election results reported in *MinCCNY.*

69. Wilkenfeld, "New York City Common Council"; Archdeacon, *New York City, 1664–1710,* 103–104, 125, 148–149; Edward M. Cook, Jr., *The Fathers of the Towns: Leadership and Community Structure in Eighteenth Century New England* (Baltimore, Md., 1976), 63–64, 80–89; Jackson Turner Main, *Social Structure of Revolutionary America* (Princeton, N.J., 1965), 213–215.

70. Gov. George Clinton quoted in *Letters of the Franks Family (1733–1748),* ed. Leo Hershkowitz and Isidor S. Meyer (Waltham, Mass., 1968), 118; Archdeacon, *New York City, 1664–1710,* 78–96, 134–142; "A Full & just Discovery of the weak & slender foundation of a most Pernicious Slander Raised against the French Protestant Refugees . . ." [1708] in *Documentary History of the State of New York,* ed. O'Callaghan, III, 427–433. Voting lists from the disputed 1701 New York City aldermanic elections are in *MinCCNY,* I, 163–178. Some evidence of residential segregation of Huguenots can be extracted from material presented in Bruce M. Wilkenfeld, "New York City Neighborhoods, 1730," *New York History,* 57 (1976): 165–182.

71. Based on surveys of *Registers of the "Eglise Françoise à la Nouvelle York"* and the ms. register of the French Church, New Rochelle, 1724–1765 (the conformist congregation), New-York Historical Society.

72. See Table 14.

73. Bonomic, *A Factious People,* 288; *Letters of the Franks Family,* ed. Hershkowitz and Meyer, xv, 114, 116–119, 124–125.

74. The undated declaration of conformity to the Church of England is in the S.P.G. papers at Lambeth Palace Library, London, v. 14, f. 284, microfilm edition by World Microfilm Publications, Ltd. See also Daniel Bondet to S.P.G., July 14, 1710, SPG mss, Letters, ser. A, v. 5, no. 135; Bondet to S.P.G., April 3, 1714, ibid., v. 9. pp. 113–117.

75. Among reports on the religious situation in New Rochelle are Daniel Bondet to S.P.G., July 28, 1712, SPG mss, Letters, ser. A, v. 7, p. 268; Robert Hunter to S.P.G., Sept. 2, 1720, ibid., ser. C, box 1; Inhabitants of New Rochelle to S.P.G., Nov. 26, 1722, ibid., ser. A, v. 16, pp. 221–222; Pierre Stoupe to S.P.G., May 18, 1725, ibid., ser. B, v. 1, pp. 362–364; Charles McCreery et al., to S.P.G., Dec. 1742, ibid., ser. A, v. 10, no. 76; Isaac Guion et al., to S.P.G., Dec. 1, 1742, ibid., ser. B, v. 19, pp. 74–75; Moses de St. Croix et al., to S.P.G., July 30, 1760, ibid., no. 176; Michel Houdin to S.P.G., Oct. 14, 1762, ibid., no. 177; Bolton, *History of the Several Towns of Westchester,* I, 634–675.

76. Daniel Bondet to S.P.G., April 3, 1714, SPG mss, Letters, ser. A, v. 9, pp. 113–117; Pierre Stoupe to S.P.G., ibid., ser. B, v. 13, p. 249; Stoupe to S.P.G., May 18, 1752, ibid., v. 20, no. 75; James de Blez et al., to S.P.G., July 30, 1760, ibid., v. 3, no. 176.

77. Aeneas Mackenzie to S.P.G., June 13, 1709, SPG mss, Letters, ser. A, v. 5, no. 18; Mackenzie to S.P.G., May 4, 1711, ibid., v. 6, no. 74; William Harrison to S.P.G., June 4, 1724, S.P.G. mss. at Lambeth Palace, London, extra volume; David de Bonrepos et. al., to S.P.G., [1733], SPG mss, Letters, ser. B, v. 1, nos. 1 and 2; Clute, *Annals of Staten Island,* 277; William T. Davis et al., *The Church of St. Andrew, Richmond, Staten Island: Its History, Vital Records and Gravestone Inscriptions*

(Staten Island, N.Y., 1925), 20–33; "Records of the Reformed Dutch Church of Port Richmond, Staten Island, N.Y.," *NYGBR*, 36 (1905): 177–184, *passim*.

78. Elie Neau to Claude Grosteste de la Mothe, [1713], SPG mss, Letters, ser. A, v. 8, pp. 474–476; Neau to de la Mothe, Nov. 26, 1713, in *The Aufrere Papers*, 209–211; *Marriages from 1639 to 1801 in the Reformed Dutch Church*, 120; "Journal of Rev. John Sharp," 424.

79. French Church of New York City, ms. consistory minutes, 1723–1766, Sept. 13, 1724; Maynard, *Huguenot Church of New York*, 129–133.

80. Louis Rou mss., New-York Historical Society, contain legal documents prepared by Rou and his attorney for the hearing before the New York Colonial Council. Some were published as *A Collection of Some Papers Concerning Mr. Lewis Rou's Affair* (New York, 1725).

81. For miscellaneous records of the elders at Trinity Church see William Berrian, *An Historical Sketch of Trinity Church, New York* (New York, 1847), 321–365.

82. Ibid. The baptismal pattern is drawn from *Registers of the "Eglise Françoise à la Nouvelle York."*

83. Drawn from a survey of the records in *Marriages from 1639 to 1801 in the Reformed Dutch Church* and "Dutch Church, Burials, 1726–1803," *Holland Society of New York, Yearbook*, (1899).

84. "Records of the First Presbyterian Church of New York," *NYGBR*, vols. 4–9 (1873–1880).

85. Minutes of the Trinity Church vestry, 1697–1708, are printed in "Early Records of Trinity Church," *Historical Magazine*, 1, 2, 4 (1872–1875); Berrian, *Historical Sketch of Trinity Church*, 321–365.

86. See the records of pew purchases and contributions to Trinity Church in Berrian, *Historical Sketch of Trinity Church*, 321–365. As in Boston and Charlestown, a number of New York City Huguenots appear to have had no regular church affiliation after 1710, but the lack of Trinity Church records makes it impossible to establish this fact.

87. New immigrant families have been defined as those whose surnames appear nowhere in the French Church records or in other New York City records prior to 1740. The baptismal pattern is drawn from *Registers of the "Eglise Françoise à la Nouvelle York."*

88. Ibid., 215, 231; Jean Hastier et al., to Venerable compagnie de pasteurs et professieurs [sic] de la Republique de Geneve, June 6, 1763, in French Church of New York, ms. consistory minutes, 1723–1766. These minutes contain several documents that name French Church elders for the 1760s and 1770s.

89. Louis Rou, "Sermons and Writings, 1704–1750," 2 vols., mss. coll., New York Public Library; W[illard] F[iske], "The 'Craftsman' on Chess: L Rou," *Notes and Queries*, 9th ser., 10 (1902): 41–43; [Fiske], *The Lost Manuscript of the Reverend Lewis Rou's 'Critical Remarks upon the Letter to the Craftsman on the Game of Chess' written in 1734 and dedicated to His Excellency William Cosby Governor of New York* (Florence, Italy, 1902); *Gentleman's Progress: The Itinerarium of Dr. Alexander Hamilton 1744*, ed. Carl Bridenbaugh (Chapel Hill, N.C., 1948), 180.

90. Maynard, *Huguenot Church of New York*, 139–154.

91. Ibid., 139–170; French Church of New York, ms. memoranda of Jacques Buvelot; ms. consistory minutes, Feb. 18, 1766.

92. Maynard, *Huguenot Church of New York*, 205–226.

Conclusion

1. The transformation of the early eighteenth-century American colonies can be appreciated in a number of diverse studies, among them Gary B. Nash, *Urban Crucible: Social Change, Political Consciousness, and the Origins of the American Revolution* (Cambridge, Mass., 1979); James A. Henretta, *The Evolution of American Society, 1700–1815: An Interdisciplinary Analysis* (Lexington, Mass., 1973); Michael Kammen, *People of Paradox: An Inquiry Concerning the Origins of American Civilization* (New York, 1972); Wendy A. Cooper, *In Praise of American Decorative Art, 1650–1820* (New York, 1980); Bernard Bailyn, *The Origins of American Politics* (New York, 1968); Jack P. Greene, *The Quest for Power: The Lower Houses of Assembly in the Southern Royal Colonies, 1689–1776* (Chapel Hill, N.C., 1963); Rhys Isaac, *The Transformation of Virginia, 1740–1790* (Chapel Hill, N.C., 1982); Richard L. Bushman, *From Puritan to Yankee: Character and the Social Order in Connecticut, 1690–1765* (Cambridge, Mass., 1967); and Michael Zuckerman, *Peaceable Kingdoms: New England Towns in the Eighteenth Century* (New York, 1970).

2. For a summary analysis of the eighteenth-century colonial economic achievement see Alice H. Jones, *Wealth of a Nation to Be: The American Colonies on the Eve of the Revolution* (New York, 1980).

3. Marianne Wokeck, "The Flow and Composition of German Immigration to Philadelphia, 1727–1775," *Pennsylvania Magazine of History and Biography*, 105 (1981): 249–278, discusses some of the impact of the changing colonial economy on the demography of the German emigration.

4. Thomas Sowell, *Ethnic America: A History* (New York, 1981) slights the importance and, sometimes, even the extent of discrimination throughout American history, a view that is both shallow and profoundly antihistorical. For the more traditional emphasis on bigotry in the colonies see Maldwyn A. Jones, *American Immigration* (Chicago, 1969), 39–63.

5. Jones, *American Immigration*, 48; Alan Tully, "Englishmen and Germans: National Group Contact in Colonial Pennsylvania, 1700–1755," *Pennsylvania History*, 45 (1978): 237–256.

6. The importance and character of ethnic tension in pre-Revolutionary New Jersey can be discerned in two quite different and excellent works: Ned C. Landsman, "Scottish Communities in the Old and New Worlds, 1680–1760" (Ph.D. diss., University of Pennsylvania, 1979), and Dennis P. Ryan, "Six Towns: Continuity and Change in Revolutionary New Jersey, 1770–1792" (Ph.D. diss., New York University, 1974).

7. Kenneth A. Lockridge, *Settlement and Unsettlement in Early America: The Crisis of Political Legitimacy before the Revolution* (Cambridge, Engl., 1981), 105–121; Kammen, *People of Paradox*, 31–56; John M. Murrin, "The Legal Transformation: The Bench and Bar of Eighteenth-Century Massachusetts," in Stanley N. Katz, ed., *Colonial America: Essays in Politics and Social Development* (Boston, 1971), 415–449.

8. Martin E. Marty, "Ethnicity: The Skeleton of Religion in America," *Church History*, 41 (1972): 5–21; Randall M. Miller, "Introduction," in Miller and Tom Marzik, eds., *Immigrants and Religion in Urban America* (Philadelphia, 1977), xi–xxii; Timothy L. Smith, "Religion and Ethnicity in America," *American Historical Review*, 83 (1978): 1155–1185; Harry S. Stout, "Ethnicity: The Vital

Center of Religion in America," *Ethnicity*, 2 (1975): 204–225; Andrew Greeley, *The Denominational Society* (Glenview, Ill., 1972), 108–126.

9. As examples, see James S. Olson, *The Ethnic Dimension in American History* (New York, 1979); Smith, "Religion and Ethnicity in America"; cf., Jay P. Dolan, *The Immigrant Church: New York's Irish and German Catholics, 1815–1865* (Baltimore, Md., 1975), 71, 83–84.

10. *Letters of the Franks Family (1733–1748)*, ed. Leo Hershkowitz and Isidor S. Meyer (Waltham, Mass., 1968), xxiii; Stephanie G. Wolf, *Urban Village: Population, Community, and Family Structure in Germantown, Pennsylvania, 1683–1800* (Princeton, N.J., 1976), 214–242; Richard M. Bernard, *The Melting Pot and the Altar: Marital Assimilation in Early Twentieth-Century Wisconsin* (Minneapolis, Minn., 1980), 115–125.

11. For superb discussions of complex motivations in emigration see T. H. Breen and Stephen Foster, "Moving to the New World: The Character of Early Massachusetts Immigration," *William and Mary Quarterly*, 3d ser., 30 (1973): 189–222, and Leo Schelbert, "On Becoming an Emigrant: A Structural View of Eighteenth- and Nineteenth-Century Swiss Data," *Perspectives in American History*, 7 (1973): 441–495.

12. Gerald F. De Jong, *The Dutch Reformed Church in the American Colonies* (Grand Rapids, Mich., 1978), 83–105, 188–210; Robert C. Ritchie, *The Duke's Province: A Study of New York Politics and Society, 1664–1691* (Chapel Hill, 1977), 144–147.

13. This subsequent discussion of the Huguenot diaspora in Europe is based on materials developed in Chapter 1.

Appendix

1. A number of different sources furnished the pertinent information for this sketch. For the Manakin settlement see James L. Bugg, Jr., "The French Huguenot Frontier Settlement of Manakin Town," *Virginia Magazine of History and Biography*, 61 (1953): 359–394; Patricia Menk, "Notes on Some Early Huguenot Settlements in Virginia," ibid., 52 (1944): 194–196; Francis Louis Michel, "Report of the Journey of Francis Louis Michel from Berne," ed. William Hinke, ibid., 24 (1916), 122–124; *Documents Chiefly Unpublished Relating to the Huguenot Emigration to Virginia and to the Settlement of Manakin-Town, . . .* Virginia Historical Society, *Collections*, n.s., 5 (1886); "The Vestry Book of King William Parish, Va., 1707–1750," *Virginia Magazine of History and Biography*, 11 (1903–04), 289–304, *passim;* and a paper by Professor Joan Gunderson of St. Olaf College, Northfield, Minnesota, given at the 1978 Northern Great Plains History Conference, entitled "The Huguenot Church at Manakin in Virginia 1700–1750."

Major sources for the Purrysburg settlement include Henry A. M. Smith, "Purrysburg," *South Carolina Historical and Genealogical Magazine*, 10 (1909): 187–219; R. W. Kelsey, "Swiss Settlers in South Carolina," ibid., 23 (1922): 85–91; Robert L. Meriwether, *The Expansion of South Carolina, 1729–1765* (Kingsport, Tenn., 1940); and Verner W. Crane, *The Southern Frontier, 1670–1732* (Ann Arbor, 1956).

On New Bordeaux see A. S. Salley, "The Settlement of New Bordeaux," *HSSCT*, 42 (1937): 38–54; Nora M. Davis, "The French Settlement at New Bordeaux," ibid., 56 (1951): 28–56; Anne C. Gibert, *Pierre Gibert, Esq., the*

Devoted Huguenot: A History of the French Settlement of New Bordeaux, South Carolina (n.p. 1976); and Arthur H. Hirsch, *The Huguenots of Colonial South Carolina* (Durham, N.C., 1928).

The only scholarly study of Campbell Town is J. Barton Starr, "Campbell Town: French Huguenots in British West Florida," *Florida Historical Quarterly,* 54 (1975–76): 532–547.

2. One of the first Manakin ministers, Philippe de Richebourg, frequently is described as lacking Anglican ordination. De Richebourg often quarreled with the Huguenot laity and with other Huguenot ministers in both Manakin and later in South Carolina, and no record of his ordination or reordination in London seems to have survived. Nonetheless, his service in St. James Santee Parish as well as his support by London's S.P.G. both suggest that de Richebourg had indeed received Anglican ordination, since neither were possible without it.

Index

HARVARD HISTORICAL MONOGRAPHS

Out of Print Titles Are Omitted

1. *W. S. Ferguson.* Athenian Tribal Cycles in the Hellenistic Age. 1932.
3. *J. B. Hedges.* The Federal Railway Land Subsidy Policy of Canada. 1934.
9. *Crane Brinton.* French Revolutionary Legislation on Illegitimacy, 1789–1804. 1936.
11. *C. S. Gardner.* Chinese Traditional Historiography. 1938. Rev. ed., 1961.
21. *O. H. Radkey.* The Election to the Russian Constituent Assembly of 1917. 1950.
27. *Marius B. Jansen.* The Japanese and Sun Yet-sen. 1954.
31. *Robert L. Koehl.* RKFDV: German Resettlement and Population Policy, 1939–1945. 1957.
32. *Gerda Richards Crosby.* Disarmament and Peace in British Politics, 1914–1919. 1957.
33. *W. J. Bouwsma.* Concordia Mundi: The Career and Thought of Guillaume Postel (1510–1581). 1957.
34. *Hans Rosenberg.* Bureaucracy, Aristocracy, and Autocracy: The Prussian Experience, 1660–1815. 1958.
36. *Henry Vyverberg.* Historical Pessimism in the French Enlightenment. 1958.
38. *Elizabeth L. Eisenstein.* The First Professional Revolutionist: Filippo Michele Buonarroti (1761–1837). 1959.
40. *Samuel P. Hayes.* Conservation and the Gospel of Efficiency: The Progressive Conservation Movement, 1890–1920. 1959.
41. *Richard C. Wade.* The Urban Frontier: The Rise of Western Cities, 1790–1830. 1959.
42. *Harrison M. Wright.* New Zealand, 1769–1840: Early Years of Western Contact. 1959.
44. *Jere Clemens King.* Foch versus Clemenceau: France and German Dismemberment, 1918–1919. 1960.
46. *James Leiby.* Carroll Wright and Labor Reform: The Origin of Labor Statistics. 1960.
47. *Albert M. Craig.* Chōshū in the Meiji Restoration. 1961.
48. *Milton Berman.* John Fiske: The Evolution of a Popularizer. 1961.
49. *W. M. Southgate.* John Jewel and the Problem of Doctrinal Authority. 1962.
50. *Edward W. Bennett.* Germany and the Diplomacy of the Financial Crisis, 1931. 1962.
51. *Thomas W. Perry.* Public Opinion, Propaganda, and Politics in Eighteenth-Century England: A Study of the Jew Bill of 1753. 1962.
52. *Ramsay MacMullen.* Soldier and Civilian in the Later Roman Empire. 1963.

53. *Charles Montgomery Gray.* Copyhold, Equity, and the Common Law. 1963.
54. *Eugene Charlton Black.* The Association: British Extraparliamentary Political Association, 1769–1793. 1963.
55. *Seymour Drescher.* Tocqueville and England. 1964.
56. *Mack Walker.* Germany and the Emigration, 1816–1885. 1964.
57. *Stephen Lukashevich.* Ivan Akaskov (1823–1886): A Study in Russian Thought and Politics. 1965.
58. *R. C. Raack.* The Fall of Stein. 1965.
59. *Charles T. Wood.* The French Apanages and the Capetian Monarchy, 1224–1328. 1966.
60. *James Holt.* Congressional Insurgents and the Party System, 1909–1916. 1967.
61. *Keith Hitchins.* The Rumanian National Movement in Transylvania, 1780–1849. 1969.
62. *Louis M. Greenberg.* Sisters of Liberty: Marseille, Lyon, Paris and the Reaction to a Centralized State, 1868–1871. 1971.
63. *Alan B. Spitzer.* Old Hatreds and Young Hopes: The French Carbonari against the Bourbon Restoration. 1971.
64. *Judith M. Hughes.* To the Maginot Line: The Politics of French Military Preparation in the 1920's. 1971.
65. *Anthony Molho.* Florentine Public Finances in the Early Renaissance, 1400–1433. 1971.
66. *Philip Dawson.* Provincial Magistrates and Revolutionary Politics in France, 1789–1795. 1972.
67. *Raymond Callahan.* The East India Company and Army Reform, 1783–1798. 1972.
68. *Francis Godwin James.* Ireland in the Empire, 1688–1770: A History of Ireland from the Williamite Wars to the Eve of the American Revolution. 1973.
69. *Richard Tilden Rapp.* Industry and Economic Decline in Seventeenth-Century Venice. 1976.
70. *Hock Guan Tjoa.* George Henry Lewes: A Victorian Mind. 1977.
71. *Marjorie O'Rourke Boyle.* Rhetoric and Reform: Erasmus' Civil Dispute with Luther. 1983.
72. *Jon Butler.* The Huguenots in America: A Refugee People in New World Society. 1983.